2016

SACRED FIRE

SACRED FIRE

A VISION FOR

A DEEPER HUMAN AND

CHRISTIAN MATURITY

RONALD ROLHEISER

IMAGE

New York

Copyright © 2014 by Ronald Rolheiser

Published in the United States by Image, an imprint of the
Crown Publishing Group, a division of Random House LLC,
a Penguin Random House Company, New York.

www.crownpublishing.com

IMAGE is a registered trademark and the "I" colophon is a trademark
of Random House LLC.

Library of Congress Cataloging-in-Publication Data
Rolheiser, Ronald.
    Sacred fire : a vision for a deeper human and Christian maturity /
Ronald Rolheiser. —First Edition.
        pages cm
    Includes bibliographical references.
    1. Spiritual formation—Catholic Church.   2. Spirituality—Catholic
Church.   I. Title.
    BX2350.3.R655 2014
    248.4'82—dc23

                        2013046344

ISBN 978-0-8041-3914-4
e-Book ISBN 978-0-8041-3915-1

PRINTED IN THE UNITED STATES OF AMERICA

Jacket design by Jessie Bright
Jacket photograph by Roc Canals Photography/Flickr Select/
Getty Images

10 9 8 7 6 5

First Edition

For my brothers,

George and Fred Rolheiser,

in gratitude.

Their generosity and sacrifice

helped provide for the rest of us,

and, after the death of our parents,

their house has always been our center.

No small thanks!

*When one reaches the highest degree of human maturity,
one has only one question left: How can I be helpful?*

—TERESA OF ÁVILA

CONTENTS

*Part Three—Radical Discipleship: The Struggle to
Give Our Deaths Away*

Some fifteen years ago, Eric Major, then the religious editor at Hodder & Stoughton, asked me to write a book on spirituality. Having taught in the area for a number of years, I seized upon the idea with enthusiasm, immediately imagining how a wide survey of contemporary spirituality might translate into a book. But Eric Major had a different idea. "I don't want a book that surveys contemporary spirituality," he said. "Those books are already out there. What I want is for you to write a book that I can give to my grown children that explains to them why I still believe in God and why I still go to church—and that I can read myself on days when I am not so sure why. I want a book on apologetics, but with a different bent."

The book, *The Holy Longing*, resulted from that conversation. And Eric Major's instincts were correct; there was a crying niche for that kind of book. The book found a huge audience, inside of all Christian denominations. But while *The Holy Longing* is a solid book, one that offers a certain basic foundation in Christian spirituality, it remains precisely that, a foundational book, a needed Spirituality 101 course, but not a graduate or final course. *The Holy Longing* is a book that is intended to help us "get our lives together," to help us achieve an essential discipleship.

But where do we go from there? What lies beyond the essentials, the basics? Where do we go once some of the basic questions in our lives have been answered, or at least brought to enough peace that our focus can shift away from ourselves to others? Where do we go once the basic questions in our lives are no longer the restless questions of youthful insecurity and loneliness? "Who am I?" "Who loves me?" "How will my life turn out?" Where do we go once the basic questions in life become: "How can I give my life away more purely, and more meaningfully?" "How do I live beyond my own heartaches, headaches, and obsessions so as to help make other peoples' lives more meaningful?"

The intent of this book is to try to address exactly those questions: How can we live less self-centered, more mature lives? What constitutes deep maturity and how do we reach that place? And, not unimportantly, what constitutes a more adult, Christian discipleship? What constitutes a truly mature following of Jesus? This book will try to answer those questions. It will try to be true to what its subtitle promises: *A Vision for a Deeper Human and Christian Maturity.*

And like *The Holy Longing,* this book too has its limits. There is still a further maturity asked of us, beyond even essential altruistic living. Beyond any degree of maturity in this life there still lies death. We are not only asked to give our lives to those whom we love, we are also asked, in a manner of speaking, to give them our deaths. How do we do that? That question will not be the focus of this book, though a chapter at the end will offer some synthetic perspectives on this. The hope is that the question of making our dying our last great gift to our loved ones will be addressed more fully in a later book.

No person is an island, and no book is a solitary effort; thus, I nurse a huge debt of gratitude to many people who helped me both to gestate these ideas and eventually to give them birth in this book. Special thanks to the many folks on whom I tested these ideas in classrooms, workshops, retreats, and in private conversations. Thanks to Gary Jansen and Doubleday for their enthusiastic reception of these ideas and their editorial suggestions. To Alicia von Stamwitz, who has given me so much creative and editorial counsel over the years and who offered these too for this project, a huge, huge thanks. To my colleague, Cliff Knighten, a deep thanks for laying a hawk's eye to the final draft and especially for his undying interest in spirituality and his constant suggestions as to whom I should be listening to and reading. A deep expression of gratitude to Robert L. Moore for letting me lean on and utilize so many of his insights. His ideas and his balance have been and remain a major source of inspiration to me. Special thanks too to Abbott Joseph Boyle and the Trappist monks at Snowmass Abbey in Colorado and to Bob Beloin, Kerry Robinson, and the Catholic community at Yale University for providing me with a nurturing space within which to write.

Finally, most of all, I want to thank my two families: the Rolheisers, that large amorphous tribe of family who supports me when I don't deserve it and puts up with me; and my religious community, the Missionary Oblates of Mary Immaculate, who through more than forty years have faithfully given me trust, a community, a job, a roof, a table, and an altar.

—*Ronald Rolheiser*
San Antonio, Texas
June 30, 2013

THE HOLY LONGING

Tell a wise person, or else keep silent,
because the massman will mock it right away.
I praise what is truly alive,
what longs to be burned to death.

In the calm water of the love-nights,
where you were begotten, where you have begotten,
a strange feeling comes over you
when you see the silent candle burning.

Now you are no longer caught
in the obsession with darkness,
and a desire for higher love-making
sweeps you upward.

Distance does not make you falter,
now, arriving in magic, flying,
and, finally, insane for the light,
you are the butterfly and you are gone.

And so long as you haven't experienced
this: to die and so to grow,
you are only a troubled guest
on the dark earth.

—GOETHE

Part One

A VISION OF DISCIPLESHIP

Three Kinds of Souls, Three Prayers

1) I am a bow in your hands, Lord, draw me, lest I rot.

2) Do not overdraw me, Lord, I shall break.

3) Overdraw me, Lord, and who cares if I break!

—NIKOS KAZANTZAKIS

DISCIPLESHIP AND THE STAGES
OF OUR LIVES

What we choose to fight is so tiny!
What fights with us is so great!
If only we would let ourselves be dominated
as things do by some immense storm,
we would become strong too, and not need names.

—RAINER MARIA RILKE, "THE MAN WATCHING"

The Seasons of Our Life and Their Interface with Spirituality

The human soul is like a fine wine that needs to ferment in various barrels as it ages and mellows. The wisdom for this is written everywhere, in nature, in scripture, in spiritual traditions, and in what is best in human science. And that wisdom is generally learned in the crucible of struggle. Growing up and maturing is precisely a process of fermentation. It does not happen easily, without effort and without breakdown. But it happens almost despite us, because such is the effect of a conspiracy between God and nature to mellow the soul.

How does it happen? What are the various barrels within which we find ourselves fermenting? How is the soul mellowed within the crucible of struggle? We mature by meeting life, just as God and nature designed it, and accepting there the invitations that beckon us ever deeper into the heart of life itself. But that is a simple cliché, more easily said than done, because as we go through the seasons of our lives the challenges we meet there can just as easily embitter and harden the soul as mellow it.

So we need to be patient with one another and with ourselves. Maturation is a lifelong journey with different phases, human and spiritual. And it has many setbacks. What can be helpful is to have a grasp of the natural seasons of our lives and how these interface with a vision of Christian discipleship and its particular stages. What are the seasons of life and what are the stages of discipleship?

A parable might help set the stage: in his autobiography, the renowned writer Nikos Kazantzakis shares a conversation he once had with an old monk named Father Makários. Sitting with the saintly old man, Kazantzakis asked him: "Do you still wrestle with the devil, Father Makários?" The old monk reflected for a while and then replied: "Not any longer, my child. I have grown old now, and he has grown old with me. He doesn't have the strength . . . . I wrestle with God."

"With God!" exclaimed the astonished young writer. "And you hope to win?" "I hope to lose, my child," replied the old ascetic. "My bones remain with me still, and they continue to resist."[1]

The lesson here is that we struggle with different forces at various times in our lives. We are always struggling and doing battle with something, but the forces that beset us change with the years. When we are young and still trying to establish an identity, these forces are very much embedded in the chaotic, fiery energies of restlessness, wanderlust, sexuality, the quest for freedom, and the sheer hunger for experience. The struggle with these energies can be disorienting and overpowering, even though they are the engines that drive us and propel us into adult life. The process of growing up is rarely serene. It is a struggle, a wrestling match with every kind of untamed energy. Everyone has his or her own tale, usually involving a lot of painful restlessness and a few shameful humiliations, of the not-so-gentle passage from childhood to adulthood.

Moreover, it is not that these energies ever go dormant or disappear from inside us; other struggles just set in and begin to eclipse them. As we sort out more who we are, make permanent commitments, and take on more and more responsibilities, we soon find ourselves beset by a new set of struggles: disappointment, tiredness, boredom, frustration, resentment. Consciously and unconsciously, we begin to sense that the big dream for our lives is over, without its ever paying the huge dividends we expected. We become disappointed that there is not more, that we have not achieved more, and that we ourselves are not more, as we sense ourselves stuck with second best, reluctant to make our peace there. All those grandiose dreams, all that potential, all that energy, and what have we achieved? Most all of us can relate to Henry David Thoreau's famous line: "The youth gets together his materials to build a bridge to the moon, or, perchance, a palace or temple on the earth, and, at length, the middle-aged man concludes to build a woodshed with them."[2] And that is a comedown that is not easily digested.

Moreover, once the sheer pulse of life, so strong in us during our youth, begins to be tempered by the weight of our commitments and the grind of the years, more of our sensitivities begin to break through, and we sense more and more how we have been wounded and how life has not been fair to us. New demons then emerge: bitterness, anger, jealousy, and a sense of having been cheated.[3] Disappointment cools the fiery energies of our youth, and our enthusiasm for life begins to be tempered by bitterness and anger as we struggle to accept our limits and make peace with a life that now seems too small and unfair. Where we once struggled to properly control our energies, we now struggle to access them. Where we once struggled not to fall apart, we now struggle not to petrify. Where we once struggled with Eros, the god of passion, we now struggle with Lyssa, the goddess of anger. And where our sympathies once were with the prodigal son, they now are more with his older brother. As we age we begin more and more to struggle with God.

Someone once quipped that we spend the first half of our lives struggling with the sixth commandment (*Thou shalt not commit adultery*) and the second half of our lives struggling with the fifth commandment (*Thou shalt not kill*). That may be a simplification, but it is a fertile image. Indeed the famous parable of the prodigal son and his older brother can serve as a paradigm for this: the prodigal son, illustrating the first half of life, is very much caught up in the fiery energies of youth and is, metaphorically, struggling with the devil; the older brother, illustrating the second half of life, struggling instead with resentment, anger, and jealousy, is, metaphorically and in reality, wrestling with God.

The point of the example is not so much to name or pinpoint what particular things we need to struggle with during the different seasons of our lives, but that there are precisely different seasons in our lives, each with distinct challenges.

This has huge implications in terms of how we understand what Christian discipleship asks of us. Simply put, the invitations that come to us from scripture, particularly from Jesus, meet us in very different ways at different times in our lives. We hear them in one way when we are young, in another in midlife, and in still quite a different way when we are old and facing death. Moreover, not all of Jesus' invitations ask for the same level of response at a given time in our lives. Some of his challenges are meant to help bring us to basic conversion, some are meant to deepen that conversion, and still others are meant to take that conversion to its full term and make us full saints. At one stage of our lives, Jesus calls us to give up *something* for God, at another stage he calls us to give up *everything*. Sometimes Jesus invites us to small conversions, and sometimes he invites us to martyrdom. Looking at the challenges of Jesus, we see that one size does not fit all!

For example, take Jesus' parable of the talents[4]: in essence, that parable warns that if we do not use our natural talents to achieve something and accomplish something in this world, we will be punished, and punished to the exact extent of what we have wasted or left unused. That warning clearly applies to us more during the first half of our lives, when we are more fragile in terms of our self-worth, are still struggling for an identity, and are still at a stage in life where success and achievement can help establish a healthy sense of self-worth, than during our later years when the human and the spiritual task is much more to let go, especially of the sense of self-worth we get through success and achievement. Success has little to teach us during the second half of life.[5] It continues to feel good, but now it is often more an obstacle to maturity than a positive stimulus toward it. Why?

How can it be that something that once was healthy for us now is unhealthy? Because the feeling of success that earlier helped positively to ground our sense of self-worth becomes, at a later stage of life, when meaning needs to be grounded in something less ephemeral, more like a narcotic keeping us from health than a medicine aiding our health. There comes a point in our lives when meaning must be predicated on something beyond the feeling we get from success and achievement. While that is ultimately true too for young people, they too may not ground their self-image on success, Jesus' parable of the talents suggests that using one's talents to the optimum can be an important part of discipleship when we are young, but should become less and less the case as we move into midlife and beyond.

There are some real dangers in not making this distinction. When we fail to distinguish among the different seasons of our lives and how these interface with the challenges and invitations that God and life send us, we are in danger of hurting ourselves in two ways: first, by trying to take on too much when we are not ready for it, and second, by not taking on enough when we are ready for it. To try to make an invitation of Jesus apply in the same way, to both halves of our lives, risks ruining its proper challenge for both halves. Let me cite just one example, a personal one:

Several years ago, I was preaching in a church on a Sunday. The gospel that day was the famous story of Jesus at the home of Martha and Mary, and Martha's infamous complaint that she was left to do the work alone, in this case the business of preparing a meal, while Mary sat idly at the feet of Jesus.[6] Jesus' reply to Martha's complaint suggests not just that Mary had chosen more wisely than Martha, but that Martha's busyness itself is something Martha should critically examine. In preaching my homily I talked about the difference between *being* and *doing* and emphasized the importance of taking our sense of worth from *who we are* rather than from *what we do*. I made the point that if we take our sense of self-worth from what we do, our successes and achievements, this eventually becomes a cancer wherein we have to keep achieving success over and over again in order to feel good about ourselves and how, when we ground our identity on our achievements, our sense of self-worth drains whenever we cannot do things that make us feel worthwhile.

To bolster that idea, I quoted Mother Teresa and Henri Nouwen, both of whom spoke and wrote eloquently on exactly this point. The substance of my message and my sources both seemed sound until, at the church door, a man, gracious and honest, gave me pause to reflect. After thanking me for the homily, he asked me this question: "Have you ever wondered at the fact that it is invariably very successful people and high achievers who, after they have achieved a lot, tell you that it isn't important to achieve anything? I think of Mother Teresa, a household name for the whole world, carrying the Nobel Prize, stepping off a plane somewhere and telling a large, adoring audience that it isn't important to achieve anything. Just be faithful. Or Henri Nouwen, after he had written fifty books and turned down teaching jobs at Harvard and Yale, telling us that it isn't important to be a success, that being is more important than doing. True, no doubt, but tell me this: from where do you get a good sense of self-worth if you are a big, fat nobody?"

His question is not facetious. It is honest and penetrating, and it highlights the importance of distinction between the different seasons of our lives. Jesus' challenge to Martha to move more from activity to contemplation, from doing to being, applies more to someone who is already established in life than to someone who is young and still struggling to establish herself. When we do not make that kind of distinction, we can lay false guilt trips on the young because we are, in fact, misusing the gospel.

We must be prudent in assigning biblical challenges and invitations. When people who are too young, or too immature, or for whatever reason are not ready to roll the dice for God try to do so, the result is invariably one of two things: depression or grandiosity, both of which initially can mask themselves as depth in the spiritual life. Of course we must be careful in discerning this. God does not call and process us generically on a conveyor belt. As already stated, one size does not fit all! Spiritual writers, beginning in scripture, have always pointed out that sometimes God can and does call very young people to the depths of maturity and the radical extremes of discipleship and service. We can think, for example, of Thérèse of Lisieux who was a doctor of the soul at age twenty-four. But that is the exception. The more general experience is that when you see someone trying to be a doctor of the soul at a very young age, you are most often seeing a neophyte in first fervor rather than a truly mature man or woman who has surrendered his or her life to God at a deep level. As well, more often than not, the fervor you see will be embedded in either grandiosity or depression. This must be gently said, rather than judgmentally stated, since the feelings of fervor that fill us when we are neophytes in the spiritual journey are a good thing, a gift from God inviting and seducing us to something deeper. But even though the feelings are good and helpful, they must be taken for what they are, not more, and not confused with full maturity, lest the gospel parable about building our house on something less than solid rock catch us full force.[7]

The Stages of Christian Discipleship— A Contemporary Interpretation

Life has its stages and so too does Christian discipleship. The key is to properly identify both and then interface them. Happily, this is happening more and more. Today there is a rich literature growing within the field of spirituality that speaks of the different stages of our lives and tries to name the appropriate spiritual and human challenges that meet us there.[8] While the language inside this literature is often new, the concept of stages within discipleship is not. Stages of discipleship are implicit in the Gospels and were made explicit throughout history in a bevy of categories within Christian theology and spirituality. Sadly, sometimes these attempts to define the various levels of discipleship were sloppy and inaccurate, biblically and theologically. For instance, to highlight perhaps the worst example, for long periods of time in Christianity there were schools of thought, sometimes nearly universal in influence, which believed that only certain people, like monks and nuns, were called to radical discipleship and full holiness, while the rest of us could be content to walk a less-demanding road.[9]

There were many other categorizations of this kind that were unhelpful and sometimes positively harmful. Unfortunately, we are still not completely free of false understandings of both the spiritual life and the stages of discipleship within it. However, that being admitted, it is also true to say that, happily, there is a better understanding today in virtually all the Christian churches apposite Christ's universal call to full discipleship. The problem is more that we are not always as clear as to all that is involved in that and what its particular stages are. What is involved? What are the stages of Christian discipleship? Or, to ask the question more widely, what are the stages of the spiritual life?

There are almost as many answers to that question as there are persons commenting within the fields of theology and spirituality; albeit, today, many of the answers are complementary rather than mutually exclusive. There is no single, normative analysis here, though some views are more accurate or more useful than others.

With this in mind, for the purposes of this book I would like to take a set of categories found in the classical mystical tradition of Christianity, particularly in the works of a mystic who was also a structural genius, John of the Cross (1542–1591), and reset them in a contemporary context and language in order to try to name and analyze the various stages of Christian discipleship in a way that is practical and is also true to both human and biblical experience. In choosing this particular set of categories, I make no claims that they are superior to or more useful than many others. They are not normative. I chose them because of my familiarity with them and because I have personally found them to be very useful in interfacing contemporary experience—my own and that of the culture—with the demands of Christian discipleship. What are those categories?

Nikos Kazantzakis, quoted earlier, understood his life's struggle and wrote his autobiography under this rubric:

Three Kinds of Souls, Three Prayers

1) *I am a bow in your hands, Lord, draw me, lest I rot.*
2) *Do not overdraw me, Lord, I shall break.*
3) *Overdraw me, Lord, and who cares if I break!*[10]

What he names here are three great struggles in life, each with a desired outcome. When I look at life, at the spiritual life, and at Christian discipleship, aided by the perspectives of classical mysticism, especially the insights of John of the Cross, I also see three great struggles not so unlike those poetically named by Kazantzakis. These struggles are both anthropological and spiritual, and each has a corresponding level of Christian discipleship. The call to follow in the footsteps of Christ takes on a unique character during each of these struggles. God does not meet us in the abstract but in our real lives. And God meets us always as fully empathetic. God's invitations to us are always ultrasensitive to where we are within our lives and what demons are besetting us there.

What are those great struggles and what are the levels of Christian discipleship? For the sake of immediate clarity, let me name them briefly and in caption: we can divide the spiritual journey into three distinct phases, corresponding to the three great struggles in our lives[11]:

ESSENTIAL DISCIPLESHIP—the struggle to get our
　　lives together
MATURE DISCIPLESHIP—the struggle to give our
　　lives away
RADICAL DISCIPLESHIP—the struggle to give our
　　deaths away

This book will be an attempt to explicate what is contained in each of these categories, though the heart of the book will focus on the second phase of discipleship, the struggle to give our lives away.

A Brief Synthesis of Each Stage

Essential Discipleship and the Struggle to Get Our Lives Together

Our first real struggle in life is the struggle to get our lives together. From our first breath onward we begin

to struggle to find our own identity and to find fulfillment and peace there. But this struggle takes on its
real poignancy only at puberty. Prior to puberty, unless our lives have been unnaturally traumatized or we
have suffered serious neglect, our lives are essentially
together. We are born in a hospital and soon taken
home to a place where we have parents, elders, a family
of some kind that is our own, and a place that is ours.
This period of our lives, childhood, is intended by God
and by nature to be a secure time. We are home, secure,
safe! Our huge anthropological and spiritual struggles
have not yet begun. But that will change, and change
dramatically, at puberty.

Simply put, puberty is designed by God and nature
to drive us out of our homes. And puberty generally
does its job, sometimes too well! It hits us with a tumult and violence that overthrows our childhood and
sends us out, restless, sexually driven, full of grandiose
dreams, but confused and insecure, in search of a new
home, one that we build for ourselves. And this is a time
of much longing and searching: searching for an identity, searching for acceptance, searching for a circle of
friends, searching for intimacy, searching for someone
to marry, searching for a vocation, searching for a career, searching for the right place to live, searching for
financial security, and searching for something to give
us substance and meaning—in a word, searching for a
home. Expressions of this longing and search are what
make up the meat of popular music, literature, and movies. Invariably, the motifs and refrains that abound there

will revolve around questions like: Who am I? Where do I find meaning? Who will love me? How do I find love in a world full of infidelity and false promises? Countless expressions of longing, of heartache, of searching; but, in the end, one focus: a burning desire for a home we once had, somehow lost, and are looking for again.

The struggle from being restlessly driven out of our first home to finding a state and a place to call home again is the journey of Essential Discipleship.

And normally we do find our way home again. It might take ten, fifteen, twenty, or more years, but, at a certain point, we land. We find ourselves "at home" again, namely, with a place to live that is our own, a job, a career, a spouse, a vocation, perhaps children, a mortgage, a series of responsibilities, and a certain status and identity. At that point, the fundamental struggle in our life changes, even though it may take years for us to consciously realize and accept this. Our question then is no longer: How do I get my life together? Rather, it becomes: How do I give my life away more deeply, more generously, and more meaningfully? At that stage, we enter the second phase of discipleship.

Mature Discipleship and the Struggle to Give Our Lives Away

Most people reach this second stage sometime during their twenties or thirties, though some of us might be in our forties, fifties, or even sixties before we cross the threshold between struggling to get our lives together as opposed to struggling to give our lives away. Moreover, for all of us, the crossover is never pure and complete. The struggle for self-identity and private fulfillment never completely goes away; we are always somewhat haunted by the restlessness of our youth and our own idiosyncratic needs, but the essential default line shifts. At a certain point, we are more fundamentally concerned with life beyond us than with ourselves.

Mature Discipleship begins, whether we are explicitly conscious of this or not, when we begin living more for others than for ourselves. For most of us this will constitute the longest period of our lives, the adult years. Imagine, for instance, someone, at age thirty, having established a career, gotten married or made a commitment to a religious or humanitarian vocation, perhaps having children, having acquired a house, and having taken on a whole series of family, community, and religious responsibilities. For him, whatever the burden, the next forty to fifty years will be fairly clear; that is, the duties and responsibilities he has taken on will pretty much dictate his life. His anthropological and spiritual task will be clear: How do I give my life away more purely and more generously?[12] Living out that struggle is what constitutes Mature Discipleship.

But this stage of raising and teaching children, running our communities and churches, and being generous adults still is not the final stage of our lives. We still have to die, and that is not a minor anthropological or spiritual task. It is the most daunting task of all. And none of us is exempt. Thus, our default line must shift yet one more time, and radically so. Henri Nouwen suggests that at a certain point of our lives, the real question is no longer: What can I still do so that my life makes a contribution? Rather, the question becomes: How can I now live so that my death will be an optimal blessing for my family, my church, and the world?[13] We must leave home a second time, and this time we face a much larger unknown.

Radical Discipleship and the Struggle to Give Our Deaths Away

As Christians, we believe that Jesus lived for us and that he died for us, that he gave us both his life and his death. What we often fail to distinguish in this, however, is that there are two clear and separate movements here: Jesus gave his life for us in one movement, and he gave his death for us in another movement. In essence, he gave his life for us through his activity, through his generous actions for us; and he gave his death through his passivity, through absorbing in love the helplessness, diminutions, humiliations, and ultimate loneliness of dying.

Like Jesus, we too are meant to give our lives away in generosity and selflessness, but we are also meant to give our deaths away, not just at the moment of our deaths, but in a whole process of leaving this planet in such a way that our diminishment and death is our final, and perhaps greatest, gift to the world. Needless to say, this is not easy. Walking in discipleship behind the master will require that we too sweat blood and feel "a stone's throw" from everybody. This struggle, to give our deaths away, constitutes Radical Discipleship. But all of this will be explicated at length later.

Grounding This in the Concepts of a Great Mystic

This way of categorizing the various levels or phases of Christian discipleship is not my own but is drawn from the writings of some of the great mystics within the Christian tradition, most particularly from John of the Cross, a sixteenth-century Spanish mystic.[14] What I have changed is basically the language and how these concepts apply in a nonmonastic and contemporary setting. But the concepts are the same.

For those familiar with the writings and concepts of John of the Cross, here is a quick co-relation: Essential Discipleship, the struggle to get our lives together, is what John of the Cross refers to as the journey through the "dark night of the senses," both as that night is experienced as pleasure and fervor and in how it is experienced as disillusionment and boredom. Mature Discipleship, the struggle to give our lives away, is what John of the Cross refers to as "proficiency"; while Radical Discipleship, the struggle to give our deaths away, is another name for what John refers to as the "dark night of the spirit."

For those unfamiliar with the classical writings of Christian mysticism, it is not important to grasp this co-relation, though my hope is that it might trigger an interest in studying some of the classical Christian mystics. But you do not need to understand the categories of John of the Cross to grasp what will be presented here. Hopefully, my extrapolation and translation of those categories will give them legs enough to stand, intelligibly, alone.

A Brief Note on the Focus of This Book

This book will not attempt to focus equally on all three phases of discipleship. Its major focus will be on the second phase of discipleship, Mature Discipleship, the struggle to give our lives away.

In a previous book, *The Holy Longing*,[15] I dealt with Essential Discipleship. Indeed the intent of *The Holy Longing* was to lay out some fundamental principles in terms of helping us get our lives together. That book might aptly be called "Discipleship 101—The Introductory Course." However, to properly contextualize Mature Discipleship, I will use Chapter Two to give a brief synthesis on Essential Discipleship.

The rest of the book will then attempt to take things further, to lay out the intermediate course, so to speak, something we might call: "Discipleship 201—The Graduate Course."

At some future date, I hope to write a full book on Radical Discipleship, on the struggle to give our deaths away. The synthetic kernel of that volume will be given in Chapter Nine of this book under the title "Anticipatory Incompletions."

ESSENTIAL DISCIPLESHIP: THE STRUGGLE TO GET OUR LIVES TOGETHER

When a baby is taken from the wet nurse, it easily forgets her and starts eating

solid food. Seeds feed on ground awhile, then lift up into the sun. So you should taste

filtered light and work toward what has no personal covering. That's how you came here,

like a star with no name. Move in the night sky with those anonymous lights.

—RUMI, "A STAR WITH NO A NAME"

The Struggle—and the Need for Two Initiations

We are, in fact, born into this world like a star without a name, and our first struggle is to acquire a name that is truly ours. To do that, we must eventually leave our wet nurse. This is our first journey.

From the minute we are born we begin to struggle to get our lives together, that is, to come to a sense of who we are, of what our meaning is, and of how we can live in such a way that our own lives remain integrated and meaningful and that our presence in the world is a positive one. From day one in our lives, every instinct in us is pressuring us in that direction. However, in our early years of childhood, despite the bumps and bruises, this struggle is more contained and more peaceful. We are children and, in normal circumstances, our lives *are* essentially together. We are at home.

But as we saw in the previous chapter, the struggle takes on a special poignancy at puberty, when, with a suddenness and near violence that literally disorients us, both our bodies and our psyches heat up with powerful energies that turn the peaceful and inquisitive child in us into the moody and restless adolescent. Our relationship to our home and our family takes on a different modality when we reach adolescence. Home no longer contains us as it did before, as the lure of friends, a bigger world, and bigger life begins to trump the security of our parents, family, and home. The family vacation, once so happily anticipated, now becomes something to be avoided. A new life with seemingly unlimited opportunities now beckons us, and it is there where we want to be, impatiently so.

Puberty is a time of major disorientation, but it is also a crucial spiritual time in our lives since it is the real beginning of our personal journey toward maturity and discipleship. And given all the tumult and disorientation that puberty brings, it is a time that begs for initiation. This time in our lives parallels the time of our infancy in terms of the need for others outside of us, elders, to help direct our energies and help protect us from ourselves.

The first moment for initiation is, of course, the time of infancy. We are born with powerful innate energies that have us reaching out unthinkingly in every direction, trying, almost literally, to take the whole world into our mouths. As babies, our energies are blind, and so we put dirt into our mouths and pull hot, steaming teakettles onto ourselves because they look inviting. But thankfully, our parents and elders patiently initiate us: they teach us what our energies are for, how to act them out in dignified ways, how to be safe, how to take care of our bodies, how to wash and dress ourselves, how to be polite and use proper manners, and how we can fit happily and safely into life. They protect us from our own energies. This is an initiation process that, for the most part, we are good at, and the end result is that, by age two, three, or four, we have a pretty nicely functioning child who knows how to conduct herself in this world. We have brought a child home.[1]

This process of initiation continues through childhood: after those early years there is school and there are daily lessons in everything from piano to football to religion. And for the next eight to ten years, until the child reaches puberty, its struggles are not cataclysmic, just the normal struggles of a child. But then, often during the course of a single summer, puberty sets in and powerful new energies beset the child, physically and emotionally, some of which constitute a real danger to the child. This time in life calls for a second moment of initiation, namely, guidance from elders in helping transform the untamed energies of an adolescent into the channeled energies of an adult.[2]

Sadly, our culture often finds itself standing flat-footed and helpless in the face of this. When our children reach that critical and dangerous phase of their lives, instead of taking them into the deep woods as previous cultures have done and initiating them into adulthood, we hold our collective breath and pray that they will make it through these tumultuous years intact, physically and morally. For the most part, we no longer have any meaningful initiation rites to help turn an adolescent into an adult. The few mini-rites that we do still have—the sacrament of confirmation, the high school graduation, the senior prom, the Quinceañera, a special weekend apart with dad or mom—do serve a certain purpose, but they hardly fit the bill as a rite that turns an adolescent into an adult. And so for us, initiation, growing up, learning how to channel all those powerful energies inside us in life-giving ways, has to happen in pieces, slowly over time, through a goodly number of inchoate rites. Thankfully, though, it does happen. We do manage to grow up somehow; at least most people do, though we pay a heavy price for our not having more explicit and effective initiation rites.

For example, anthropologists who study initiation

rites in tribal cultures tell us that in some of those cultures the rites are so severe and demanding that sometimes a young man or woman does not survive the rite, but dies during the initiation. Our present sensibilities are horrified by that. We cannot imagine allowing something like that to happen, elders subjecting their adolescents to trials and ordeals that can lead to their deaths. Yet they lose few young people during those initiations, while, in our own cultures, thousands of young people die every year trying to self-initiate, trying to find their own way into adulthood.[3] There is a tragic irony here: we are horrified by what seems to us primitive and cruel, even as thousands of our young people die unnecessarily and prematurely because they have no one to help them sort out the meaning of their own energies. But that is the struggle, and none of us is exempt.

What are some images that might help us understand this journey?

Images for the Struggle

BIBLICALLY, this might be understood as the *struggle of the prodigal son*, our wrestling with the devil, our struggle with the powerful propensities within our youthful energies toward pleasure, sex, affluence, power, and false freedom, MYSTICALLY, this can be called the *dark night of the senses*, our struggle to walk through both pleasure and disillusionment so as to break our natural motivation to act for what brings pleasure into our own lives. ANTHROPOLOGICALLY, this can be described, as it just was, as the *struggle to leave home and to find one's way back home again*. Finally, POETICALLY, this journey might be called what Goethe called it, the *holy longing*, namely, the struggle to understand and transform the fire of our deepest eros into a fire that ultimately brings us to our true meaning and puts our lives at the service of God and others.[4]

What, more specifically, are these untamed energies of youth that drive us out of one home in search of another?

The Untamed Fiery Energies of Our Youth

Youthful restlessness, loneliness, sexuality, and longing can appear to be all of one piece, and, indeed, that is how they are generally experienced in our lives, as an inchoate restlessness that will not let us sit comfortably at home on a Friday night. Analytically, however, this generic energy can be broken down into various interpenetrating pieces, and for purposes of self-understanding that can be very helpful. So we can look at that huge ball of heat that hits us full force in our youth and ask ourselves: What are its specific pieces? For the purposes of this book, I would like to single out seven aspects of this energy, each of which, without some initiation and mentoring from responsible elders, constitutes a danger in our lives, but with proper initiation becomes a wonderful life-giving force in our lives.

i) Eros . . . the Sheer Pulse for Life

For many of us today, the word *eros* has a very narrow meaning and connotes sex, and sex in a very restricted sense. We speak, for instance, of an erotic film or book, meaning that it contains graphic sex scenes. And so the term *eros,* for the most part, is a pejorative term inside of our daily vocabulary and especially inside of spiritual literature. That is an unfortunate development, both because we rob an archetypal word of is richness and especially because we then think of our erotic energies as antithetical to our spiritual ones.

Eros was the mythical Greek god of love, and his name eventually began to be used in literature and Greek philosophy as a rich word to connote the deepest pulse within life itself, encompassing all aspects of love: friendship, care, romance, emotional obsession, sexual attraction, pragmatic planning and arranging, and altruism and self-sacrifice.[5]

There is no word more apt than *eros* to describe the deepest energy and fire inside us, especially as this makes itself felt in our youth. The mythic god of love is inside us, with all his grandiosity, hungers, thirsts, and lusts. We feel this as a powerful pulse for life, as a buoyancy that trumps every death wish, as an irresistible greed for experience, as a relentless pressure within our sexuality, as a desire to taste things, to know all things, to be known by others, to be everywhere, and as a desire for heroism and martyrdom. Thomas Aquinas once asked the question: What would fully satisfy our human hungers? His answer: Everything! All Being! Our full human hungers would be quenched only when and if we knew everything, loved everything, and were known and loved by everything. And when we are young and in the fever of grandiosity and idealism that enflames us at puberty, the pulse for life in us is strong enough to have us believe, against all the practical limits of our lives, that it can happen, that it can all somehow be ours, that we can have a life that is huge and grand and noble.

Overall, this is a wonderful life-giving energy inside of us that is too soon dulled and depressed within our adult years. That is why young people can be so much fun to be around, despite their immaturity. In our youthful years this pulse for life is so strong that it enables us to carry deep wounds with a resiliency that will later be more difficult for us to access. In essence, the powerful eros of our youth keeps us *preneurotic* and helps us stave off much of the anger and depression that so often besets us in midlife and beyond.

To cite an example: I remember coming to the Oblate Seminary in western Canada at age eighteen and joining about forty other young men, all under the age of twenty-five. For seven years—the course of our preparation for ordination—we lived together in very close quarters in an undersize house with very limited contact with the outside world. We were very much a world to ourselves. Yet despite the fact that we were all immature, those were seven wonderful, special, and fun-filled years in my life. We argued and fought, especially on the sports field and sometimes in the classroom, and worked through the normal jealousies and personality clashes; but overall, each of us looks back with fondness on those years. We were able to do what we did precisely because we were young and the pulse of life in us was strong enough to stave off neurotic anger and depression. We were young men, still preparing for life. Today, all these years later, all of us are much more mature, but if we tried to live together now in that same situation, we would soon kill one another. Now we are mature, but the pulse of life in us has been sufficiently dulled and depressed to leave ample room for our neuroses, those horrible errors of childhood, which William Stafford once described as storming out to play through the broken dyke of our disillusionment.[6] And that broken dyke is precisely the now-dulled and depressed pulse for life that was once strong enough inside us to shelter us from our own wounds. Immaturity has its upside, and that is why it is a struggle to get our lives together.

ii) Sexuality . . . Its Brute Force Inside Us

A cynic once said that, while love makes the world go round, sex makes the earth move! It also keeps the world populated. We are all powerfully, incurably, and wonderfully sexed; this is also part of the conspiracy between God and nature.[7] Sexuality lies right next to our instinct for breathing, and it is always present in our lives, but it hits us with a near violence in our youth.

Spiritual literature tends to be naive and in denial about the power of sexuality, as if it could be dismissed as some insignificant factor in the spiritual journey, and as if it could be dismissed at all! It cannot be. It will always make itself felt, consciously or unconsciously. Nature is almost cruel in this regard, particularly to the young. It fills our youthful bodies with powerful hormones before we have the emotional and intellectual maturity to properly understand and creatively channel that energy. Nature's cruelty, or anomaly, is that it gives someone an adult body before that same person is adult in his or her emotions and intellect. There are a lot of physical and moral dangers in a still-developing child walking around in a fully adult body. Further, today this is being exacerbated by the fact that we are reaching puberty at an ever younger age and are marrying at an ever later one. This makes for a situation, almost the norm in many cultures, where a young girl or boy reaches puberty at age eleven or twelve and will get married about twenty years later. This begs the obvious question: How is his or her sexuality to be emotionally and morally contained during all those years? Where does that leave him or her in the struggle to achieve Christian discipleship?

Admittedly, nature seems almost cruel here, but it has its own angle. Its fundamental concern is to get each of us into the gene pool, and all those powerful hormones it pours into our bodies at adolescence and all those myriad ways in which it heats up our emotions have the same intent—nature wants us to be fruitful and multiply, to perpetuate ourselves and our own species. And nature is uncompromising here: at every level of our being (physical, emotional, psychological, and spiritual) there is a pressure, a sexual one, to get us into the gene pool.[8] And so, when you next see a young man or woman consciously or unconsciously strutting his or her sexuality, be both sympathetic and understanding. You were once there, and nature is just trying to get him or her into the gene pool. Such are its ways, and such are its propensities, and God is in on the conspiracy.

Of course getting into the gene pool means much more than physically having children, though that is a deep imperative written everywhere inside us that may be ignored only in the face of some major psychological and moral risks. There are other ways of having children, though nature all on its own does not easily accept that. It wants children in the flesh. But the full bloom of sexuality, as we will see later, takes on other life-giving forms. We are all familiar with the line: *Have a child. Plant a tree. Write a book.* There are different ways to get into the gene pool, and all of us know persons who, while not having children of their own and neither writing a book nor planting a tree, are wonderfully life-giving women and men. Indeed, the religious vow of celibacy is predicated on that truth. Sexuality also has a powerful spiritual dimension, though that is less evident to an adolescent.

But irrespective of age and maturity, we must never be naive to the sheer, blind power of sex. Dealing with the brute and unrelenting power of our sexuality lies at the root of many of our deepest psychological and moral struggles. This takes on many guises, but the pressure always has the same intent: nature and God keep an unrelenting pressure on us to get into the gene pool, that is, always to open our lives to something bigger than ourselves and to remain cognizant of the fact that intimacy with others, the cosmos, and God is our real goal. It is no great surprise that our sexuality is so grandiose that it would have us want to make love to the whole world. Is that not our real goal?

Dealing with sexuality constitutes one of the great struggles in getting our lives together and achieving a basic essential discipleship. It is no secret that today one of the major reasons why many young people, and indeed people of all ages, are no longer going regularly to their churches has to do, in one way or the other, with their struggles with sexuality and their perception of how their churches view their situation.

iii) Restlessness . . . Our Congenital Insatiability

"In the torment of the insufficiency of everything attainable, we learn that ultimately in this world there is no finished symphony."[9]

Karl Rahner wrote those words, and they describe the experience of everyone, young or old. Ultimately, this life cannot give us everything for which we yearn. We are always somewhat frustrated, unfulfilled, diseased, out of rhythm, and restless. As the biblical writer Qoheleth puts it, from the beginning of life until the end, we are out of sync with the rhythm of the seasons because we have a "timelessness" inside of us that simply cannot make peace with the limited rhythms of this world.[10]

However, while we all suffer from restlessness, this

is a disease that particularly inflicts the young, not just because of the overabundance of sexual hormones in their bodies, but because they are in a time of their lives during which they are tearing up roots and trying to plant those roots elsewhere. Being rootless helps enflame restlessness. As well, today information technology has made it possible for a young person to have a sense of being connected to the whole world in a way that was neither possible nor imaginable before. While that sense of connection to virtually everything that is important is making for a highly informed young person, it is also habitually overstimulating that person's restlessness, akin to the restlessness we often feel at big parties and gala events where everyone is present to everyone and yet we feel present to nobody. There is a strange anomaly here: the bigger the celebration, the more the connection, the greater the restlessness. The poet Jill Essbaum, in a poem titled "Easter," laments that, for her, Easter is a depressing time because its celebration of abundant new life almost taunts her by reminding her how nonabundant her own life is and how "everyone I've ever loved, lives happily just past my able reach."[11] The way information technology connects us to all that is happening in our world and its overabundance of life often triggers that same kind of depression within young people, and, most often, this will be felt as painful restlessness.

Moreover, where this restlessness particularly affects the struggle of a young person to get his or her life together is in the areas of choice and commitment. Every

choice is a renunciation, and often a series of very painful renunciations. Thus, choosing is always difficult.
To choose to marry one person is to not marry anybody else. An overstimulated restlessness makes choice
and commitment very difficult for many young people
today, particularly in the areas of marriage and fidelity.

A huge part of the struggle to get our lives together is
a coming to peace with our own restlessness.

iv) Loneliness . . . Our Distance from Intimacy

Loneliness is not the same thing as restlessness. We all
suffer from restlessness, but as we mature, find a home,
find a marriage partner, have children, find a vocation,
find faithful friends, and find ourselves overbusy and
overtired from all the responsibilities we have to carry,
we also find ourselves less lonely. We no longer have the
need to always be with others. Indeed, often the opposite is generally true, we begin to crave solitude. That is
because we now have intimacy in our lives, perhaps not
the emotional or sexual intimacy we crave in our daydreams, but we have real people who care for us, need
us, and rely on us.

That is generally less true for those who are young
and are working through those transition years of leaving the intimacy of their homes to try to establish a new
home for themselves. Despite all the friends, partying,
and electronic connections, this is often a time of fierce
loneliness: Who ultimately does love me? Will I meet my
soul mate? Whom will I marry? Who will be my family?
Who will be faithful to me?

The struggle to find intimacy, particularly the intimacy we once had in the security of home, is a huge part of the struggle to get our lives together and eventually to walk behind Jesus in discipleship.

v) Insubstantiality . . . the Struggle for Meaning, Personal Identity, Significance, and Self-Worth

A man I know who likes playing the court jester is fond of lamenting: "Life is hard for me because I have to deal with the *magnitude of me*!" I cite this quip because for all of us the opposite is forever true; we have to deal with the *insubstantiality of me*. We are not born into this life with a clear sense of who we are, an easy sense of self-worth, a solid sense of security, and a sure conviction that we are wanted, loved, and lovable. In biblical terms, we are born *anxious*.

Scripture scholars tell us that, for Jesus, the opposite of faith was not doubt or unbelief, but anxiety, being anxious. We see this, for instance, in the famous parable of the lilies of the field,[12] where Jesus invites us precisely beyond the anxiety that forever gnaws at us deep down and triggers in us the propensity to secure life for ourselves, to try to guarantee our own security, and to try to assure by our own efforts that we are lovable and have significance. One of our deepest struggles in life is dealing with the unconscious anxiety inside of us that pressures us to try to give ourselves significance and immortality. There is always the inchoate gnawing: do something to guarantee that something of your life will last. It is this propensity that tempts us to try to find meaning and significance through success and accumulation. But in the end it does not work, irrespective of how great our successes have been.

As scripture also tells us, only God can give us significance and immortality. Jesus teaches this everywhere, but nowhere is that message more clearly and more gently put than in an incident in the Gospels where his disciples come back from a mission full of joy and enthusiasm about the successes they had achieved and share their enthusiasm with Jesus. He shares in their joy, but then gently reminds them that their real joy should lie not in their successes, which are ephemeral and cannot always be achieved, but in the fact that their names are written in heaven, that God is giving them an eternal significance far deeper than any they can create for themselves through their achievements.[13]

However, that is not easy simply to accept, even for those who have achieved great things and found that those successes did not do for them what they had expected they would. And for a young person, insecure and still longing to achieve something of significance, this is a great struggle.

vi) Inchoate Moral Desire . . . the Struggle for Moral Rectitude

All of us, unless we are psychopaths or have been deeply corrupted, are incurably moral. Inside of us there is irrepressible pressure for moral rectitude. While this is strong in everyone, it is particularly strong in us when we are young and still idealistic, before our wounds begin to depress this energy and make us cynical. Sometimes, as for instance in the case of a bully or anyone who appears highly insensitive, it appears to be absent, but in these cases it has simply been unhealthily channeled.

However, like all the other fiery energies that heat up our bodies and emotions when we are young, this energy, if it is not properly initiated and directed to genuine, life-giving outlets, is dangerous inside a person. If this energy is not initiated and properly directed, the young person will be overly prone to get caught up in fads, in hype, in political correctness, in false religion or false politics, in cults, or worse still, in the type of things we see in mass shootings on university campuses and school yards, where the moral fervor of a person drives him to murder and suicide for some perverse moral reason.

We see misdirected, uninitiated moral fervor too in suicide bombers, when individuals believe that, by destroying innocent lives, they are being martyrs for God and truth. That is the ultimate analogate of misguided moral rectitude. But we all suffer from it to some degree, of which the countless moral indignations we swallow every time we listen to those who do not espouse our political or religious views should be enough to convince us. Everyone has a cause and everyone needs a cause because we have an irrepressible moral pressure inside. And for a young person, confused and struggling with a massive ball of fiery uninitiated energy inside him or her, dealing with that inchoate moral desire can be a huge struggle.

vii) Inchoate Nostalgia . . . to "Come Home," to Roots, to
Moral Companionship, to a Soul Mate, to Quiet,
to Solitude

In the end whether we know it or not, all of these struggles are about one thing, finding our way back home
again. What we all want at the end of the day is home,
ease, rest, someone to be comfortable with, someplace
to be comfortable in, a home, eternal rest. But as we saw,
this is not easy, especially for a young person who has
just left home and is unsure of where and with whom he
or she will again find home. The energies of our youth
drive us out, and in that restlessness we search in many
places, and sometimes, as the popular song has it, in all
the wrong places, for that home we have lost and are
trying again to find. But the point of the search is clear:
we are looking for a soul mate, for someone or something to take us home.

Initially, there is usually no sense of desperation; we
are young and the years still stretch endlessly ahead.
But eventually, a certain panic and desperation sets in,
which we feel more cruelly on weekends and around
major holidays when everyone else, it seems, has someplace to go and something exciting to do, and we are
painfully alone. Allow me to share a couple of stories to
help illustrate this.

My youngest brother tells this story: one Friday afternoon at his office, he and some coworkers were talking
about what they planned to do that evening, the beginning of the weekend. Several of his coworkers shared
how they planned to meet various friends and hit some

of the more trendy nightspots in the city. My brother, happily married for more than twenty-five years, shared rather timidly that he and his wife planned simply to order in some pizza and watch a movie together. "That must sound boring to you!" he volunteered. "Not at all," said one of the young, single women in his office. "We do all the things we do—restaurants, nightclubs, and the social scene—only so that sometime and, God willing, sooner rather than later, we can be where you are now, content at home on a Friday night, with pizza and a movie and someone to make a home with."

My second story is similar: some years ago, teaching a summer class at an American university, I assigned as reading material Christopher de Vinck's book *Only the Heart Knows How to Find Them: Precious Memories for a Faithless Time*.[14] The book is a series of wonderful, idealistic essays on the joys that he himself, a restless writer, has found in his marriage, with his wife and children, and in the quiet comfort of his own home. A week into the class, a young woman, about thirty years of age, walked into my office with de Vinck's book in her hand, tears in her eyes, and this story: "Father, I have lived a hot-blooded youth and have slept my way through a couple of states, always thinking that I was somehow finding and tasting life. But what I really want is what this man has! A home, someone to love me, a place of that kind of comfort!"

In short, that is the search for Essential Discipleship, the struggle to get our lives together. Deeper than our wanderlust and desire for adventure is the desire to find our way back home. Ultimately, we want the adventure only so that we can savor it and tell it around the fireplace at home.

Canadian poet Dennis Lee articulates the strength of our longing for home in a poem titled "Juniper and Bone."

Old momma teach me moonlight
Old momma teach me skin
Old momma teach me rhythm
When the ocean crashes in

And take me to the heartland
And teach me how to fear
Old momma teach me hunger
At the turning of the year

Old momma teach me music
Made of juniper and bone
Old momma teach me silence
To the certainty of stone.[15]

The Temptations That Beset Us on the Journey

Youthful energies bring with them a bevy of temptations. Most of these are obvious: the desire for pleasure, sex, affluence, power, and freedom. Inside of every young person there is a prodigal son or a prodigal daughter just itching to set out on a journey away from the Father's house. For most of us, moral and psychological sensitivities keep that itch mostly in check, but we would be

lying if we said that we did not have powerful temptations in other directions. Youth will be youth, and many
of its struggles are more than sufficiently documented.
But today, certainly within secularized cultures, *two*
particular struggles might be highlighted:

First, as already mentioned, is the fact that so many
of our youth struggle with commitment. The reasons
for this are many and complex. It is too simple to blame
it all on a false notion of community and freedom since
many young people are very communitarian and, of-
tentimes more so than middle-aged and older persons,
want constant companionship and someone ever present with them. The problem lies more in an overstimulated restlessness and grandiosity that makes choosing,
at least in terms of permanent commitment, very difficult. We all struggle to "will the one thing."[16] As Henri
Nouwen so graphically put it: We want to be saints but
we also want to experience all the sensations that sinners experience.[17] In youth the struggle to "will the one
thing" often takes on a particular difficulty around the
issue of permanent commitment.

Second, perhaps more true inside of highly secularized cultures than elsewhere, youth today struggle with
something that might be termed the *puer-syndrome* or
puella-syndrome (*puer* and *puella* being the Latin terms
for *boy* and *girl*). Inside of some analytic circles these
terms have taken on the connotation of the "eternal
boy," Peter Pan, and the "eternal girl," Tinkerbell. Indeed, today many of us have as our ideal of adulthood:
the eternal boy, forever youthful and swinging free and

noncommitted through the skies; and the eternal girl, forever free of body fat and stretch marks, perpetually turning heads as she walks into a room. Adulthood is not identified with being an elder, a parent, a grandparent, or any duty-bound adult, with gray hair, body fat, stretch marks, and responsibilities that, many days, weigh so heavily on one's time and energy so as to push one's looks and personal development a little further down the agenda.[18]

Simply put, there are many pressures inside of our culture today that want to keep us forever young, forever free, and forever the adolescent in a way that prevents us from ever fully growing up, from making the transition from adolescent to elder. So often boys remain boys, not men, and girls remain girls, not women. That is the not-so-subtle ethos of most secularized cultures, and it is strongly, often unhealthily, promoted and reinforced by the fashion industry and Hollywood (where the leading stars are growing ever younger and ever slimmer, or at least are being projected in that light). And that leaves us with a problem: Peter Pan and Tinkerbell are, in the end, children who never carry any responsibilities or carry anybody or anything beyond their own youthful bodies. Mature adults carry the young, and they also carry all the responsibilities that make our families, communities, neighborhoods, churches, and governments work. It's the wisdom of God and nature that eventually makes for gray hair, body fat, and stretch marks, all of which are a struggle for many of our youth today.

Robert L. Moore, an expert in both psychoanalysis and spirituality, has brilliantly dissected this, showing how today the ideal images for self-understanding for both men and women are no longer the classical, archetypal ideals of adulthood, namely, being an *elder*, a *knight*, a *magus*, and a *lover*. Instead, too often, our ideal is the adolescent version of these archetypes: rather than being an *elder*, an adult parent or grandparent, we want to be the *admired child*; rather than being the *knight*, who is a team player and puts his sword and muscle at the service of the king, we want to be the *hero*, singularly admired and singularly defining the cause; rather than being a *magus*, positively contributing our intelligence to the community, we want to be the *trickster*, the immature iconoclast, the cynical wit whose intelligence is forever baffling the community or mocking it; and rather than being the mature *lover*, who can create delight for others and be a life-giving friend, we want to be the *adolescent romantic*, whose personal loneliness trumps everything else.[19]

It is not easy making the transition from adolescence to adulthood. Many temptations lure us off that path. Fortunately, though, nature and God are persistent and lay their own traps and enticements to lure us into adulthood. Puberty drives us out of our first home, and though it may take ten or twenty years, most of us eventually find our way back home again, to a new home, one that we have created for ourselves. What does that new home look and feel like? That will be described in detail in the next chapter. The purpose of this chapter has been more to name and describe the struggle to get there—the struggle to get our lives together and begin to walk behind Jesus in essential discipleship.

A Brief Overview of Essential Discipleship

Up to this point, I have been using mainly the language of the human sciences to describe our struggle to get our lives together. We will now shift languages and try to describe that same struggle in religious and Christian terms. How do we struggle to get our lives together religiously? How do we struggle to become essential (if not yet fully mature) disciples of Christ?[20]

The answer to that will be brief here since my entire book *The Holy Longing* is an attempt to lay out the fundamentals of Christian discipleship. I will not try to summarize all that is contained there, but rather simply try to name again the key elements of an essential discipleship of Christ.

So we can ask ourselves, at what point are we following Christ essentially? If we were brought to trial in a court of law and accused of being a Christian, what characteristics would we have to exhibit for there to be enough evidence to convict us? That is an important question because today there is much confusion about what lies at the center of the practice of the Christian faith and what lies at the periphery, about what is negotiable and what is demanded, about what is essential and what is accidental. What are the essentials of a basic Christian discipleship?

As stated and elaborated in *The Holy Longing*, a healthy following of Christ will rest on four foundational pillars.[21] These are revealed clearly in the Gospels and are prescribed by Jesus and the other New Testament writers as nonnegotiable demands of Christian discipleship. At one point in his ministry, Jesus puts the demands for following him into a simple formula: *pray, fast, and give alms.*[22] However these elements, named as the essentials of discipleship, must be understood in the way he meant them. For Jesus, prayer meant not just praying privately but also keeping the commandments and being involved in some kind of communitarian prayer, the celebration of his word and the Eucharist. Fasting meant an asceticism that included a fasting from bitterness of heart. And alms giving meant justice as well as charity. Hence, if we unpack more fully what is contained in Jesus' formula for discipleship, we can name four constitutive elements: i) *private prayer and private integrity*; ii) *charity and justice*; iii) *involvement within an ecclesial community*; and iv) *forgiveness and mellowness of heart.*

What, in essence, does Jesus ask of us apposite to each of these?

i) Private Prayer and Private Integrity

In spelling out the demands of discipleship, Jesus clearly asks several things of us: first, that we have a relationship to both his Father and to him "in secret," in private.[23] Obviously, to establish and maintain that, we will need to pray, honestly and deeply, in private. This invitation is everywhere in the Gospels and is everywhere present in all the Christian churches. As Christians, we are asked to cultivate an intimacy with Jesus, in private, as the ultimate basis for our Christian discipleship. This has taken on special emphases within the mystical tradition within Christianity, within Roman Catholic devotional practices, and within Evangelical churches in their insistence on the centrality of a personal relationship to Jesus Christ. But it is everywhere present in Christian theology and spirituality. Moreover, it is especially present in the Gospel of John as one of the major themes of his entire gospel. For John, intimacy with Jesus, as portrayed in the "beloved disciple," trumps everything else in terms of discipleship. No serious Christian scholar or pastor questions the centrality of this invitation from Jesus, even as some scholars and pastors fear that this is sometimes overemphasized, to the detriment of other aspects of discipleship. The reverse fear, of course, is also well-founded; in some churches and in some circles of spirituality there is an insufficient emphasis on private prayer and private morality.

Second, tied to Jesus' invitation to meet him in private in the depths of our hearts, is the concomitant invitation to keep the private depths of our hearts honest and integral. Simply stated, Jesus tells us that "if anyone loves me, he or she will keep my commandments."[24] In the Gospels, fidelity to keeping the commandments is one of the major criteria to discern whether or not our private prayer is real or whether it is an illusion, or, worse still, a form of rationalization. Our prayer is honest only when our lives back it up.

Hence, we are essentially following Jesus only when, among other things, in our lives there is some regular effort at private prayer and that effort is matched by a regular effort to keep the commandments and keep our private morals intact. Private prayer and private morality are one of the nonnegotiable demands inherent within Christian discipleship.

ii) Charity and Justice

Jesus' human origins lie in Judaism, and he stood and taught within their prophetic tradition of charity and justice. Hundreds of years before his birth, the great Jewish prophets had already coined this mantra: "The quality of your faith will be judged by the quality of justice in the land; and the quality of justice in the land will be judged by how the weakest and most vulnerable groups in society ('widows, orphans, and strangers') fared while you were alive." Jesus inherited a religious tradition that already emphasized outreach and actions to the poor as a nonnegotiable demand within any true religious practice. The idea was that our standing with God depended not just on our private prayer and integrity but also on how we stand with the poor. Indeed, the Jewish prophets made it clear that God favored the poor.

Jesus took this even further. He endorsed the idea that God favors the poor,[25] but added the notion that God is *in* the poor, that we meet God in the poor, and that how we treat the poor is (with no escape clauses) how we treat him.[26] In effect, Jesus told us that nobody will get to heaven without a letter of reference from the poor.[27] This, although clear in the Gospels and in the Jewish scriptures, is often either misunderstood or rejected by many sincere Christians.

Jesus' invitation that his disciples be both charitable and just is commonly misunderstood or, perhaps more accurately stated, is *under*-understood. How so? What Jesus asks of us here is not just that we be generous of heart and give in charity to the poor, though he does ask for that. He asks for more. Charity, as we know, can sometimes operate independently of justice, especially of social justice. Jesus does not just ask us to give in charity to the poor, he also asks us to work at correcting all the social, political, and economic structures that disadvantage the poor and help keep them poor.[28] Charity seeks to give directly to the poor so as to help alleviate their poverty, Justice seeks to correct the structures that help create that poverty. And Jesus asks us to do both.

For a variety of reasons, many sincere Christians struggle to accept the latter part of that challenge, namely, that private charity alone is not enough and that Jesus asks us also to work at social justice. Why the struggle? Because social justice always has direct political and economic implications so that it can never be fully extricated from political and social ideologies, and this embedding forever leaves it as less than pure. However, despite that perennial handicap, it must still be accepted as part of Jesus' nonnegotiable demands for discipleship. Indeed, it is sobering to note that scripture scholars point out that in the Christian scriptures, one out of every ten lines deals directly with the physically poor and the challenge to respond to them. In the Gospel of Luke, that becomes every sixth line, and in the Epistle of James that challenge is there, in one form or another, in every fifth line. It is impossible to ignore that following Jesus demands that we practice both charity and justice, and this demand is just as nonnegotiable as is the demand of private prayer and private integrity. Evolution works through this principle: the survival of the fittest. One of the essential elements of Christian discipleship demands that we work for this principle: the survival of the weakest and the gentlest.

iii) Involvement Within an Ecclesial Community

Christianity is constitutively communal. Jesus calls us to follow him not just as individuals but also in a community. Indeed, the community itself forms part of Christ's body and how we relate to one another is as important as how we relate to God. For Jesus, the two great commandments—to love God and to love each other—form one whole, so that it is impossible to say with validity: I love God, but hate my brother or sister.[29]

And loving one another is not an abstract thing for Christians. At a point it means praying together, worshipping together, having fellowship with one another, working with one another to be of service to the poor and to the world in general, and considering one another brothers and sisters. In a word, that means church. Christianity is constitutively communal, and that means it is also constitutively ecclesial. For Christianity, community is part of its essence. Simply put, Christian discipleship is not something that you can do alone; it is something that you do with others, inside a community. One cannot be a disciple of Jesus and say: "I'm a Christian, but I can pray just as well at home!" Christian discipleship demands community, ecclesiology, church. The search for the Christian God is not just a private quest but is a communal endeavor, and that means being a disciple of Jesus always demands connection with some concrete historical community, a church.

This, of course, is a struggle for many people today, as is evident in the growing separation between ecclesiology and spirituality, where more and more people are searching for God but want little or nothing to do with their churches. There are many reasons why this is happening, ranging from the excessive individualism within our cultures to a lot of dissatisfaction with our churches, but however weighty the reason, the attempt to walk the road of Christian discipleship alone or on our own terms leaves us limping badly in following the footsteps of Jesus. Being with others regularly, within a community of worship, fellowship, and service is one of the essential, nonnegotiable elements of Christian discipleship.

iv) Forgiveness and Mellowness of Heart

"The last temptation is the greatest treason, to do the right deed for the wrong reason."[30] Those are words from T. S. Eliot, and they aptly describe a major challenge in Christian discipleship: we must do the right things, but we must also do them for the right reasons. Essential Christian discipleship asks that we have a private relationship to Jesus, that our private lives reflect that relationship, that we practice both charity and justice, that we be involved in some ecclesial community, and also that we do all of these things with a mellow, forgiving heart.

We can see what is at stake here by looking at the older brother of the prodigal son. On the surface his devotion to his father lacks nothing, as is evident in his bemoaning the celebration being given for his younger brother. He protests that his own life is blameless and a paradigm of filial devotion. He has kept all the commandments, has never left his father's house, and has done all the required work. The irony is that he fails to notice that he is not, in fact, *inside* his father's house, but is standing outside of it and being gently invited in by his father. What is keeping him outside, since, after all, he is doing everything correctly? Bitterness and anger. A bitter, unforgiving heart is just as much a blockage to entering God's house as is any moral transgression. We can be scrupulously faithful and still find ourselves standing outside of God's house and outside the circle of community and celebration because of a bitter heart. To be a saint is to be fueled by gratitude, nothing less. Christian discipleship is as much about having a mellow and forgiving heart as it is about believing and doing the right things. But this is not an easy thing to accept.

Irrespective of our ecclesial or political ideology and

ethos, liberal or conservative, we all tend to write off this demand as a nonnegotiable in regards to Christian discipleship. Invariably, we tend to rationalize it away by pointing to the weight and urgency of our causes, be they dogmatic or moral. We see this, in its worst example, in suicide bombers, who are religiously convinced that their cause is so important that they can be martyrs, for God, by destroying dozens or perhaps even thousands of innocent lives. When the case is this extreme, we see more easily what misguided religious fervor looks like and how important religiously it is to have a mellow and forgiving heart. But we are not as perceptive in seeing the rationalizing suicide bomber inside ourselves when, for the sake of God and truth, our own religious and political discourse is laced with bitterness, anger, jealousy, demonization, lack of respect, lack of graciousness, and lack of elementary Christian and human charity. We also tend not to recognize it in the embittered moralizing that sometimes emanates from our ecclesial communities. A mellow and gracious heart is not a negotiable Christian virtue. It is an essential demand of Christian discipleship.

We began this section by asking the question: How do we struggle to get our lives together religiously and in terms of Christian discipleship? The fiery energies of youth, particularly in a highly secularized culture and inside an historical situation within which the Christian churches have not always lived up to their own ideals, will not always find or clearly distinguish the essentials of Christian discipleship and will often struggle as well to accept them and acquiesce to them, even if they are found. The struggle from puberty to adulthood is a mammoth one, religiously as well as anthropologically.

Some Guidance from a Spiritual Master for Making This Journey

John of the Cross, the great Spanish mystic, in a very succinct passage in his book *The Ascent of Mount Carmel*,[31] offers five valuable counsels that he suggests will help, in effect, move someone from immaturity to maturity. To better grasp the meaning of these counsels, however, it can be helpful to extrapolate them from their rather narrow historical context and reset them into a wider setting, our own lives today. John wrote these counsels for professional contemplatives, monks and nuns, who were trying to grow more mature in their lives, primarily through the exercise of prayer. For 99 percent of us, that is not our context, both in that we are not living in monasteries and in the fact that our primary duty in life is not formal prayer. Hence, in reading John of the Cross, and many other spiritual classics from the desert and monastic traditions, we need to keep that in mind.

What are John's five counsels?

    i)   His first counsel is that we should study the life of Christ, meditate on it, and try in every way to bring our own lives into conformity with his teachings.

ii) His second counsel is that we then try, more deeply, to imitate Christ by striving to imitate his motivation. Our actions are less important than is the reason that we do them. Christ acted not because it brought him pleasure or ultimately enhanced his own life; he acted for a higher reason: to do his Father's will, to try to bring more life into other peoples' lives. That too must become our motivation.

iii) After we have made the decision to try to imitate Christ's motivation, the third counsel invites us to discern whether we are or are not rationalizing by seeing if the same difficulties and pains that flowed into Christ's life begin to flow into our own. Hence, John cautions us to be suspicious if the cross of Christ does not begin to find us.

iv) His fourth counsel invites us to relativize ourselves by no longer giving in to our natural instinct to seek to be the center of attention. For John, we move toward maturity by striving to be a listener rather than the one seeking to be listened to, by striving to give our attention to others rather than seeking to be the center of attention, and by striving to be the one who is blessing others rather than being the one seeking the blessing.

v) Finally, his fifth counsel, much in the line of the famous Prayer of Francis of Assisi, invites us to move toward maturity by a dialectical road. The poem he writes as an invitation to this is self-explanatory:

To reach satisfaction in all
desire satisfaction in nothing.
To come to possess all
desire the possession of nothing.
To arrive at being all
desire to be nothing.
To come to the knowledge of all
desire the knowledge of nothing.

To come to enjoy what you have not
you must go by a way in which you enjoy not.
To come to the knowledge you have not
you must go by a way in which you know not.
To come to the possession what you have not
you must go by a way in which you possess not.
To come to be what you are not
you must go by a way in which you are not.[32]

A Brief Synopsis

The journey, both anthropological and spiritual, from puberty to adulthood is meant not just to bring us home again, but it is also meant to bring us to initial maturity. But how might initial maturity be defined, both in human and in Christian terms?

In human terms, initial maturity might be defined as having broken the pleasure principle as the basic source of motivation in our lives so that, now, our motivation for acting is more for the good of others than for ourselves.[33] When we reach that stage, we cross, as we saw, a threshold where a basic default line in us shifts from *struggling to get our lives together* to *struggling to give our lives away.* The journey to cross that threshold is our first, great anthropological struggle in life, and it begins in earnest at puberty and ends on that day when our motivation for doing things is more concerned with others than with ourselves.

Religiously, in terms of Christian discipleship, initial maturity might be defined as having drunk in the person and teachings of Jesus to a sufficient degree that we struggle, within the limits of our present lives, to cultivate a personal relationship to him, keep our moral lives essentially in line with his teaching, practice both charity and justice in our lives, have some kind of regular involvement within an ecclesial community, and work with some deliberateness to keep our hearts mellow, gracious, and forgiving. The journey toward that goal also takes on a special poignancy at puberty and ends when the fiery energies of our youth bend, at least in essence, to the essential demands of Christian discipleship.

And that lands us on a new shore, with a new task, and with a new struggle, namely, adult discipleship and the struggle to give our lives away.

Part Two

MATURE DISCIPLESHIP: THE STRUGGLE TO GIVE OUR LIVES AWAY

As Jesus and his disciples were on their way, he came to a village where a woman named Martha opened her home to him. She had a sister called Mary, who sat at the Lord's feet listening to what he said. But Martha was distracted by all the preparations that had to be made. She came to him and asked, "Lord, don't you care that my sister has left me to do the work by myself? Tell her to help me!" "Martha, Martha," the Lord answered, "you are worried and upset about many things, but only one thing is needed. Mary has chosen what is better, and it will not be taken away from her."[1]

If you can't get out of something, get more deeply into it!

SOME PERSPECTIVES FROM CLASSICAL SPIRITUALITY AND THE HUMAN SCIENCES

Not even Jesus found "the ready."

Jesus called Nathaniel . . . Nathaniel lacked openness. Nathaniel wasn't ready.

Jesus called Philip . . . Philip lacked simplicity. Philip wasn't ready.

Jesus called Simon, the Zealot . . . Simon lacked non-violence. Simon wasn't ready.

Jesus called Andrew . . . Andrew lacked a sense of risk. Andrew wasn't ready.

Jesus called Thomas . . . Thomas lacked vision. Thomas wasn't ready.

Jesus called Judas . . . Judas lacked spiritual maturity. Judas was definitely not ready.

Jesus called Matthew . . . Matthew lacked a sense of social sin. Matthew wasn't ready.

Jesus called Thaddeus . . . Thaddeus lacked commitment. Thaddeus wasn't ready.

Jesus called James the Lesser . . . James lacked awareness. James wasn't ready.

Jesus called James and John, the sons of thunder . . .
James and John lacked a sense of servanthood.
James and John were not ready.
Jesus called Peter, the Rock . . . Peter lacked courage.
Peter was not ready . . . .

The point, you see, is that Jesus doesn't call the
ready. Jesus calls the willing.[2]

A New Task and a New Struggle

Jesus doesn't call the ready; he calls the willing! That is a consoling thought because the heavy responsibilities of adulthood and the narrow gate of discipleship generally call us before we are really ready. Thankfully, we are at least somewhat willing because maturity is often imposed on us by conscription, as the circumstances and responsibilities of our lives drag us protesting into generosity and adulthood. And so it happens that at some stage of our lives, often when we are still in our twenties, we find ourselves shouldering a whole series of adult responsibilities, carrying the load, as the ones who have to raise the young, do the work, pay the bills, and make sure the planet keeps running. Like Martha in scripture, we are in charge of the hospitality and of cooking the supper. Moreover, when we look ahead, we see that this will be the situation, and our situation, for the next forty to sixty years, the longest period of our lives.

This season of our lives, all those years when the work and responsibilities land on our shoulders, is meant to be the life-giving season of our lives, the time where we give our lives away in love and service as spouses, parents, grandparents, uncles, aunts, godparents, providers, teachers, pastors, and supportive friends. This is the second level or phase of discipleship, Mature Discipleship. Classical mystical writings call this phase of our lives and discipleship "proficiency"[3]; suggesting that we are now proficient, essentially at least, at life and at spirituality. Those same writings go on to say that during all those years of proficiency the question that drives our lives and our energies needs to be focused beyond ourselves and beyond our own struggle for identity, meaning, and comfort. The question that drives our lives needs then to be: How do I now give my life away more generously and more purely? How do I do this better? Living for something beyond ourselves is what is being asked of us during all these years. But we are rarely ready. It is comforting to know we need only be willing!

This chapter will attempt two things: it will provide some images for self-understanding for this phase of our lives, and then, at greater length, it will name and examine the major demons we wrestle with during this time. It will draw mainly upon anthropological and psychological perspectives, though insights from the classical mystical tradition, particularly from John of the Cross, will also be utilized. Subsequent chapters, indeed the rest of this book, will deal explicitly with the Christian challenges that meet us there.

How might Mature Discipleship be defined? What is the struggle to "give our lives away"?

Images for the Struggle

Biblically, the prototype for Mature Discipleship is the active ministry of Jesus, though we can single out some salient incidents, such as his washing his disciples' feet at the Last Supper, as particularly illustrative of what it means to give your life away. *Anthropologically,* mature living is identified with being an *elder,* with being someone who helps carry life rather than with being a child or a student who still needs to be carried.

Though the focus of this book is on Christian life, Hindu spirituality, ancient and rich, offers a valuable paradigm within which to understand Mature Discipleship. It understands life as having five basic stages: (i) First, we are a "child," and our task then is to play, learn a language, and learn proper respect and manners. (ii) Childhood ends when we become a "student"; and this, for Hinduism, refers to all the years that we spend in preparation for marriage and a career. (iii) We cease being a student when, through marriage or a career, or both, we take on adult responsibilities and become a "householder," that is, someone whose task it now is to live for others. (iv) We remain a householder until our later midlife when, at about the time we become grand-parents, the invitation is to become a "forest dweller," namely, someone who graduates from the responsibilities of being the provider, the one who shoulders all the responsibilities for the family and the community, to someone who now withdraws from fully active life to do inner work so as to discern how he or she wants to spend the final years of his or her life and how to prepare for that. (v) The last stage of life in Hindu spirituality is the stage of becoming a "sannyasin," a holy beggar, namely, someone who has in effect dropped out of normal life and now lives a life of extreme simplicity and radical dependence upon others for his or her livelihood.[4]

Mature Discipleship: What It Looks and Feels Like

The mature stage of our lives is easy to describe since most everyone who is reading this is probably in that stage of life. Essentially, it looks like this: you are now a "householder" in that you have a home, a status, a family, a mortgage, a career, a vocation, and a whole—often crushing—series of responsibilities and duties. If you are through your years of searching for and preparing for marriage and a career, you are in the mature, life-giving stage of your life.

What does that feel like? On the surface it can feel pretty bland, or flat, or overpressured, or disappointing, so that, reflectively, we do not feel very much at all, out-

side of longing for a vacation away from all the responsibilities and duties that beset us. But more deeply, as we
go through those years, what ultimately lies underneath
in terms of our inner energies?

Despite all of the things we wrestle with, and these will
be described shortly, if someone were to photograph our
deepest insides, we would look surprisingly good. What
that photo would reveal is that the pleasure principle, as
the source of our motivation, still makes itself strongly
felt, but it is no longer the ultimate decision-making voice
inside of us. Higher concerns now trump the pleasure
principle, at least in our major decisions, and there is a
healthy anxiety inside us about contributing something
to make our families, our churches, and our world better.
The photo would also reveal that, despite the dissatisfac-
tions and frustrations in our lives, we have an essential
identity, we know who we are, and we (unless we are
acting out in infidelity) have an essentially integrated
sexuality, namely, one that lets us sleep at night and stay
within our commitments during the day. And finally, the
photo would reveal that, despite all the restlessness that
still gnaws away inside of us and despite all the efforts we
make at keeping ourselves young, we have an essential
life-giving capacity beyond adolescent self-focus, and we
are basically comfortable beyond the tumultuous restlessness of youth. We can sit home in relative calm with pizza
and popcorn on a Friday night. The photo would show
that, essentially, we have found a home. However, if the
camera went yet deeper, it would reveal that, beneath this
essential comfort, there is an inchoate, nagging disquiet

that is just stirring enough to let us know that someday, though not quite yet, there are still some deeper things to sort out and a deeper journey to be made.

That is the good news! But there is an underside, like an iceberg. The part that appears above the surface is impressive, but there is so much more to explore if we penetrate the depths. This can be exciting. And it can be dangerous. What is the other side of the picture? What are the demons that perennially beset us during the adult years of our lives?

The Long Loneliness—The Struggles of Life-Giving Adults

James Hillman once said that a symptom suffers most when it doesn't know where it belongs![5] That is just as true for our emotional and spiritual ailments as it is for our physical ones. It can be hugely helpful for our self-understanding to have the things that ail us be properly named and put into proper perspective. One of the things that made Henri Nouwen such a powerful spiritual writer is that he was able to shine a flashlight into his own personal struggles and then describe those struggles in a way that let his readers name and bring to light their own deep and sometimes shameful struggles. Good spiritual writing, among other things, should help introduce us to ourselves.

With this in mind, let us attempt to name and describe the major struggles that come with the territory as we live through the long years of maturity. When the classical mystics describe the struggle of *proficients,* they highlight six particular demons that beset us during this time.

i) Some Lingering Canaanites: A Partially Unbroken Pleasure Principle That Wants Revenge

Mature Discipleship is predicated on having, essentially, broken the pleasure principle as the basic source of motivation in our lives; but "essentially broken" does not, at least in this life, ever mean completely broken. Selfishness, narcissism, and the idiosyncratic preference never fully go away. Beaten back by the maturity we have found to base our decisions upon something beyond our own advantage, the pleasure principle goes underground, takes on new guises, and asserts itself in subtler garb. But it is always there waiting to recapture its old ground.

The Jewish scriptures give us a rich metaphor for this, the image of having to kill off all the Canaanites after having taken the Promised Land. On the surface, the text reads this way: Israel, after having conquered the Promised Land, is asked by God to kill all the original inhabitants of the land, the Canaanites. Taken literally, this is a horrible command, one that would erase our very concept of God's goodness and impartiality. God, seemingly, commands the Israelites to kill every Canaanite in the land—including all the women and the children, and even their cattle and domestic pets. Does God actually do this?

Clearly, this must be read metaphorically and archetypally. Nobody really dies in a metaphor. This is a drama that is meant to take place inside the soul of every person once one has converted and begins to move into one's new life, the Promised Land. The "Canaanites" are a metaphor for one's old life and one's old habits. Unless they are killed off, every one of them, they will regroup and eventually recapture our souls. People in Alcoholics Anonymous programs easily understand this: if you hope to keep your sobriety you need to clean out your liquor cabinet of all the Canaanites—all the beer, all the scotch, all the bourbon, all the gin, all the rye, and all the brandies. You cannot keep drinking even one of them. The Jewish scriptures simply give us this metaphor inside a hard image. Jesus employs the same metaphor inside a softer image: new wine needs new wineskins!

Classical spiritual writers warn us that, after we have broken the pleasure principle and reached a mature level of discipleship, the old temptations will resurface with a vengeance, just in subtler forms. Put metaphorically, the Canaanites will forever be trying to take back the Promised Land, namely, our maturity. Forewarned is forearmed.

What dangers do they warn us most specifically about here?

Their first warning concerns the danger of reverting to immaturity because of the longing for another honeymoon. Our route to maturity generally involves a honeymoon or two. Honeymoons are real, are powerful, and afford us, this side of eternity, with one of the better foretastes of heaven. Because of that, they are not easy to let go of permanently. Inside of every one of us there is the lingering itch to experience that kind of intensity yet one more time, and that itch is made stronger by the fact that our commitments, including our marriage, can often seem bland and flat when measured against the intensity of a honeymoon. One of the demons that we must wrestle with after we have made lifelong commitments is the powerful temptation to experience yet another honeymoon. Infidelity in marriage, among other things, is often triggered by this temptation.

Contemporary psychology has its own insights to contribute here. It warns of a number of things that can derail our maturity and send us back into a new adolescence; but, instead of speaking of yearning for a second honeymoon, it speaks of midlife crisis.

As well, sexuality remains an issue. A marriage commitment, a religious vow of celibacy, or a private commitment in conscience to keep our sexuality within moral and Christian bounds does not take away the raw, relentless power of sexuality. Despite our maturity, it will always make itself felt. For many of us this will not necessarily take the form of some overt sexual acting out, such as engaging in an affair or masturbation, or viewing pornography. Indeed for many, as we age, the press of our sexuality will not even be felt very strongly, or at all, as explicit sexual desire. But the pressure of our sexuality will always be there, and if it is not consciously dealt with, it will show itself in its shadow in some form: in the

misuse of power, in bitterness and anger, in some drinking or eating disorder, in embittered moralizing about
sex, in a denial and an unhealthy fear of sex, or, quite
commonly, in a depression where one's sexual thermostat
is simply turned off so that we no longer feel any genuine
delight in our gender or sexuality, or in life in general.

Moreover, our sexuality presents us with yet another
problem during our adult years. We are psychosomatic
creatures, not pure spirits. And so what happens inside
of our minds and hearts and souls strongly affects what
happens inside of our bodies and our sexuality. There
are some cryptic lines that appear a number of times in
the writings of John of the Cross that warn us that as
we grow spiritually "the spirit will begin to flow into
the senses."[6] What this means is that as we go about
our relationships and everyday activities in our adult
years, our grandiosity is either being stimulated, when
we meet warmth and affirmation, or depressed, when
we meet coldness and rejection. In either case, what we
feel will not just stimulate or depress our minds; it will
do the same thing to our bodies and sexuality. Our relationships and activities, even when we are mature and
committed, will still, perennially, stimulate or depress
us so as to have a strong effect on our bodies and on
our sexuality.

What does that look like? For some of us this will
make itself felt as the perennial temptation to temper-
amental promiscuity, namely, the propensity to fall in
love with many different people, even as we are techni-
cally faithful in our commitments; for others this will

trigger temptations to act out in some sexual way; for still others it will lead to professional dishonesty in that situations that in truth satisfy some sexual need are defined as pastoral or professional; and, for some, denial will kick in and we will not recognize or accept these feelings as in any way sexual but will abandon them to work themselves out unconsciously in unhealthy ways, leaving us to deal with the consequence, some form of depression. Naïveté is not our friend here.

Moreover, there is a particular danger here for those who, whatever their vocation or profession, are so successful that they receive huge doses of affirmation, privately and publicly. Almost daily the media will tell us yet one more story of some major religious figure, or politician, or rock star, or athlete whose sexual acting out has led to a fall from grace. We might be more sympathetic than gleeful. The spirit flows into the senses. So much adulation, if not grounded in some healthy way, will invariably overstimulate a person's grandiosity and, with that, his or her sexuality. The dangers here are many, and not just for celebrity religious and public figures, but for all of us. Again, naïveté and denial are not our friends here. Unlike celebrities, sexuality never leaves the room.

ii) The Death of the Honeymoon—a New Kind of Loneliness

In our adolescent years we are lonely, but that loneliness is still part of an innocence, idealism, and yearning that believes that someday we will find a great love who will

take our loneliness away. That yearning drives us out-
ward, and when we do find love, during the course of
the honeymoon, it does take our loneliness away. But all
honeymoons end, not because they are unreal or false,
but because they eventually do their work. The death
of our honeymoon strips us of an illusion and shows us
what lives behind it, genuine reality and real limit. This
triggers a number of deep changes inside us. What happens here?[7]

Simply put, during a honeymoon, we are not truly in
love with an individual person; we are in love with love
itself, with the powerful energies love is releasing inside
us, and with the archetypal energy being carried by the
person with whom we are honeymooning. For example,
the young Jack who falls in love with the young Jennifer
is not, at this stage, in love with her, though he thinks
and feels he is. He is in love with love itself and with
the archetype of femininity that Jennifer is carrying. In
effect, in loving her he is loving all women, is loving
femininity itself, and is loving half of the Godhead. For
this reason, at this time in his life, Jennifer is enough
for him. She can take away his loneliness because she is
carrying half the human race and half of God.

But in the end, Jennifer is just a singular individual
woman, perhaps even an exceptional and noble one.
She, all alone, cannot carry all that Jack is seeing in her,
all femininity and half the Godhead. She alone cannot
take another person's loneliness away. Thus, no matter how good the honeymoon and no matter how good
Jennifer, eventually reality will break through and Jack

will see and realize that he married one, singular, limited human being—Jennifer, not femininity and half of God. This will necessarily cause a certain amount of disillusionment in him which, while laden with some dangers, is a good thing. He has not fallen out of love with Jennifer, but with his own fantasy of love, though he may well confuse the two. The upside is that, for the first time in his life, he is seeing Jennifer as she is, as her own person, with both her goodness and her faults, the archetypal energies she carries and her very real limits. At this point, as opposed to the honeymoon, *love becomes a decision*, which means that Jack, should he choose now in the clear light of day to recommit himself to Jennifer, is acting, perhaps for the first time in his life, for value itself, for something beyond the idiosyncratic preference, for something beyond himself. That is a new level of maturity or, more accurately, the real beginning of maturity.

But this will bring with it a new loneliness, that of seeing and accepting the actual limits of our own lives, a pain intertwined with accepting our own mortality. When the honeymoon dies, the big dream is over and we realize that we can defy gravity and make love to the whole world only in our dreams, because, in reality, our lives come down to this singular person, this singular family, this one city, this too-small house, this less-than-fulfilling job, this irritating mortgage, these nonfamous friends, and this less-than-perfect body. Reality has broken through, and we see a very limited horizon at the end of the tunnel.

That realization will bring with it a nur
tations. We have already spoken of the lo
ond honeymoon. That temptation will now
Psychologists speak of the midlife crisis. That tou
now be a tempting invitation. Classical mystical writers
highlight boredom and having to settle into dour duty
as the particular demons that will beset us during the
long years of generativity. Indeed, John of the Cross says
repeatedly that, after our honeymoon, be it a honeymoon in either emotional or religious fervor, for many
of us, our single greatest struggle during our adult years
will be with simple boredom and lack of excitement and
emotional stimulation in our lives. Honeymoons are
stimulating, but we go home from them. Home might
bring its security and comforts, but it cannot match the
excitement of a honeymoon, especially during some of
its most duty-bound seasons. Mature Discipleship provides us with a lot more stability than excitement. The
long years of being the responsible, duty-bound Martha
bring with them their own kind of loneliness and their
own particular temptations.[8]

iii) Resentment of Duty and a Joylessness Bordering on Anger

The years of our maturity are the heavy working years
of our lives. These are the years, as has already been
stated, when the major responsibilities fall on our shoulders. Like the biblical Martha, the supper gets cooked
only if we do the cooking and the mortgage gets paid
only if we earn the money. We are in charge. We are

responsible. We carry the car keys, the house keys, and the debt for both. The major load is on our shoulders, and sometimes it feels as if we are on a treadmill with no way of stepping off. Consequently, all too often, despite the privilege of being young, being healthy, and being in charge, it is easy to feel burdened, taken for granted, unappreciated, and used by others. Like Martha in scripture, it is easy to feel resentment because we seem to be doing all the work while others are getting more of a free ride.

That is the feeling that can weigh us down for long periods during our adult years, and can make us fall asleep to something that we will wake up to only when it is too late, namely, that these years when we are young and healthy and in charge are the best years of our lives. There is something worse than having too much to do, and that is having nothing to do or too little to do of importance. We will be a lot more awake to that fact when we sit in a retirement home, stripped of youth, health, and our car keys, knowing that all those years when we thought we were being taken for granted were years of privilege that were laden with a potential for joy that—because of our unawareness of privilege—we never quite picked up on.

If you had your life to live over again, would you do anything different? We all know accounts of people who, in retirement, were asked this question and replied that, given the chance again, they would try to enjoy it more. Many are the persons who deeply regret that during the healthiest and most productive years of their lives they were too driven and too unaware of the richness of their own lives to appreciate and enjoy what they were doing. Instead of privilege, they felt burden; instead of gratitude, they felt resentment; and instead of joy, they felt anger. One of the demons we wrestle with during our adult years is the resentment of Martha, that is, a joylessness bordering on anger for, ironically, being burdened with the privilege of health, work, and status. Vincent de Paul is reported to have once said: It is more blessed to give than to receive—and it is also a lot easier. That is not something we generally appreciate during the tiring years when we are trying to live selfless lives.

iv) Workaholism: Beginning as Conscription and Ending as Escape

The demands made on us in our adult years bring with them the perennial temptation to become a workaholic. If we are sensitive persons, we will wrestle constantly with the pressure to surrender ourselves to too many demands and to become overcommitted. It begins in goodwill and innocence, but it inevitably transmutes into something else. Initially, we give ourselves over to all these demands because this is what is asked of us; but, as more and more time goes by, that commitment becomes less altruistic and more self-serving.

First off, though we are generally blind to this, it becomes an escape. We remain busy and preoccupied enough that we have an inbuilt excuse and rationalization so as not to have to deal with relationships, be that to our families or to our God. Being weighed down constantly with work and duty is a burden, but it is also a great protection. We do not get to smell the flowers, but neither do we have to deal with the deeper things that lurk under the surface of our lives. We can avoid the unresolved issues in our families and our psyches. We have the perfect excuse! We are just too busy. Generally, our society supports us in this escapism. With most other addictions, we are eventually sent off to a clinic, but if we are addicted to our work, we are generally admired for our disease.

Along with this there is also the danger of taking more and more of our meaning from our work rather than from our relationships. As we become more and more immersed in our work, to the detriment of our relationships, we will naturally begin too to draw more and more of our meaning and value from our work, and, as numerous spiritual writers have pointed out, the dangers in this are many, not least among those is the danger that we will find it harder and harder to find meaning in anything outside of our work. Old habits are hard to break. If we spend a good number of years drawing our identity from working hard and being loved for being anything from a professional athlete to a mom, it will not be easy simply to shift gears and draw our meaning from something else.

Classical spiritual writers are unanimous in warning about the danger of overwork and of becoming overpreoccupied with our work. That is a huge danger lurking right within our own generosity.

v) Acedia and the Noonday Devil

Very often when we feel weighed down with sadness and depression we can, if we analyze things a bit, point to something that helped trigger that sadness: a death, a breakdown in a relationship, frustration with our work, the bitterness of a colleague, an issue with our health, overtiredness, or even just the weather. Often we can point to something that is taking the sunshine away. The Desert Fathers spoke, however, of a certain sadness that can beset us for no apparent reason. They called this "acedia" and "the noonday devil" and distinguished it from other kinds of sadness for which we can pinpoint a reason. In their view, the "noonday devil," unlike the devil who strikes at crisis times, hits in broad daylight, when there is seemingly no reason to be sad.[9]

Evagrius Ponticus, a Desert Father, writing some seventeen hundred years ago, gives a colorful description of the devil who strikes at high noon:

> The demon of acedia—also called the noonday demon—is the one that causes the most serious trouble of all . . . . First of all he makes it seem that the sun barely moves, if at all, and that the day is fifty hours long. Then he constrains the monk to look constantly out the windows, to walk outside the cell, to gaze carefully at the sun to determine how far it stands from the ninth hour [lunchtime], to look this way and now that to see if perhaps [one of the brethren appears from his cell]. Then

too he instills in the heart of the monk a hatred for the place, a hatred for his very life itself, a hatred for manual labor. He leads him to reflect that charity has departed from among the brethren, that there is no one to give encouragement. Should there be someone at this period who happens to offend him in some way or other, this too the demon uses to contribute to further hatred. This demon drives him along to desire other sites where he can more easily procure life's necessities more readily find work and make a real success of himself . . . . He joins to these reflections the memory of dear ones and of his former way of life. He depicts life stretching out for a long period of time, and brings before the monk's eye the toil of the ascetic struggle and, as the saying has it, leaves no leaf unturned to induce the monk to forsake his cell and drop out of the fight.[10]

What brings on the "noonday devil"? Anything can trigger its entry: a hot sun at noon, rain, an old song on the radio, a beautiful face in a crowd, a reunion party, a half-forgotten lullaby, somebody else's good fortune, a farewell hug, the simple mention of a significant other's name, a sorting through of old photographs, a wedding or a gala event that should ideally bring us joy, or an ordinary weekday morning. Everyone is prone to be beset by the noonday demon, regardless of age, but we are particularly vulnerable during our adult years when we are in those long middle innings when the freshness of the beginning has long since worn off and it seems we have little to look forward to except the lunch hour.

This demon is a close cousin to the demon of boredom that John of the Cross highlights so strongly. Many of the classical spiritual writers warn us strongly of its power during our adult years; but the good news, as Evagrius himself tells us, is that "no other demon follows close upon the heels of this one (when he is defeated) but only a state of deep peace and inexpressible joy arise out of this struggle."[11]

vi) The Drama of the Gifted Child and the Deep Struggle to Forgive

More than thirty years ago, Alice Miller wrote a famous piece that she titled *The Drama of the Gifted Child*.[12] In her view, in simple words, this is the drama of the gifted child: first off, the gifted child is not necessarily the child prodigy. The gifted child is the opposite of the daredevil who fears nothing, particularly what other people think of him or her. The gifted child is the sensitive child, the good child anxious to please, to measure up, and not disappoint others. The gifted child is you! And you pay a price for your sensitivity.

None of us have perfect childhoods. All of us, as children, suffer some lack of affirmation, lack of love, lack of being properly valued, and some positive cruelty and unfairness. These experiences cut deep and leave deep scars in our psyches. However, prior to midlife, the life force is so strong in us that we can more easily live with those wounds, even the very deep ones. However, sometime in midlife, often during our thirties, our wounds begin to break through and create a certain drama inside of us, namely, an awareness of the depth of our own wounds and a concomitant sense of how those wounds took their origin in incidents of unfairness, cruelty, and abuse that we suffered and how, now, we have little or no recourse to deal with that unfairness. And so it is easy, at this point in life, for bitterness and anger to begin to color our lives. For Miller, it is not a mystery that our adult years will find us dealing with a lot of anger and bitterness. And for her, the drama can be resolved only through grief, tears, and eventual forgiveness.

As we pass through our adult years, what we wrestle with continues to shift, and, generally, at a point, we find ourselves wrestling more with the demons of the older brother than with the demons of the prodigal son. I remember some years ago, talking to a woman in a church, a faithful Christian, wife, and mother, who confessed that now, just as she was entering her fifties, all kinds of angers were beginning to seep through in her life, angers that confused her since she had not had to deal with them before and she loved the people with whom she was perennially angry. "What's wrong with me?" she pleaded. "Why am I dealing with all this anger just now in my life?" What I tried to make her aware of was that it was no accident that this would be her struggle at fifty, that this came with the turf, and that this was her real religious struggle, the hugest one we all have to overcome before we die.

As we age, we can slim our spiritual and psychological vocabulary down to very few concepts, but one of these is forgiveness. As we age we need to forgive— forgive those who hurt us, forgive ourselves for our own mistakes, forgive life for having been unfair, and then forgive God for seemingly not having protected us—all of this so that we do not die bitter and angry, which is perhaps the greatest religious imperative of all.

The Religious Faults of Mature Adults

There is an old axiom that says: "It is not a question of whether you are a sinner or not, but only a question of 'What is your sin'?" There is an important truth in that. This side of eternity, we never can fully rid ourselves of our faults. They simply take on new and subtler guises, but they never fully disappear. There are always more moral battles to be fought. Up to now, we have been speaking of our major struggles during our adult years. But what are major faults during those years? What faults invariably come with the territory?

Many classical spiritual writers devote a section of their teachings to what they call "the faults of those already advanced beyond first conversion." That refers to us, during our adult years. What faults do we tend to exhibit during those years?

Classically, spiritual writers have often broken our moral struggles down into a battle with a number of innate propensities that they called the seven deadly sins.

The list of that infamous seven varies slightly through history, but generally these seven deadly sins were named pride, envy, wrath, sloth, greed, gluttony, and lust. The notion is that we struggle with each of these throughout our entire life, except those struggles take ever subtler forms as we mature. What forms do they tend to take during all those years when we are trying to live unselfishly?

i) Pride

How pride lives in us during our adult years is probably best described, as Jesus describes it, in the famous parable of the Pharisee and Publican.[13] The Pharisee, who is vilified in this story, is proud precisely of his spiritual and human maturity. That is a subtle form of pride of which it is almost impossible to rid ourselves. As we mature emotionally, morally, and religiously it becomes almost impossible not to compare ourselves to others who are struggling and feel both a certain smugness that we are not like them and certain disdain for their condition. Spiritual writers describe the fault in this way: pride in the mature person takes the form of refusing to be small before God and refusing to recognize properly our interconnection with others. It is a refusal to accept our own poverty; namely, to recognize that we are standing before God and others with empty hands and that all we have and have achieved has come our way by grace more so than by our own efforts.[14]

During our adult years pride often disguises itself as humility as a strategy for further enhancement. Thus it takes Jesus' invitation to heart: Whoever wants to be first must be last and be the servant of all! Then, as we are taking the last place and being of service, we cannot help but feel very good about ourselves and nurse the secret knowledge that our humility is both superiority over others and something for which we will later be recognized and admired.

As well, as we mature, pride will take on this seemingly noble face: we will begin to do the right things for seemingly the right reasons, but we are deceiving ourselves because, in the end, we are still doing them in service to our own pride. Our motivation for generosity is often more inspired by the desire to feel good about ourselves than by real love of others. For example, a number of times during my years of ministry, I have been tempted to move to the inner city to live among the poor as a sign of my commitment to social justice. It took a good spiritual director to point out to me that, at least in my case, such a move there would, no doubt, do a lot more for me than for the poor. My moving there would make me feel good, enhance my status among my colleagues, and be a wonderful thing inside of my curriculum vitae, but would not, unless I would more radically change my life and ministry, do much for the poor. Ultimately, it would serve my pride more than it would serve the poor.

The British Carmelite nun Ruth Burrows cautions that this same dynamic holds true in terms of our motivation for prayer and religious practice. Again, sometimes our motivation has more to do with our own pride than with real faith and generosity. Thus, she writes: "The way we worry about spiritual failure, the inability to pray, distractions, ugly thoughts and temptations we can't get rid of . . . it's not because God is defrauded, for he isn't, it's because we are not so beautiful as we would like to be."[15]

And pride, invariably, brings with it a harsh or condescending judgment on others. We see this latter aspect, pride as a harsh or condescending judgment of others, most strongly perhaps in the period shortly after first conversion; when young lovers, recent religious converts, and neophytes in service and justice, still caught up in the emotional fervor of the honeymoon, think they alone know how to relate to one another, to Jesus, and to the world. Their fervor is admirable, but their pride and judgment of others invariably spawn an arrogance and elitism. But God and nature conspire together to ensure that the grind of the years will eventually restore humility.

ii) Envy and Jealousy

Jealousy is often the straw that stirs the drink, irrespective of our age and maturity. Scripture scholars remind us that there are two commandments against jealousy, while even idolatry and adultery each get only one. More recently, anthropologists like René Girard have advanced theses that propose that the ultimate roots of all violence and war lie in envy. Like pride, envy is very difficult to shed. Like pride too, it has many guises. How does it show itself in a mature adult?

One of the ways that envy manifests itself in the mature adult is in the form of feeling threatened, however subtly, by the talents, achievements, and beauty of others. Put crassly, at this stage of our lives, little people do not threaten us, talented people do! In essence, we feel diminished by other people's greatness and find ourselves nitpicking and looking for flaws rather than blessing the talents and achievements of others. We can do an inventory on ourselves apposite the sin of envy by asking ourselves these questions: How often in a given day do I praise another as opposed to criticize another? How often do I nitpick, and why do I nitpick? Why do I find it much easier to be empathetic with someone who is hurting as opposed to sharing truly in someone's good fortune? Why do I experience a secret glee upon hearing about the fall from grace of a celebrity? Why do I struggle to bless younger people? When did I last truly praise a younger person of the same sex?

Another way envy can manifest itself in the mature is in the envy of the older brother of the prodigal son, namely, in an unconscious envy of the amoral that inevitably shows itself in embittered moralizing and the resentment that others who are not as faithful as we are get to enjoy God's free love just as much as we do. Jesus addresses this explicitly in his parable about the vineyard workers who came at different hours, warning that we can end up having everything and enjoying nothing because we are watching what everyone else is getting.[16]

iii) Wrath and Anger

As we saw earlier, as we age and mature, the wounds of our childhood begin to break through more and more. With that come strong feelings about the unfairness of our lives and concomitant feelings of anger. While these are psychologically understandable, full maturity asks that we face, with more courage, anger's deepest root, namely, lack of patience with ourselves, others, and God. Wrath and anger are very much rooted in lack of patience.

Moreover, the root of some of our angers, however subtly they manifest themselves in our adult years, lie not in our wounds but in our selfishness. Ruth Burrows plainly states that "there is a bitterness which is an infallible indication of selfishness."[17] In a similar vein, Thérèse of Lisieux suggests that we experience "broken hearts" because we are seeking ourselves inside a relationship.[18] Hence, we see that, after initial conversion, wrath and anger express themselves more as impatience, bitterness, and a sense that life has not been fair to us.

iv) Sloth

Sloth, as it is commonly conceived, connotes simple laziness and lack of ambition. For most adults, this is not an issue; in fact, ambition and an addiction to work is the greater danger. How then does sloth take other guises inside of us?

More commonly in adults, sloth takes the form of postponing and evading our true responsibilities. For instance, we are slothful when we procrastinate and put off having to deal with a moral or relational issue in our lives. The classic example here is the newly converted Saint Augustine who put off dealing with his sexuality by praying: "God, make a chaste Christian, but not yet!" We are slothful when we utter that prayer—"Yes, but not yet!"—about issues we do not yet want to face, be they in the area of sexuality, anger, getting serious about our prayer lives, or being open to forgive a certain person. John of the Cross has a colorful expression for this kind of sloth. He calls it *hebetudo mentis*, a certain dullness of mind that we contract through laziness and a distracted, inattentive spirit.[19]

We are also slothful when we distance ourselves from the more radical demands of adult responsibility and Christian discipleship and settle in for second best rather than striving for the higher bar. Ironically, we often hide our sloth by working hard so as not to have to face the more challenging task of doing our inner work.

v) Greed

When we think of greed, the picture that most easily comes to mind is that of someone being addicted to accumulating wealth and possessions and then hoarding that all for himself, Scrooge and the naive man in the Gospels who kept building bigger barns. Albeit the desire to own things and make things secure for ourselves never entirely leaves us, greed, for an adult, usually takes a subtler guise. What we hunger for and want to accumulate for ourselves is not so much houses, yachts, and fat bank accounts, though in honesty we would love those as well. Rather, what we want to accumulate is experience, status, and reputation. More than we want people to recognize us for our money, we want them to recognize us for our good name, our achievements, and our knowledge. The greed to be known and admired eventually trumps the greed for money.

vi) Gluttony

Every addiction is a manifestation of gluttony; and perhaps among all our sinful propensities, gluttony is the one that is the most shameful to admit. Why? Because when we think of gluttony, we tend to think of a certain childish lack of discipline and self-control. But gluttony is a bigger story.

Our propensity for gluttony takes its root in more than just our baser instincts. One of the reasons why our appetites are so wide, huge, insatiable, and hard to control lies in the fact that we have the image and likeness of God inside of us. Moreover, God's image inside of us is not just a beautiful, Andrei Rublev icon stamped inside of our souls. Rather, God is fire, infinite fire, and that infinite fire with its godly appetites is also inside us. And so it is not a mystery that we are prone to addictions. Our hearts and minds want to be everywhere, like God, and drink up the whole world and make love to it.

Gluttony is a word that describes all the various kinds of shortfalls we have in channeling our infinite appetites. At a baser level, it generally manifests itself in some lack of control in relationship to food, drink, sex, entertainment, and perhaps today in an inability to control information technology in our lives. How does it manifest itself at subtler levels? We simply develop other addictions that look and feel noble rather than shameful. For example, as a culture today, we struggle to keep the busyness and pressures of our lives in proper check so that we can enjoy proper leisure time. This is often a form of gluttony. Here is how Wayne Muller puts it. He begins with a famous quote from Thomas Merton warning about the dangers of overwork. "To allow oneself to be carried away by a multitude of conflicting concerns, to surrender to too many demands, to commit oneself to too many projects, to want to help everyone in everything, is to succumb to violence." Whenever this happens, Muller warns,

> Life has become a maelstrom in which speed and accomplishment, consumption and productivity have become the most valued human commodities. In the trance of overwork, we take everything for granted. We consume things, people, and information. We do not have time to savor this life, nor to care deeply and gently for ourselves, our loved ones, or our world; rather, with increasingly dizzying haste, we use them all up, and throw them away.[20]

Gluttony and addictions take varied and subtle forms during our adult years.

vii) Lust

Lust in its wide sense refers to any inordinate desire. We can lust for anything from sex to spirituality. Commonly, though, we associate lust with excessive and self-centered sexual desire, that is, with sexual desire that is either too impatient or too self-centered, or both, to properly respect the object of that desire. As mature adults we would, of course, like to believe that we have outgrown lust. However, given the sheer power of sexual desire within us, it is hard for us, even when we are mature and committed to properly respecting sexual boundaries, ever to be free from lust. Who has never had a lustful sexual fantasy?

However, as we mature, lust takes on more subtle modalities. Perhaps we no longer suffer from crass sexual desire, but that does not mean that lust has disappeared from our lives. Where does lust appear in our lives even after we have brought our sexual actions and fantasies into essentially moral bounds? Lust then remains in us in a lack of purity of heart. What does this mean?

Perhaps a good place to start by way of explanation would be with a much-maligned text in the Gospels in which Jesus tells us that if we even look on someone with lust, then we have already committed adultery in our hearts.[21] What is the real challenge here?

The challenge is to live in purity of heart. That is lust's opposite. And what is purity of heart? To be pure of heart is to relate to others and the world in a way that respects and honors the full dignity, value, and destiny of every person and every being on the planet. To be pure of heart is to see others as God sees them and to love them with their good, not our own, in mind. To be pure of heart is to see others in a way that fully respects their sexuality. Purity of heart is purity of intention.

But that is hard to do, even when we are mature. Lust gets in the way: given the raw power of sexuality inside us and the power of our human drives and yearnings, it is hard enough always to keep our actions pure, but it is even more difficult, and rare, to have a pure spirit, a pure heart, pure daydreams, and pure intentions. Our hearts want what they want and pressure us to where we can easily feel a certain repugnance for the very word *purity*. That repugnance, however, is based largely on a misunderstanding. Purity is not a deadening of the heart, a stripping away of our sexuality, but a deeper maturity that lets our sexual energies flow out in a more life-giving way. Purity of heart does not mean that we will not have any sexual fantasies. It means that those fantasies will not be lustful. When we are mature, our problem with lust, to quote James Hillman, lies less in controlling lustful fantasies than in understanding their transpersonal nature as a cosmic dynamic.[22]

A Certain Disquiet Underneath

Because work and responsibilities keep us so busy and preoccupied during our adult years, and because we are generally relatively youthful and healthy during this period of our lives, save for particular occasions that expose our vulnerability, we tend not to deal very explicitly with our own mortality during these years. Our death seems as something far off, and the cares and joys of the present mostly trump any explicit anxiety about when, where, or how we will die, and how we plan to manage that. And that is how it should be. Jesus himself cautions us not to second-guess the present by having undue anxiety about the future. Life is meant to be lived and enjoyed, free from unhealthy fears of death.

And so we go through our adult years with our anxieties focused mostly on our relationships, our kids, our families, our jobs, our mortgage, our grandkids, our retirement plans, the woes of our favorite sports teams, and the deck we still need to build off the living room. These are healthy anxieties, manageable ones, and ones that do not rock us in our boots. But beneath these manageable anxieties, there will be, as we stated earlier, an inchoate, nagging disquiet that is just stirring enough to let us know that someday, though not quite yet, there are still some deeper things to sort out and a deeper journey to be made.

What is that deeper journey? Beyond Mature Discipleship lies Radical Discipleship, the struggle to give our deaths away, to make our leaving of this life our last, and perhaps greatest, gift to our loved ones, our churches, and our society. At what point in our lives should we begin more explicitly to focus on this final journey? The answer to that question is huge and complex and constitutes the substance for another book. That journey is the one which John of the Cross calls the "dark night of the spirit." Chapter Nine will attempt to give a brief outline of this last journey.

A Brief Synopsis

Mature Discipleship is the struggle to give our lives away, after we have attained initial maturity. This generally constitutes the longest period of our lives, our "householder" years—those thirty, forty, fifty, or sixty years between landing solidly somewhere in adulthood and looking at retirement and what lies beyond. Our basic anxiety during these years needs to be around the questions: How do I do this better, more generously? How do I make a deeper, more life-giving contribution? These questions define both our human and spiritual task during these years. But how do we go deeper? How do we respond more generously still? The remaining chapters of this book, drawing largely from the deep wells of the Gospels and subsequent Christian spirituality, will attempt to articulate some of the invitations and challenges that beckon us to give our lives away in a more adult, more generous, more noble, and more life-giving way.

SOME GENERAL INVITATIONS
FROM SCRIPTURE

Powers Hapgood, an American who lived during the early and mid-twentieth century, was Harvard educated and inherited a factory. But he gave the factory to the workers and was later, just after World War II, arrested for protesting for the poor. In court, the judge asked him: "Mr. Hapgood, you are Harvard educated, why would anyone of your advantages choose to live as you do?" Hapgood replied: "Because of the Sermon on the Mount, sir."[1]

Give your life to something larger than yourself and pleasure—to the largest thing you can: To God, to relieving suffering, to contributing to knowledge, to adding to literature, to something else. Happiness lies this way, and it beats pleasure hollow.[2]

Gospel Invitations Inviting Us to Be
More Generous and Life Giving

The struggle for maturity, to give our lives away in an ever more generous way, is a lifelong endeavor. In this life, we never fully arrive. There is always more work to be done, and God respects that. Thus, when we look at the invitations for conversion in the Gospels, we see that, while they all ask the same thing of us in the end, they meet us at different moments in our journey, and those moments help define and shape the depth and specificity of the invitation. For example, at one moment in our lives, Jesus' words can be understood as inviting us to basic conversion. Later on, those same words can be understood as inviting us to a much more radical commitment; and, still later, those same words can be understood as inviting us to martyrdom. The invitations of Jesus come to us in a very particular way for every particular situation within which we find ourselves. So it is helpful to ask the question: Which of Jesus' invitations to deeper conversion have particular bearing upon our lives when, in essence, we are already good people who are not yet full saints?

This chapter will examine and highlight six invitations that come to us in the Gospels that have a more particularized bite during those years of our lives when we are already generous but not yet fully saints. The subsequent chapter will highlight two other invitations that are intended to bring us to yet an even deeper maturity.

Challenges from Jesus to a Deeper, More Generous Discipleship

Our adult years constitute the longest period of our lives, and, as we saw, we will have to wrestle with many demons during those years. Crises of every kind will find us. But in terms of growing in maturity and discipleship, these crises enter our lives not just as challenges to us to retain our balance and stability but, especially, as invitations to stretch our hearts and minds into deeper understanding, deeper compassion, deeper generosity, and deeper maturity. In essence, these crises also include within themselves an invitation for us to move from being good people to becoming great people.

What follows are six invitations from the Gospels, each of which hits us more particularly within a certain crisis in our lives, and invites us to go deeper, to find stability again at a new place, and to open our hearts and our eyes in a new way. As well, each of these invitations is particularly pertinent in terms of handling the demons that beset us within our adult years. Within these invitations, therefore, we find the key principles for a more adult discipleship.

What are these six invitations to deeper maturity and discipleship?

i) To Look for Christ on the Road to Emmaus
During a lecture at the University of Louvain, Edward Schillebeeckx was once asked this question: If you had to submit one biblical text that you felt named our faith

situation today, what would that text be? His answer: "The disciples walking on the road to Emmaus on Easter Sunday." He then went on to explain himself in words to this effect: the disciples walking toward Emmaus are deeply discouraged, their once-firm faith has been shattered, but they are walking with Jesus and yet are unable to recognize him. The situation of today's Christians in our secularized cultures is basically the same: we are walking on the road to Emmaus, discouraged, our youthful faith crucified, talking with Christ, but unable to recognize him. As adult Christians today we often find ourselves living in that time between Good Friday and Easter Sunday, when the God we were raised on has been crucified but a sense of the resurrection has not yet sufficiently illumined our imaginations so that we can recognize the God who is walking beside us.[3]

Most of us are familiar with the well-known story of the disciples meeting Jesus on Easter morning on the road to Emmaus. The story is recorded in the Gospel of Luke and is very rich in both symbol and challenge.[4] Allow me to recast it, in essence, and then add some commentary:

On the morning of the first day of the week, two disciples are walking away from Jerusalem toward the village of Emmaus, some seven miles away. As they are walking they are discussing how Jesus had been crucified just two days earlier in Jerusalem. As they converse in this way, Jesus approaches them on the road, but they do not recognize him. He asks them why they are so discouraged and downhearted, and they respond by telling him that he, Jesus, must be the only person in Jerusalem who has not heard of what happened in Jerusalem on Friday. Jesus asks them: "What did happen?" They answer by saying that Jesus, whom they had believed was the messiah, was crucified and with that, as well, their hope. They tell Jesus that some women in their company have reported that Jesus was resurrected, but they do not believe them. They share that their faith and hope in Jesus is now in the past tense. Then, in the harshest words he will use in the entire Gospel of Luke, Jesus calls them "senseless and foolish," and, referring to the scriptures from which they took their faith, he explains to them how in a true understanding of what the messiah must be it makes sense that the messiah should be crucified. Their hearts burn within them as they hear this, even as they do not yet really understand it, nor do they recognize Jesus. When they stop for the evening, Jesus stays with them, and, while they are eating, he breaks the bread as Eucharist and offers it to them. Then their eyes are opened, and they recognize him as the Christ; he disappears from their sight, and they, with new vision, faith, and enthusiasm, return to Jerusalem that same night and announce to the other disciples that they have seen the risen Christ.

This story is replete with symbolism, invitation, and challenge. It is also an exceptional piece of literature. What is its real content?

Some of its richness emerges when we simply parse the language: Luke begins by setting the story "on the first day"; but for him, that does not just refer to Sunday, the first day of the week, but also to the day of the resurrection when, for Christians, the world starts over. For Luke, "the first" day here refers back to the first day of the original creation. He is telling us that the world is starting over. Time is beginning anew. This is the new "big bang."

But the two disciples, discouraged by the crucifixion, do not know this, and so they are walking away from Jerusalem toward Emmaus. The symbolism here is important: They are walking *away* from Jerusalem *toward* Emmaus. "Jerusalem," for Luke, represents three things: the faith dream of the disciples, the church, and the place of the crucifixion. "Emmaus," on the other hand, represents a place of escape, of worldly consolation.[5] Thus, in symbol, Luke is telling us this: the two disciples in this story are *walking away* from their faith dream, away from the church, and away from the place where Christ has been humiliated, and they are walking toward a place of human consolation. That too, perennially, is ever our temptation when our world of faith and values collapses. But the disciples never get there! Jesus appears to them on the road, listens to their discouragement, and, by restructuring their imagination and consequently their faith, he has them returning to their faith dream and their church on that same day, with the humiliation of the crucifixion now integrated into their understanding.

How does Jesus do this? The exchange of conversation, as Luke records it, is rich in symbol and gives us some clues:

Jesus meets the two disciples (and scholars suggest that this was a man and his wife) and asks them why they are so downhearted. One of them answers by telling Jesus that he, Jesus, must be the only person who is ignorant of what has just happened, the crucifixion. Luke does not want us to miss the irony in this. Jesus is, in fact, the only person who *does know* what has happened. But Jesus plays naive and has them explain to him their interpretation of the crucifixion. In their interpretation, the crucifixion was understood as a humiliation so great that it is impossible to integrate it into their faith. It effectively ends their faith and hope. To this, Jesus responds harshly, calling them "foolish and senseless." Why? Because, as Jewish believers, they would have been familiar with the Psalm that says: "The fool says in his heart that there is no God!"[6] And in their inability to integrate the crucifixion into their vision of God, they were saying in their hearts precisely what the foolish say; namely, that given this kind of humiliation, there can be no God.

Then, beginning with their own understanding of scripture, Jesus restructures their imagination in a way that lets them see that not only can this humiliation be integrated into their vision of faith, it is indeed the key piece to help integrate everything else. However, initially they grasp this only inchoately, at a certain gut level; their heads are still largely in the dark. It is only later, when they celebrate the Eucharist, that they can integrate the teaching into their conscious imagination. And what is the teaching?

That the humiliation of the cross is the deep secret that not only unlocks a proper understanding of Christ but also unlocks the depth of human wisdom. Moreover, and this is Luke's central point in this story, in our journey of discipleship, we will, any number of times, have to undergo a certain dynamic of crucifixion and resurrection in our faith: our vision of faith and hope will be crucified and humiliated. God, Christ, and the church, as we understand them, will die in our experience. In the discouragement that ensues we will be tempted to walk away from our faith, our church, our hope, our Christ, and our God, toward some place of consolation. But somewhere on that road, as we walk toward consolation, Christ will appear, in a new guise, and we will be unable initially to recognize him. Eventually, however, that encounter will restructure our imagination and our faith so we will recognize Christ in a new and much deeper way, and that recognition will turn us away from the place of consolation, "Emmaus," and send us back to our dream of faith and our church, "Jerusalem."

The key in all of this is our ability or inability to recognize Christ when he meets us on the road. Why did the original disciples not recognize him? Christian theology has often answered this in an inept way by suggesting that the lack of recognition was due to the fact that Jesus, in his resurrected body, would have looked very different physically than in his preresurrected body. That may well be true and would be an important part of the story had Aristotle or some other Greek thinker written this gospel. Luke, however, writing out of a Hebrew mind-set, was making another point. His point was rather that the disciples did not recognize Jesus because, given their mind-set, it was impossible for them to see Christ in one who had been so humiliated in the crucifixion. Dying in this way made him, in their faith eyes, the "excluded one," the one outside of God's blessing. Their faith had trained their eyes to see and recognize only a Christ who fit their understanding and imagination. A crucified Jesus did not fit into that understanding and thus was unrecognizable to them, even as he was chatting with them.

This is an experience that we will all undergo at various times during our adult lives: for all of us there will come times when everything that is precious to us religiously will get crucified and we will find ourselves discouraged, shattered religiously, and tempted to walk toward some place of consolation. God, Christ, and church will still be very much alive in our lives, but we will not be able to recognize them because our eyes and hearts will have been trained to see God, Christ, and church only in the way that they were integrated into our lives *before* this crisis beset us. But as the mystics say, this is not a crisis of faith but a crisis of the imagination, a particular dark night of the soul within which we have to sort through a death of what is precious to us religiously so as to receive God, Christ, and church into our lives in a new and deeper way.

Deeper maturity and a more faithful discipleship are found on the road to Emmaus, when discouraged, in darkness, and tempted, we let our imaginations be restructured by a deeper vision of what God, Christ, and church mean.

ii) To Remain, Like Peter, Committed When Everything in Us Suggests That We Walk Away

One of the major trials within mature discipleship is that of fidelity, of remaining steadfast and loving within our commitments over the long haul, after our initial emotional fervor has waned and some disillusionment has set in. The challenge then will be to act out of value rather than out of feeling and to act out of trust rather than out of understanding. Allow me one such illustration from the Gospels, the invitation to Peter to remain committed to Christ in the face of major questions and a major disillusionment.

The incident takes place in John's Gospel at the end of Jesus' discourse on the bread of life.[7] Jesus ends that homily with the words "Unless you eat the flesh of the son of man and drink his blood, you can have no life in you."[8] These words deeply shocked his audience, most of whom were Jewish and could only understand his words to mean cannibalism. This precipitated a crisis in Jesus' ministry. John reports that many of his disciples drew back and no longer followed him, finding his words intolerable. With most everyone deserting him, Jesus turns to the twelve apostles and asks them: "Do you also want to leave?" Peter answers on their behalf with the words: "Lord, to whom shall we go? You have the words of eternal life."[9]

Peter's answer is a paradigm for maturity and sustained commitment. In essence, this is his situation, and this is his answer: he has just heard Jesus say something that he cannot understand, and what he does understand he cannot accept. Jesus' words do not sound like life; they sound like death. In the face of this, Peter is asked: "Do you want to walk away like the others?"

In effect, in colloquial language, this is his answer to Jesus: "Yes, I would like to walk away! Except that I know better! What I have just heard, I don't get—and what I get, I don't like! Except I know, deep down, that I am better off not getting it with you than getting it some other place!"

I offered those words in class one day to some students, and a man immediately quipped: "That sounds like my marriage!" A number of students laughed, but the man protested: "That's exactly the point: anyone who has ever been in a commitment for a long time, be it a marriage, in a religious vocation, or some service to the community, knows that there are days and seasons when your commitment looks like death and you'd like to walk away . . . except, except, you are smart enough to know that, long range, this commitment is bringing you life!"

In his autobiography, *Surprised by Joy,* C. S. Lewis

recounts the night when he, as an adult convert to Christianity, first knelt down and admitted to himself and confessed to God his faith in Christ. He knelt down, he writes, not with enthusiasm, with a heart and mind bubbling with emotion. He knelt down, rather, "as the most dejected and reluctant convert in all England." And one might ask, given that reluctance, why would he ever choose to kneel? He knelt down because, to quote his own words, he had come to realize that "the hardness of God is kinder than the softness of men, and His compulsion is our liberation."[10] That is the same reason why Peter chose to remain with Jesus even after Jesus' words confused and upset him. Peter, like Lewis, knew "God's compulsion."

What is "God's compulsion"? It is an intuitive sense, rooted in something deeper than thought or feeling, of what we need to do to find and sustain authentic life within ourselves. For example: Daniel Berrigan was once asked in an interview: "Where does faith live? Is faith more in the head or in the heart?" His answer was colorful, crass, and deadly accurate: It's in neither, he replied. "Faith is rarely where your head is at. Nor is it where your heart is at. Faith is where your ass is at!" In saying this, he was not trying to be fanciful but was trying to highlight a major truth about faith and maturity—namely, that our commitments, our actions, our charity, and our moral actions, much more so than our thoughts and feelings, ultimately determine whether we believe or not. Passing strange but strangely true, the posterior is invariably a better indication of where we stand with faith and love than are the head and the heart. Our actions speak more truly than do our words and feelings. We know this from experience.

We all have had the experience of being inside certain commitments (marriage, family, church) where, at times, our heads and our hearts are not there, but we are there! The head tells us this does not make sense; the heart lacks the warm feelings to keep us there. But we remain there, held by something deeper, something beyond what we can explain or feel. What is that? It is God's compulsion, the intuitive sense inside of us that tells us not what we would like to do or what we think it would be wise to do, but what we have to do.

During the long years of maturity when boredom, the longing for a second honeymoon, midlife crisis, misunderstanding, disillusionment, and numerous other things eat away at our fidelity like rust on iron, we can find ourselves, on any given day, standing like Peter before Jesus, with every reason of head and heart to walk away, but knowing at a deeper place inside of us that, for us, real life depends upon staying the course. When we honor that deeper place inside us, real life will flow into us.

This poses, of course, an important question: How do we discern inside of ourselves what we really want? If someone is paralyzed in coming to a decision because he or she cannot decide between different roads that might be taken, a good counselor will ask the question: What do you really want to do here? That is the key question, but both the counselor and client must be sure to consider that question on three levels: What do I think is *the wisest thing to do* here? What would *I most like to do* here? What do *I have to do* here? The first two questions are important and should be carefully discerned, but life-giving decisions are often contingent upon our most carefully weighing the last question.

iii) To Walk as Both "Son of David" and as "Lord," Inside the Regions of Tyre and Sidon

One of the tensions we will experience as we grow in maturity and depth in discipleship is that of torn loyalties. As we grow in sensitivity we will find that who we consider as family, as compatriot, and as brother or sister in faith will also grow. New tensions will arise in us, and new misunderstandings will surround us as we find ourselves stretched and torn beyond our old loyalties, yet with an unwillingness to abandon those old loyalties. When that happens in our lives we will find ourselves, in terms of a gospel image, standing with Jesus inside pagan territory, talking to a Syrophoenician woman, and feeling torn between being a loyal child of our faith tradition and being a universal instrument of salvation for our God.

Here, in essence, is the pertinent gospel image that depicts that situation:

> At a certain point in his ministry, Jesus leaves the Jewish regions within which he is preaching and withdraws to the notoriously pagan region of Tyre and Sidon. There he is approached by a

Syro-Phoenician woman who addresses him in this way: "Son of David, have pity on me and cure my daughter." Initially, Jesus gives her no reply. But as she persists in her pleading, Jesus says to her: "I was sent to the lost sheep of the house of Israel, and to them alone. It is not right to take the children's bread and throw it to the house dogs." The woman, rather than being put off by this reply, simply rephrases her plea: "Lord, even the dogs eat the scraps that fall from the master's table." Upon hearing this, Jesus says to her: "What faith you have! Let it be done as you wish." And he heals her daughter.[11]

The setting of this gospel passage is already a major homily: Jesus is in a pagan country, one within which he stands before a different ethnicity and a different religion and is drawn into a dialogue by a woman, someone of a different gender. It is not a stretch of the imagination to submit that this is exactly where our churches and we, as adult disciples, stand today. We are in new territory wherein the questions of ethnic plurality, other religions, and gender are central and impossible to ignore. The present tensions in our world that have to do with our relationships to other ethnic and religious groups, to Islam in particular, along with the tensions in our churches surrounding the question of women, should be more than enough to alert us to the fact that our old loyalties are being stretched. But there is still more to this gospel incident than its symbolic setting.

For our purposes of wanting a model of how to act inside of torn religious loyalties, this is how this incident might be extrapolated and recast today into our own lives. I will use a Roman Catholic example, but, no doubt, this will translate easily into the experience of other churches: imagine that you are in charge of running a baptismal-preparation program in your local congregation. Eight candidates present themselves, and you, along with a team of other parishioners, lead them through a nine-month preparation process, beginning in September and culminating with the candidates being baptized at the Vigil service on Holy Saturday. You prepare your eight candidates well, and on the early evening of Holy Saturday you are in the church helping prepare the celebration and offering last-minute support for your eight candidates, when a woman you have never seen before approaches you and asks: "Are you in charge of the baptismal program here?" You respond in the affirmative, and she asks you: "I would like to be baptized here tonight!" Then you, like Jesus, might well say: "It's not possible. I'm running a Roman Catholic program, and we have a number of criteria you have to first meet. You aren't ready. You skipped the prescribed preparation program! If we baptized you, it would not be fair to those who spent all these months in preparation! Come back in September and we can see about getting you into our next preparation process." But then the woman surprises you with these words: "I'm sorry, I guess I didn't address you properly. Let me rephrase this: Are you simply a Roman Catholic running a program for your own church's benefit, or are you also a person who is a universal instrument of salvation for everyone, Roman Catholics and everyone else? And if you are the latter, well, then I am one of yours as much as these other eight candidates whom you've prepared." Now, if you are like Jesus, you might say: "Wow! You skipped all the preparation, but I can see from your answer that you have more than enough faith to be baptized. Get in line, and we will baptize you first!"

The point of this story is not, of course, how pro-grammatic or nonprogrammatic we should be in our pastoral practices. There is a deeper tension at play here: what is highlighted is the tension within Jesus between his loyalty to his identity as the Jewish Messiah and his loyalty to his wider identity as a universal instrument of salvation for all peoples. The woman pleads her case to him twice, but under a different rubric each time; Jesus finds himself unable to help her in one instance but able to help her in the other. This tension is subtly contained in the dialogue:

The Syrophoenician woman, a non-Jew, approaches Jesus and addresses him by invoking his Jewish title: "Son of David." And up to this point in the Gospels, this is very much how Jesus defined himself, namely, as the Jewish Messiah. Appealed to under this rubric, he refuses her request, protesting that he has been "sent to the lost sheep of the house of Israel, and to them alone" and that she is not one of the people he has been sent to save. Moreover, she has skipped a thousand years of religious preparation. And so the woman changes the way she addresses him in her second plea. She does not appeal to him as the "Son of David." In her second plea she appeals to him as God's universal instrument of salvation for everyone, Syrophoenicians no less than Jews, those who have been religiously prepared and those who have not. What she is doing, in effect, is calling Jesus to a wider loyalty by appealing to another identity that Jesus is already carrying.

Jesus was the Jewish Messiah, the "Son of David," but he was also God's universal instrument of salvation for all peoples, "Lord." And as is evident in this passage and other places in the Gospels, this constituted a tension, both in him and within his followers. On the one hand, Jesus is fiercely loyal to his identity and mission as "Son of David," and, on the other hand, he is also fiercely loyal to his wider identity and mission as "Lord." And as we can see from his encounter with the Syrophoenician woman, there were certain things he could not respond to as "Son of David" that he could respond to as "Lord." But as we also see from this encounter, he was fiercely loyal to both identities.

And that tension, torn between loyalties but remaining faithful to both, is the real point of this story. In this story, Jesus models for us how we should carry this tension within our own lives, because, like him, we also stand before the world with two competing identities and two competing loyalties:

On the one hand, we are all "Sons or Daughters of David." Each of us has a specific religious identity. For example, in my case, as "Son of David," I am a

Roman Catholic, subject to the creeds and the teachings of scripture, subject to the pope, subject to my local bishop, subject to Roman Catholic canon law, and subject to numerous other ecclesial and liturgical rubrics and regulations. And I must be loyal to that identity. I am not free simply to disregard my own church's teachings and rules according to pastoral need or personal whim. Thus, at one level, I have been sent to minister to the lost sheep of Roman Catholicism. But that is not my only identity and mission.

On the other hand, I am also called to be "Lord." Beyond my specific religious identity and denominational affiliation, I am called to be a universal instrument of salvation to the whole world. All others, regardless of faith or religious denomination, are also my sheep, just as much as those within Roman Catholicism. And I must also be fiercely loyal to this identity and mission. I am not free simply to disregard this mandate according to pastoral need or personal whim. I am also sent out to minister to the whole world, irrespective of faith and religion.

It is the same for every one of us. One part of us is called to minister to our own, and that brings with it its own set of rules; another part of us is called to minister to the whole world, and some of the house rules no longer apply then.

That is a major tension to carry, and, too often, we resolve it on the basis of ideological preference; namely, if I am a conservative, "Son of David" forever trumps "Lord," and I will then answer all pastoral and ecclesial

issues the way Jesus initially answered the Syrophoenician woman. Conversely, if I am a liberal, "Lord" forever trumps "Son of David," and I answer all pastoral
and ecclesial issues the way Jesus answered the woman
after her second pleading. But what this story models
for us is that we should not resolve this tension via a
prefabricated decision that is based upon our personal
ideology: conservative in my makeup, a conservative
solution; liberal in my makeup, a liberal resolution.
Rather, like Jesus, we should hold the tension and remain loyal to both sides as we make the decision. Allow
me a personal example:

During my early years of ministry, I worked under
a wonderful archbishop who, both in his own ministry
and in his instructions to others, modeled how this tension is meant to be carried. On several occasions, confronted by a very difficult pastoral situation, I phoned
him for advice. How should I handle this? His answer
was always the same: in a gentle, yet clear voice, he
would say: "Father, you know the mind of the church.
You know my mind. You also know canon law and our
diocesan regulations. But you are also looking at these
people and their particular pain. God has put you there.
Keep everything in mind, and then do what needs to be
done. Just tell me afterward what you decided. I might
not agree with you, but you need to make the decision."
In effect, he was telling me: be loyal to both of your
identities as you make this decision.

While this episode in the Gospels appears as a minor
incident within Jesus' ministry, it teaches a critical les-

son because so much of the tension between conservatives and liberals within religious circles can, in fact, be boiled down to the archetypal poles represented in this story: conservatives intuit and honor the truth of what is contained in being "Son of David"; liberals intuit and honor the truth that is contained in being universal "Lord." The Gospels want us to intuit and honor both truths.

Deeper maturity will bring with it the tension of stretched loyalties. Jesus, in his encounter with the Syrophoenician woman, offers us a model of how to properly carry that tension.

iv) To Respond to the Invitation to Be Perfect as Our Heavenly Father Is Perfect and to Look Frantically for the Lost Coin

As we journey through our adult years, the hope is that we continue always to grow in maturity and generosity. But what is the ultimate goal of our growth? How do we envisage *full bloom*? Jesus defines this for us when he says: "Be perfect as your heavenly father is perfect."[12] The ultimate goal is perfection itself.

However, this presents an immediate problem. Perfection, as it is commonly understood, is a human impossibility. Our commonsense notion of perfection comes from Greek thought, where something is thought to be perfect only if it is flawless, without any blemish whatsoever. A perfect complexion would have no flaws, as would a perfect moral life. But that is a human impossibility and is not, in fact, what Jesus is asking of us. Jesus' framework of thought was more Hebrew than Greek, and inside that framework perfection does not have the commonsense connotation of flawlessness. Rather, Jesus' concept of perfection is very much identified with compassion, so much so that sometimes the Gospels simply name it as compassion. Compassion is an attainable goal. Hence, Jesus challenges us: *be compassionate* as your heavenly father is compassionate.

How might that be defined? The dictionary definition of compassion is not particularly helpful here because the subordinate clause, as your heavenly father is compassionate, specifies the word in this case. How is God compassionate?

Jesus defines it this way: God, he says, lets his sun shine on the bad as well as the good. God's love does not discriminate; it simply embraces everything. Like the sun, it does not shine selectively, shedding its warmth on the vegetables because they are good and refusing warmth to the weeds because they are bad. It just shines, and everything irrespective of its condition receives its warmth.

This is a stunning truth: God loves us when we are good, and God loves us when we are bad. God loves the saints in heaven, and God equally loves the devils in hell. They merely respond differently. The father of the prodigal son and of his older brother loves both equally, one in his weakness and the other in his bitterness, and his embrace is not contingent upon their conversion. He loves them even inside their distance from him. And we are asked to love in the same way. That is what it means to be perfect, compassionate, in the biblical sense. But how do we do that?

Perhaps another question needs first to be asked: If God loves us equally when we are bad and when we are good, then why be good? This is an interesting question, though not a deep one. Love, understood properly, is never a reward for being good. Goodness, rather, is always a consequence of having been loved. We are not loved because we are good, but hopefully we become good as we experience love.

And so we return to the question: How can we be compassionate as God is compassionate? How do we, like God, embrace indiscriminately? How do we let our love shine on the bad as well as the good, without saying that nothing matters, that it is okay to live in any way and do anything? How do we love as God loves and still hold true to who we are and what our values are?

We do so by holding our personal and moral ground in a gracious and loving way even as we let our love and understanding embrace everything. And for this, we have Jesus' example. He embraced everyone—sinners and saints alike—without ever suggesting that sin and virtue are unimportant. Indeed, a truly loving embrace says the opposite. It highlights the difference. For example, imagine that your college-age daughter comes home for a weekend, along with her boyfriend. You already know that they are living together, but the awkward question still arises: Do you challenge them to sleep in separate rooms while they are at your house? You do, and you do so unambiguously: you tell your daughter, gently but unequivocally, that while they are under your roof and unmarried, they will sleep in separate rooms. She objects: "That's hypocritical—my values aren't the same as yours, and I don't believe this is wrong in any way!"

Your response is the nondiscriminating, yet discriminating, compassion of God: you hug your daughter and tell her that you love her, that you know that she is already sleeping with her boyfriend, but that she may not do so in your house, under your roof. Everything inside of your body language, your embrace, and your person will clearly communicate two things: "I love you, you're my daughter; I will always love you, no matter what. But I don't agree with you on this matter." Your embrace does not say "I agree with you!," it simply says "I love you!" and the affirmation of your love, even as you hold your personal and moral ground, will perhaps, more than anything else you can offer her, invite her to reflect upon your moral ground and why you hold certain things so deeply.

This kind of embrace, which radiates God's compassion and understanding even as it holds its own moral ground, is asked of us not just in families and friendships, but in every area of life. Whether we are Catholic or Protestant, Evangelical or Unitarian, Christian or Jew, Jew or Muslim, Christian or Muslim, prolife or prochoice, liberal or conservative, we all must find the compassion and empathy to be able to embrace in a way that expresses love and understanding even as that embrace does not say that differences are of no importance.

There is a time to stand up for what we believe in, a

time to be prophetic, a time to draw a line in the sand, a time to point out differences and the consequences of that, and a time to stand in strong opposition to values and forces that threaten what we hold dear. But there is also a time to embrace across differences, to recognize that we can love and respect each other even when we do not hold the same values, when what is common eclipses our differences. There is a time to be compassionate as God is compassionate, to let our sun shine indiscriminately on both the vegetables and the weeds without denying which is which.

One of the signs of deeper maturity is precisely the capacity to radiate this kind of compassion, to mirror God's nondiscriminating embrace. But this is not easy because sometimes things separate us from others in ways that seem to demand that we make our compassion selective. We are divided from one another by, among other things, language, race, ethnicity, gender, religion, politics, ideology, culture, personal history, temperament, private wounds, and moral judgments. It is hard, in the face of all this, to see people who are different from us as full brothers and sisters, as equally important citizens of this world, and as loved and valued by God in the same way we are.

And so we often live in distrust of one another and demonize one another, seeing danger in every difference. We then either actively oppose one another or simply steer clear of one another and caution our loved ones to steer clear as well. Consequently, we live in a world in which various groups stay away from one another:

liberals and conservatives, Protestants and Catholics, Jews and Arabs, Arabs and Christians, Muslims and Buddhists, black and white races, prolife and prochoice groups, feminists and traditionalists. The list is unending. How can we be compassionate as God is compassionate within all of this?

Jesus gives us a model for compassion in his gesture of washing his disciples' feet. The biblical text is found in John's Gospel[13]: In this gospel, Jesus does not institute the Eucharist at the Last Supper. Instead, where the other Gospels have Jesus taking the bread and wine and offering it to his disciples as his body and blood, John's Gospel has Jesus taking up a basin and towel and washing his disciples' feet, in the face of their protests. What does this gesture mean?

It has various levels of meaning: at one level, it is a gesture of humility, the master washing the feet of his servants, the master taking the mantle of privilege and reversing it into the apron of service. This is the meaning that Christian iconography and popular piety have generally drawn from the text. While that is correct, it does not go far enough. This is a gesture of humility, but of a particular kind of humility, one that stretches us beyond the differences that normally separate us. This can be educed from the background of this text.

Scholars estimate that this text was written as least sixty to seventy years after Jesus' death. John, who is seen as its author, would have been the only apostle still alive, and he would have been a very old man, perhaps over ninety years of age. What makes this important is that he would have already seen sixty to seventy years of church life. And church life then was like church life now: they fought about most everything, and especially they fought about the Eucharist. By the time the Gospel of John was written, there were already, not unlike today, a variety of practices around the Eucharist and all kinds of disagreements about it. Hence, what is highlighted in John's Gospel about the Last Supper is not the institution of the Eucharist with bread and wine, but one of the major meanings of the Eucharist, namely, a reaching across distances that divide us, through the basin and the towel.

The gesture of Jesus washing his disciples' feet is one of the salient biblical images of what it means to be compassionate as God is compassionate. What Jesus is doing with this gesture is reaching across the divide, every kind of divide that separates us from one another, to let God's embrace enfold everyone equally. Let me risk a bold example:

In our secularized societies today, no moral issue divides us as much as that of abortion. It is a deep divide that separates us, the sincere from the sincere. What is to be done apposite the issue of abortion? If the ninety-year-old apostle John were here today, I suspect that he would suggest that in the face of this division, we bring out some basins and towels and have prochoice and prolife groups, liberals and conservatives, wash one another's feet. If that were done sincerely, there would be a real chance that our society might finally begin the kind of conversation that is needed to end abortion, given that in the end nobody really wants it. But that is quite a stretch, and it is meant to be. The biblical gesture of washing someone else's feet does not just invite us to the clean, feel-good, humility we experience after serving a meal in a soup kitchen, wonderful as that is. It invites us too to a compassion that feels messy, that is, to a compassion that, like the sun, sheds its light on friend and foe alike in a humility that does not always feel good but rather has us swallowing hard as we lay a gentle hand and an understanding heart on someone who bitterly disagrees with us.

That kind of embrace, across great ideological divides, demands precisely a deep act of humility. And that deep act of humility itself demands an insight and an inner strength that normally escape us. How do we find the vision and the inner strength to reach across a painful divide? We find it by, metaphorically, taking off our "outer garment" so as to be in touch with our deepest inner reality. What is implied here?

We wear more than physical clothing to cover our naked selves; we cover our nakedness too with a specific ethnicity, language, religious identity, culture, political affiliation, ideology, set of moral judgments, and a whole gamut of private wounds and indignations. These are in essence our outer garments. But we also possess a deeper inner garment. Our real identity lies underneath. How so?

The text that describes Jesus' washing the feet of his disciples is carefully prefaced with these words: "Jesus knowing that the Father had put everything into his hands, and that he had come from God and was returning to God, got up from the table, and took off his outer garments."[14]

When John is describing Jesus "taking off his outer garment," he implies more than just the stripping off of some physical clothing, some outer sash that might have gotten in the way of his stooping down and washing someone's feet. In order to let go of the pride that blocks any human being from stooping down to wash the feet of someone different from himself, Jesus had to strip off a lot of outer things (pride, moral judgments, superiority, ideology, and personal dignity) so as to wear only his inner garment. What was his inner garment? As John mystically describes it, his inner garment was precisely his knowledge that he had come from God, was going back to God, and that therefore all things were possible for him, including washing the feet of someone whom he already knew had betrayed him.

That is also our own inner garment, the reality that lies deepest beneath our race, gender, religion, language, politics, ideology, and personal history (with all its wounds and false pride). What is most real is that deep down, beneath these other, outer, things, we are imprinted with the dark memory, the brand of love and truth, the inchoate knowledge that, like Jesus, we too have come from God, are returning to God, and therefore are capable of doing anything, including loving and washing the feet of someone very different from ourselves. Our inner garment is the image and likeness of God inside us, and when we are in touch with this, we can find the strength to wash one another's feet across any divide: liberal–conservative, prolife–prochoice, Catholic–Protestant, Jew–Muslim, Muslim–Christian, black–white, man–woman, and begin to feel sympathy for one another beyond our wounds and differences.

Sometimes in our better moments we already do that. Unfortunately, to have one of our better moments usually takes a great sadness, a tragedy, or a death. Mostly, it is only in the face of mutual helplessness and sorrow, at a funeral or in the face of tragedy, that we are capable of forgetting our differences, putting away our outer garments, and seeing one another as brothers and sisters.

Deep maturity invites us, at various critical times in our lives, to put aside our placards, without denying the worthiness of the cause, and take up a basin and towel so as to embrace in compassion someone separated from us by a bitter divide.

One final point on being compassionate as God is compassionate: biblical compassion demands that we never be content, either as a family or a church, while some of our members are separated from us. The compassion of God leaves no room for writing off anyone else as lost or as good riddance. This is everywhere present in Jesus' message, though poignantly so in the parable of the woman with the ten coins.[15]

Here is the parable: a woman had ten coins and lost one. She became extremely anxious and agitated about the loss and began to search frantically and relentlessly for the lost coin, lighting lamps, looking under tables, and sweeping all the floors in her house. Eventually, she found the coin, and her joy in finding it matched her agitation in losing it. She was delirious with joy, called together her neighbors to share in her joy, and threw a party whose cost far exceeded the value of the coin she had lost.

Why such anxiety and such joy over the loss of a coin and the finding of a coin whose value was that of a dime? The answer lies in the symbolism of numbers: in her culture, nine was not a whole number; ten was a whole number. Both the woman's anxiety of losing the coin and her joy in finding it have little to do with the value of the coin but with the value of wholeness; a certain wholeness in her life had been fractured and only by finding the coin could it be restored. And so you might recast the parable this way:

A woman had ten children, which constituted her family. With nine of them, she had a good relationship, but one of her daughters was alienated from her and from the family. Everyone else came regularly to the family table, but this one daughter did not. The woman could not find rest in that situation; she needed her alienated daughter to rejoin them. She tried every means to reconcile with her daughter, and, one day, in a miracle of miracles, it worked. Her daughter reconciled with her and came back to the family. The family was whole again; everyone was back at the table. The woman was overjoyed, withdrew her modest savings from the bank, and threw a lavish party to celebrate the great grace that her family was whole again.

Mature compassion demands that, like that woman, we are meant to be solicitous, not able to rest, lighting lamps and searching, until our families, churches, and communities are again whole and those who will no longer sit at a table with us are back in the fold. Nine is not a whole number, and neither is the number of those who are normally at our family or church tables. We need to be constantly uneasy: Who is not at the table with us? Who no longer goes to church with us? Who feels uncomfortable worshipping with us? Who will no longer join us in a conversation over morality or politics? The hard question is: Are we comfortable with the fact that so many people can no longer join us at our family, church, moral, or political tables?

Sadly, today, too many of us are comfortable in families, churches, and communities that are far, far from whole. Sometimes, in our less-reflective moments, we even rejoice in it: "Good riddance! Love us or leave us! She was not a real Christian in any case! His views are so narrow and bigoted, it's just as well he is not here! We are better off without that kind! There's more peace this way! We are a purer, more faithful church because of her absence!"

But this lack of a healthy solicitude for wholeness compromises maturity and Christian discipleship. We are compassionate as God is compassionate only when, like Jesus, we remain in tears for those "other sheep that are not of this fold" and when, like the woman who lost one of her coins and would not sleep until every corner of the house was turned upside down in a frantic search for what was lost, we too set out solicitously in search of that lost wholeness.

v) To Live the Baptism of Jesus and Not Just of John

John Shea once wrote a haunting poem about John the Baptist. The poem begins with the Baptist in prison, hearing the dancing above his head and knowing that this is soon to culminate in his being beheaded. Strangely, he is not too upset. Herod is about to give Herodias's daughter half his kingdom, and John feels that he might as well die in the bargain, given that he is only half a man and half a prophet. Why does he feel himself as only half a man? He is only half a man because, as Shea's poem puts it, he can do only a half job:

> I can denounce a king, but I cannot enthrone one.
> I can strip an idol of its power, but I cannot reveal the true God.
> I can wash the soul in sand, but I cannot dress it in white.
> I can devour the word of the Lord like wild honey,
> but I cannot lace his sandal.
> I can condemn sin, but I cannot bear it away.
> Behold the Lamb of God, who takes away the sin of the world.[16]

John the Baptist is aware of both his strength and his impotence. He can point out what's wrong and what should be done, but after that he is helpless, with nothing to offer in terms of the strength needed to correct the wrong. That is indeed only a half job, a half prophecy: it can denounce a king by showing what is wrong, and it can wash the soul in sand by blasting off layers of accumulated rust and dirt; but ultimately, it cannot empower us to correct anything. Something else is needed. What?

Anyone who has ever tried to overcome an addiction

can answer that question. A clear head, a clear vision of what is to be done, and a solid resolution to leave a bad habit behind is only a half job, a first step—an important one but only an initial one. The tough part is still ahead: Where to find and sustain the strength needed actually to change our behavior and give up a bad habit? Those who have ever given up an addiction will tell you that, in the end, they did not do it by willpower, or certainly not by willpower alone. Grace and community were needed, and they were what ultimately provided what willpower alone could not.

At one point in the Gospels, Jesus tells his disciples that it is easier for a camel to pass through the eye of a needle than for a rich person to enter the kingdom of heaven. The disciples are stunned, and Peter responds by saying: "If that is the case, then it is impossible!" Jesus appreciates that reaction and adds: "It is impossible for humans, but not for God." Anybody who is in recovery from an addiction knows exactly what Jesus means by that. They have experienced it: they know that it is impossible for them to give up the object of their addiction—and yet they are giving it up, not by their own willpower but by some higher power: grace.

The Gospels speak of this as a baptism, and they speak of two kinds of baptisms: the baptism of John and the baptism of Jesus, adding that John's baptism is only a preparation for Jesus' baptism. What's John's baptism? It is a baptism of repentance, a realization of what we are doing wrong and a clear resolution to correct our bad behavior. What is Jesus' baptism? It is an entry into grace and community in such a way that empowers us internally to do what is impossible for us to do by our willpower alone.

But how does this work? Is grace a kind of magic? No. It is not magic, but all psychic, emotional, and spiritual energy is, by definition, beyond ordinary phenomenological understanding. Simply put, that means that we cannot ever fully lay out its inner plumbing and explain how it works. There is a mystery to all energy. However, what we can lay out empirically is its effect. Spiritual energy works. Grace works. This has been proven inside the experience of thousands of people (many of them atheists) who have been able to find an energy inside of them that clearly does not come from them and yet empowers them beyond their willpower alone. Ask any addict in recovery about this.

Simply put, too often, as mature adults, we are still trying to live out our lives by John's baptism alone, that is, by sheer willpower. That gives us a valuable insight into what is wrong in our lives and what is wrong in the world, but leaves us mostly powerless to actually change what is wrong. There is no salvation through willpower alone. Years of trying to change our lives without real results should have taught us that. What we need during our adult years is something that can empower us beyond our own strength, a fire beyond our own, a baptism into grace and community.

vi) To Wait in the Upper Room with Other Disciples

There is an axiom attributed to Peter Maurin, the man who helped Dorothy Day found the *Catholic Worker* that goes something like this: "When you don't know what else to do, keep going to meetings because Pentecost happened at a meeting!"

He is right. Pentecost did not happen to a solitary man or woman, praying on a mountaintop, in a church, in a desert, or under a tree. It happened to a group of men and women at a church meeting. Moreover, it did not happen at a triumphal church meeting, where men and women were sure of themselves as they praised God in confidence. It happened at a church meeting where men and women, frightened for their future, were huddled in fear, confusion, and uncertainty, but were gathered in faith and fidelity despite their fears. This is how scripture describes it.

At the end of Luke's Gospel, just before he departs this earth, Jesus gives a rather shaky group of followers this counsel: return to the city and don't leave until you feel yourself clothed with power from on high! We find out later, in the Acts of the Apostles, how his followers interpreted this; that is, they met and, frightened and uncertain of their future, waited together in an upper room until they experienced the new fire of Pentecost.[17]

As we struggle to sustain our commitments and move to deeper maturity within our various faith circles today, perhaps few metaphors are as penetrating, as fertile a field for reflection, and as descriptive of what is actually happening as is this image of waiting in the Upper Room. What is contained in this image, more precisely? This picture: a formerly confident but now somewhat deflated group of disciples are huddled together, confused and out of energy, needing to be recharged anew, unsure of what they are waiting for, but waiting nonetheless for something new to happen to them, for new fire, for a new vision and a new energy from beyond.

In many ways, that describes both the faith and the ecclesial situation of many men and women today, regardless of religious denomination. Like the first followers of Jesus, immediately after his departure, they also no longer know what they should be doing. Their faith and values too have been crucified. So much of what used to work no longer does. They are finding it ever harder to pass their faith on to their own children, to fire the religious and romantic imagination of their culture, and to make a religious and moral dent of any kind in the ever hardening secularity within ordinary consciousness. What should they be doing in the face of declining church attendance, the growing agnosticism of the world, and the ecclesial indifference of so many of their own children?

Biblically, this is the answer: return to the city and remain in the Upper Room! What is meant by that? In Luke's Gospel, as we saw, "the city" refers to Jerusalem, which itself is an image for the church and the faith dream that Jesus had instilled. To walk away from Jerusalem, as the disciples were doing in walking toward Emmaus, was to walk away from the church and from their faith dream. And so the invitation to mature disciples today is the same as it was for that first generation of disciples who were fearful and confused as they faced Jesus' departure: Return to the city, return to your faith dream! Go and wait with one another in the Upper Room!

Thus, our faith circles, church services, and ecclesial meetings are, in effect, the Upper Room. And that Upper Room has many modalities: beyond our regular church services we have ecclesial meetings of every kind, Bible studies, ecumenical meetings, religious congresses, pastoral institutes, catechism classes, social justice commissions, institutes on spirituality, religious retreats, international synods on missiology, small faith-sharing groups, and men and women everywhere praying in churches, kitchens, and monasteries, asking for a new fire from beyond. All these activities, all these things we do in our faith circles, put us into the Upper Room.

And, like the original Upper Room in Jerusalem, our venues too are generally humble, church basements and church foyers, with bad chairs, bad lighting, and bad dishes. The Upper Room is not glamorous, not a Leonardo da Vinci painting. It always looks like the meeting room in your local church. But it is there that Pentecost happened and will continue to happen. And so Jesus' advice to today's struggling believer is still the same as it was to a group of uncertain and shaky disciples at the time of his Ascension: return to the city and wait in the Upper Room! Or, as Peter Maurin put it: "When you don't know what else to do, keep going to meetings because Pentecost happened at a meeting!"

SOME PARTICULAR INVITATIONS FROM SCRIPTURE

There is only one sorrow, the sorrow of not being a Saint.

—LEON BLOY[1]

From Goodness to Greatness

All of us know many good people, women and men who are honest, generous, courageous, and faith filled. By and large, the world is a good place. But among all those good people, only a select few stand out as truly exceptional in both their humanity and their virtue. Many of us are good, few among us are great. Indeed persons of the equality of Mother Teresa stand out as singular and exceptional within a whole generation. Why? What distinguishes them from others? What distinguishes goodness from greatness? What takes maturity to a higher level? What fuels the highest generativity within Christian discipleship? What makes someone a full saint?

This will not be a full answer to those questions, nor a systematic one. This chapter will attempt to answer these questions by examining two invitations that come to us in the Gospels, which invite us to move from goodness to greatness, from being a saint in progress to being a saint in actuality, from being a good-hearted woman or man to being a Mother Teresa or a Dag Hammarskjöld. Those invitations, as we will also see, beckon us beyond the sorrow of not being a saint. What are those invitations?

The Invitation to the Rich Young Man

i) The Invitation

If one were to look for a text in the Gospels within which Jesus invites a good person to take the next move so as to become a great person, one would be hard-pressed to find a more explicit example than the invitation that Jesus offers to a rich young man.[2] We have rarely picked up on the depth of this invitation because we have tended to vilify this young man when, indeed, nothing in the text gives us cause. He is not some morally lax person, in need of basic conversion. Rather, he is already mature and solidly committed in faith and virtue. He is a good person who is not yet fully a saint. He stands in our place. His question to Jesus is indeed

our question, and Jesus' invitation to him is indeed the
invitation before which most mature, faithful persons
daily stand. What is his question and what is the invitation that Jesus offers him?

It would be interesting if we could be reading this
text for the first time, instead of being overfamiliar with
it. The danger in our overfamiliarity is that we do not
pick up on the sincerity and depth of this man, nor identify with him, because we already know that he is rich
and that he will turn down Jesus' invitation, when, in
fact, we do not learn either of these until the very end of
the story. Would that we could unlearn what we know
and look at this story with fresh eyes, because perhaps
no one in the Gospels more clearly represents the habit-
ual struggle of the mature, committed man or woman
than does this young man. Jesus' invitation to him is
Jesus' invitation to every good man or woman to move
from goodness to greatness. What is his story?

In essence it runs this way: one day a young man
comes up to Jesus, respectfully acknowledges him, and
asks him this question: "Good Master, what must I do
to possess eternal life?" Jesus answers by referring to
the scriptures and reminding him of something that as
a faith-filled believer he already knew: "Love the Lord
your God with all your mind, your heart, and your
strength, and love your neighbor as yourself, and to
keep the commandments." The young man responds: "I
have been doing this since my youth." Jesus looks at him
and loves him, accepting the truth of his answer, and
says to him: "You lack one thing. If you would receive

eternal life, go sell *everything* that you have, give the money to the poor, and come and follow me." But the young man cannot accept the invitation, blocked by his riches, and goes away sad.

ii) Two Images for an Interpretation

What has just transpired here? Let me offer two stories by way of interpretation, one taken from the Desert Fathers and the other from a contemporary setting.

There is a famous story taken from the writings of the Desert Fathers, which might well be a homily on this gospel passage. It reads this way: "Abbot Lot went to see Abbot Joseph and said: 'Father, according as I am able, I keep my little rule, and my little fast, my prayer, meditation and contemplative silence; and according as I am able I strive to cleanse my heart of bad thoughts: now what more should I do?' The elder rose up in reply and stretched out his hands to heaven, and his fingers became like lamps of fire. He said: 'Why not become all flame?' "[3]

What does it mean to "become all flame"? A second story, from a present-day setting, can perhaps be illustrative here: some years ago, I was preaching a retreat to a group of priests. One evening, after our conference, five of them invited me to join them for something they termed "a support-group meeting." We met in a small breakout room. They had set out some finger foods, pretzels, beer, and scotch on a table, but they didn't get to them for nearly an hour. The first hour was taken up with each of them making a searing, honest, detailed confession to the whole group of all they had done wrong since they last met, from failures in reaching out to the needy, to resentments and anger within their ministry, to acts of private indulgence. Only after each priest in turn had made his confession did they turn to the food, the drink, and the socializing.

As we were socializing, the leader of the group explained to me how this group had come together. "I started this group four years ago," he shared, "because I needed to do something in my own life. I was a good priest, but I wasn't a great priest, and I can name the reasons for both. I was a good priest: I went to the seminary in sincerity, did my studies as best I could, and was ordained and ministered as best I could. Early on in my ministry, the bishop assigned me to four rural parishes, and the workload was crushing. I had meetings almost every night and was on the road most of the time. But I did it! I was generous to a fault. And the people loved me for it. They thought I was Francis of Assisi. I was a good priest, but I wasn't a great priest. I had no illusions about that. I had a number of things I leaned on to handle my tension. While I did all that work, I did it with a lot of resentment, carrying lots of anger inside me. I complained a lot. And because I was working so hard, I began to compensate in terms of my lifestyle. I was always tired and didn't have much of a life outside my ministry, so I began to lean on the creature comforts available to me. My salary isn't great, but I had little else to spend it on, so I bought the best of everything. I went on expensive holidays, and if I went out to eat, I bought the best steak in the house and the most expensive wine on the menu, because I felt tired and felt this was owed to me. I bought the best in liquor and every kind of electronic gadget, music, and video. None of these things were bad, but they were, unconsciously, becoming compensatory. And finally, worse than resentment and lifestyle, I sometimes handled my tension through masturbation. I was doing all this good work, but I had no illusions that I was Mother Teresa. And the irony was that these compensations made everything else work; they were my way of coping with tension.

"That all began to change with my father's death. I much admired him. Driving home from his funeral, crying in the car, I made a resolution that, if I was going to be a priest, I was going to be a *great* priest! No more compensations, no more slipping into mediocrity! But I was naive. I had to learn what everyone who has ever overcome a bad habit has to learn, namely, that you cannot correct your life by willpower alone, you need grace and community. So after I realized that I didn't have the strength to give up my bad habits all on my own, one by one, I talked my closest priest friends into doing this with me. Now we meet regularly, every week when we can, and we try to do this together. We want to be priests whose lives are fully transparent, so that when people see us, what they see is truly what they get! We call ourselves a group for "radical sobriety," though none of us has ever had a problem with alcohol; but none of us has ever had full sobriety either. Full sobriety is full transparency, and full transparency is full honesty."

Others in the group shared about their entry into the group and each had a similar story: "I was a good priest, but not a great one! Being in this group is an attempt to move myself beyond a certain mediocrity that I was stuck in." One of the priests who shared his story, the youngest in the group, made this comment: "I only joined this group two years ago, and doing what we are doing is the hardest thing I have ever done in life. Not the confession to the others, since I trust them, but being thirty-eight years old and trying to live like Mother Teresa. That's hard." Then he added: "But it's also the best thing I have ever done! I have never been this happy."

There was indeed a quality of happiness within and among them that was palpable. They were happy men, happy priests. It is significant to note that, after turning down Jesus' invitation, the rich young man went away *sad;* not bad, just sad. He came to Jesus as a rich, sad young man and he went away as a rich, sad young man. He did not lose anything, except an opportunity. What was his sadness? The sadness of not being a saint: "There is only one sorrow, the sorrow of not being a Saint."[4]

It is not an imaginative stretch to connect the invitation that Jesus offers to the rich young man to these stories. The rich young man comes to Jesus much like Abbott Lot came to Abbott Joseph: He, in effect, is asking Jesus: "I keep the rules, I say my prayers, I am doing most everything right. What more should I be doing?" And Jesus' answer is that of Abbott Joseph: "Why not become all flame?" The story of the five priests helps

explicate what it means concretely to become all flame
and what it means to move from goodness to greatness.
What does it mean?

The priest who founded this group of men, in speaking of his own need for conversion, shared this image:
"I sometimes picture my soul as a mansion with thirty
rooms. I had given twenty-seven of them to God, but I
had kept three for myself. Conversion for me meant giving up those final three rooms. Sometimes too I quantify
that: I had given up about 90 percent of my life to God,
but I had kept back 10 percent. The difference between
being a good priest and being a great one is just that,
keeping back 10 percent, holding back on three rooms!"
To become all flame is to give up the last three rooms.

That, nearly perfectly, describes the rich young man
standing before Jesus. In essence, he is telling Jesus: "I
have given up almost everything for God. What more
must I do?" Jesus' answer is simple and direct: "Give up
the rest! You have given up almost everything, and that
is good. But now, to move beyond your present sadness
to a deeper joy, you have to give up *everything*! Half
measures and three-quarter measures no longer do it for
you; you have to give it all up!"

And that too is the invitation to everyone who, while
already generous and good, is not yet a full saint. What
is still lacking in the lives of most mature adults? What
separates most of us from someone like Mother Teresa?
What takes someone across the threshold of goodness
to the household of greatness? Metaphorically speaking,
we need to become all flame. Concretely, that means

giving over those last, clung-to, areas of our lives, those last three rooms, that last 10 percent that we are still keeping for ourselves because we need those compensations to enable us to handle our tensions. And the sadness that so subtly clings to us like an odor, even in our goodness and generosity, is there because, like the rich young man, we are still walking away from the full invitation. We are still holding something back, still holding on to some of our own riches.

There is a poem by Margaret Halaska that captures this brilliantly, both in terms of our resistance to handing over all the rooms in our house to God and God's infinite patience in dealing with us. The poem is titled "Covenant," and it reads as follows:

The Father
knocks at my door
seeking a home for his son:

Rent is cheap, I say.

I don't want to rent. I want to buy, says God.

I'm not sure I want to sell,
but you might come in to look around.

I think I will, says God.

I might let you have a room or two.

I like it, says God, I'll take two.
You might decide to give me more some day.
I can wait, says God.

I'd like to give you more,
but it's a bit difficult. I need some space for me.

I know, says God, but I'll wait. I like what I see.

Hm, maybe I can let you have another room.
I really don't need that much.

Thanks, says God, I'll take it. I like what I see.

I'd like to give you the whole house
But I'm not sure—

Think on it, says God, I wouldn't put you out.
Your house would be mine and my son would live in it.
You'd have more space than you'd ever had before.

I don't understand at all.

I know, says God, but I can't tell you about that.
You'll have to discover it for yourself.
That can only happen if you let him have the whole house.

A bit risky, I say.

Yes, says God, but try me.

I'm not sure—
I'll let you know.

I can wait, says God. I like what I see.[5]

iii) The Strength to Do It

But the gospel story of the rich young man is not yet finished, there is still a further invitation within it. After the young man has declined his invitation, Jesus turns to his disciples and says: it is easier for a camel to pass through the eye of a needle than for a rich man to enter the kingdom of heaven. And his disciples are stunned by this. Peter expresses their shock by saying, If that is the case, then it is impossible. Jesus welcomes this response and says: In fact, it is impossible, for humans, all on their own, but nothing is impossible for God![6] What Jesus is affirming here is what the founder of that priests' group expressed when he said: "I had to learn what everyone who has ever overcome a bad habit had to learn, namely, that you cannot correct your life by willpower alone, you need grace and community." It is impossible to live out greatness on only the strength of our own willpower. We need grace and community. We become saints only with the support of others.

Like the rich young man, every mature man or woman stands with this invitation always in front of him or her, offered by an infinitely patient God who likes what he sees. Full human maturity and full generativity as a disciple of Jesus lie in accepting that invitation, in becoming pure flame, in handing over those last rooms in our house.

The Invitation to Ponder as Mary Pondered

i) Mary as the Paradigm of Maturity and Discipleship

The second biblical invitation to move from goodness to greatness, from being a saint in progress to being a saint in actuality, is the invitation to ponder as Mary, the mother of Jesus, pondered. This is modeled for us in the Gospels where Mary is held up for us as the paradigm of Christian discipleship.[7] Indeed in the Gospels, during Jesus' earthly life, most everyone gets it wrong; the authorities, the crowds, the disciples, and even the apostles. Most everyone tends to misunderstand, to miss the point and betray. Unlike those others, Mary singularly gets it right. She shows what a true disciple should be and should do.

But the Gospels present this rather subtly. Indeed, at times they almost seem to denigrate her role. For example, on one occasion, while Jesus is speaking to a group, someone comes up to him and tells him that his mother and his family are looking for him. Jesus replies by asking, "Who is my mother? Who are my brothers and sisters?" and then answers, "Whoever hears the word of God and keeps it is mother and brother and sister to me."[8] In another instance, he is speaking when a woman in the crowd raises her voice and says: "Blessed is the womb that bore you and the breasts that nursed you!" Jesus answers her: "Rather blessed are those who hear the word of God and keep it."[9]

Superficially, in both cases, Jesus seems to be distancing himself from his mother and playing down her importance. The opposite is true. What Jesus is doing in these texts is downplaying his mother's biology in order to highlight her faith. When he states that whoever hears and keeps the word of God is his true mother, the first person whom he is naming is his own mother, given that she was the first person to hear the word of God and fully keep it. Hence, Jesus' exchange with the woman who praises his biological mother might be recast this way: "You must have a wonderful mother!" "Indeed, I do, but in a much deeper way than you suppose. All mothers are wonderful in their biology, but mine is even more wonderful in her faith!" In the Gospels, Mary is the first person to hear the word of God and keep it, and thus the first true disciple.

ii) The Notion of Pondering

The one quality that perhaps most deeply exemplifies Mary's faith and discipleship is contained in a single phrase predicated of her: *she pondered*. Mary pondered while the others did not. What does it mean to ponder in the biblical sense?

We need to make an immediate distinction here: one can ponder in the Greek sense and one can ponder in the Hebrew sense. Pondering in the Greek sense might aptly be defined by an expression that comes to us from the Greek philosophy: the unexamined life is not worth living. Our commonsense notion is very much tied to that notion of pondering, where to ponder means to try to think something through in all its depth and implications. One pictures, for example, Rodin's famous sculpture *The Thinker,* someone sitting in a chapel or on a mountainside, intensely reflecting on something, mulling it over, considering all its various angles. But this would be what the word would mean had the Gospels been written by Aristotle. But the Gospels, while written in Greek, are Hebrew thought, and there, pondering has a different, more existential, connotation. Simply put, to ponder, in the Hebrew sense, meant to hold, carry, and transform tension so as not to give it back in kind, knowing that whatever energies we do not transform we will transmit. What does this mean concretely?

Perhaps it can best be captured in an image, the image of Mary standing under the cross. As Jesus was dying, the Gospels tell us that Mary, his mother, stood under the cross. What is contained in that image? What is in this picture that invites us to more than simple admiration, piety, or sympathy? This is a mystical image, and it is anything but pious. What is Mary doing while standing under the cross?

On the surface it appears that she is not doing anything at all. She does not speak, does not try to stop the crucifixion, and does not even protest its unfairness or plead Jesus' innocence. She is mute, seemingly passive, overtly not doing anything. But at a deeper level she is doing all that can be done when one is standing under the weight of the cross, she is holding and carrying the tension, standing in strength, refusing to give back in kind, and resisting in a deep way. What is meant by this?

Sometimes well-intentioned artists have painted Mary as prostrate under the cross, the wounded mother, helplessly distraught, paralyzed by grief, an object for sympathy. But that does not honor what happened there nor teach its lesson. Prostration, in this situation, is weakness, collapse, hysteria, resignation. In the Gospels, "standing" is a position of strength. Mary "stood" under the cross. She was strong there. Still, why the silence and why her seeming unwillingness to act or protest?

In essence, what Mary was doing under the cross was this: her silence and strength were speaking these words: "Today, I can't stop the crucifixion; nobody can. Sometimes darkness will have its hour. But I can stop some of the hatred, bitterness, jealousy, and heartlessness that caused it—by refusing to give it back in kind, by transforming negativity rather than retransmitting it, by swallowing hard, in silence, and eating the bitterness rather than giving it back in kind."

Had Mary, in emotional and moral outrage, begun to scream hysterically, shout angrily at those crucifying Jesus, or physically tried to attack someone as he was driving the nails into Jesus' hands, she would have been caught up in the same kind of energy as everyone else, replicating the very anger and bitterness that caused the crucifixion. What Mary was doing under the cross, her silence and seeming unwillingness to protest notwithstanding, was radiating all that is antithetical to crucifixion: gentleness, understanding, forgiveness, peace, light, and courage.

And that is not easy to do. Everything inside us demands justice, screams for it, and refuses to remain silent in the presence of injustice. That is a healthy instinct, and sometimes acting on it is good. We need, at times, to protest, to shout, to throw ourselves literally into the face of injustice and do everything in our power to stop it. But there are times too when things have gone so far that shouts and protests are no longer helpful, darkness is going to have its hour, and all we can do is stand under its cross and help absorb its bitterness by refusing to participate in its energy. In those situations, like Mary, we have to say: "I can't stop this crucifixion, but I can stop some of the hatred, bitterness, jealousy, brutal heartlessness, and darkness that surround it. I can't stop this, but I will not conduct its hatred."

And that is not the same thing as despair. Our muted helplessness is not a passive resignation, but its opposite. It is a movement toward the only rays of light, love, and faith that still exist in that darkness and hatred. And at that moment, it is the only thing that faith and love can do. As the book of Lamentations says, there are times when the best we can do is put our mouths to the dust and wait![10] Sometimes too, as Rainer Maria Rilke says, the only helpful thing is to absorb the heaviness: "Do not be afraid to suffer, give the heaviness back to the weight of the earth; mountains are heavy, seas are heavy."[11] That is not passivity, resignation, or weakness; but genuine, rare strength.

That is what it means to ponder, in the Hebrew sense. This is what is predicated of Mary when the Gospels tell us that she "pondered these things."

iii) A Poem to Ponder

When the state of Texas carries out executions, it does them at a place called Huntsville. Michael Maginn, an Irish writer, once wrote a poem within which he brings together two poignant images: Mary pondering under the cross and a small group of Christian women standing outside the death chamber in Huntsville. The poem reads like this:

Huntsville

(for protesters and counter protestors)

At Huntsville, Walker County,
God fearing citizens congregate with zealous enthusiasm,
To celebrate the Black Mass of capital punishment,
eye for eye, tooth for tooth, life for life.

Ugly mayhem in the prison parking lot
As the killing hour approaches:
Rival protestors confronting each other,
Placards screaming across the blistering yard.

A small huddle of women
Stand to the side with candles, speaking softly,
Supporting one another, shouting no bitter slogans,
Silently absorbing cat calls and angry invective.

Like the women at the foot of the cross
at another execution.

Lord,

May we never add a single drop

To the negative, destructive energies

That swirl around us every day,

Threatening to engulf us.[12]

iv) The Opposite or Pondering—Amazement

Sometimes things are more fully understood when we see them in contrast to their opposite, and that is true here. What is the opposite of pondering? Biblically, the opposite of pondering is "amazement, to be amazed." What is amazement?

In the mid-1990s, a novel by Robert Waller, *The Bridges of Madison County,* took America by storm. It was the number one, best-selling book for an entire year and eventually was turned into a popular film of the same title. The story runs like this: a photographer for *National Geographic* is driving around in rural Iowa, looking for a set of historic bridges he has been commissioned to photograph. He is lost and eventually drives to a farmhouse to ask for directions. As chance would have it, the unlucky husband has just left for a week to attend a cattle show, and his wife answers the door. There is instant karma, soul connection. They both feel it. She invites him for dinner, and before the meal is over they have fallen in love, deeply and irrevocably. Before the evening is over, they are also in bed with each other.

What is wrong with this picture? People can fall in

love instantly, deeply, and permanently at first glance.
It takes only fifteen seconds for the whole world to
change. What is wrong is that we are supposed to believe that something sublime has taken place, something
so profound and deep that the rest of us can only contemplate it in envy. But that is the fallacy. When two
people who have known each other less than six hours
make love with each other, how sublime can that be? Is
that not tantamount to gestating a baby in six hours,
writing a doctoral thesis in six hours, or doing a painting or writing a novel at one sitting and purporting it to
be a masterpiece? How sublime can something be when
there has not first been some sublimation (at least for
more than a couple of hours)? What we have here is an
instance of what the Gospels call "amazement." What
is this?

The Gospels record a number of instances where
Jesus does or says something that catches people by surprise. The evangelists then tell us: "And the people were
amazed." Invariably, almost immediately, Jesus says:
"Don't be amazed!" He has a deep suspicion of amazement. Why? Because he knows that the same people
who are so impressed with him one day so as to want to
make him king need very little altering of circumstance
to begin the chant: "Crucify him!"

What is amazement? We are amazed in the biblical
sense when we simply let energy flow through in the same
way as a wire conducts an electrical current, when we
simply take in the energy of the group around us or the
energy of spontaneous emotion and, without holding,

carrying, or transforming it, act on it as it flows through us. That can sometimes be harmless or even good, at a rock concert or a football game, but it can also be mindless, negative, and dangerous. Amazement lies at the root of hype, ideology, groupthink, mob mentality, gang rapes, and crucifixions. Crowds do not think: they act out of a blind energy, and that carries immense dangers. Indeed, scripture scholars tell us that in the Gospels, most every time the word *crowd* is used, one could supply the adjective "mindless."

To ponder, biblically, is the opposite of this. We ponder when we do not let the energy of the crowd or of spontaneous emotion simply flow through us and become the basis for our actions. Instead, we hold and carry and transform that energy so as to not mindlessly retransmit it. And this capacity lies at the root of deeper maturity and deeper virtue. For example, examine this challenge from Jesus:

At the very heart of his moral teaching, lies this statement: "Unless your virtue goes deeper than the virtue of the scribes and Pharisees, you will not enter the kingdom of God."[13] It is easy to miss the challenge in this text because we too easily think of the hypocrisy of the scribes and Pharisees that Jesus sometimes highlights. But in this instance, he is not referring to their faults but to their virtues, and, indeed, they were very religious and moral. What was their virtue? They held themselves, and very strictly too, to two great moral pillars: the Ten Commandments and the ideal of justice. To be virtuous for a scribe or a Pharisee meant keeping the Ten Commandments and being strictly just with your neighbor. So why is this inadequate?

Because in the end, this can still be done in amazement, by giving energy back in kind. We can keep all the commandments and be just to our neighbor without having to love our enemies or having to forgive one another. Justice is predicated on fairness, an eye for an eye, and that of itself does not demand forgiveness or that we love our enemies. Hence, I can be a just man without having to transform many of my spontaneous energies. For example: If someone comes up to me and says: "I like you!" it will trigger the kind of energy in me that will make for the spontaneous response: "I like you too!" Conversely, if someone comes up to me and says: "I hate you!" the energy this triggers in me would lead to a response in kind: "I hate you too!" This is the reaction when we simply let energy flow through us like a conduit. There is no virtue in this.

Jesus tells us that real virtue lies at a deeper place: "You have learnt how it was said: You must love your neighbor and hate your enemy. But I say to you: love your enemies and pray for those who persecute you; in this way you will be children of your Father in heaven, for he causes his sun to rise on bad men as well as good, and his rain to fall on honest and dishonest men alike. For if you love those who love you, what right have you to claim any credit? Even tax collectors do as much, do they not? And if you save your greetings for your brothers, are you doing anything exceptional? Even the pagans do as much, do they not? You must therefore be perfect just as your heavenly Father is perfect."[14]

In offering this challenge, Jesus is offering the litmus test for maturity and Christian discipleship: Can you love an enemy? Can you forgive a murderer?[15] He is also stretching us humanly and morally to a deep place that we cannot reach unless we ponder in the biblical sense; that is, unless, like Mary pondering, we take the raw and blind energies that flow through us and hold and carry and transform them before acting on them. Deep virtue demands of us that, like Mary standing under the cross, we transform hate-filled energy so as not to give it back in kind.

v) The Difference Between Amazement and Wonder

Amazement, defined in this way, needs however to be sharply distinguished from wonder and awe. Wonder and awe are healthy while amazement is not. What is the difference? Wonder and awe stop the flow of energy passing through us; amazement facilitates it. A quip from a famous comedian might be helpful in explaining the difference. George Carlin once made this comment on why he had such a congenital distrust of religious neophytes who claim to be "born again": "They talk too much, pure and simple! When I was born, I was so stunned that I couldn't speak for two years! If someone has a religious experience and shuts up for a couple of years, I will take him seriously!"

There is an important distinction captured in that. Wonder and awe do us good precisely because they stun and mute our spontaneous energies. They literally paralyze us so that we become reflective by conscription. Amazement does the opposite. It turns us into mindless cheerleaders, irrespective of what is right or wrong or what we actually value. We see the difference between amazement and wonder in the way Zechariah and Mary react differently to the angel, Gabriel, when he appears to them: as the Gospel of Luke writes this up,[16] Gabriel appears first to Zechariah and informs him that his wife, Elizabeth, despite being postmenopausal, will conceive and bear a son. Zechariah, knowing this is a biological impossibility, voices the appropriate questions, and Gabriel, seemingly unhappy with his questions, mutes him for the next nine months. A very short time later, the same angel appears to Mary and announces to her that she, though a virgin, will have a son. Mary voices almost the identical concerns that Zechariah voiced, but she is not muted or silenced. Why? She did not need to be silenced because she *pondered* the angel's greetings, she self-muted; she met Gabriel's words with awe and wonder rather than with amazement. Awe and wonder are the biblical antithesis of amazement.

vi) The Efficacy of Pondering—"Taking Away the Sins of the World"

The Gospels depict Mary as pondering and, in a subtle but clear way, hold that up as the key mature action that someone can do to help take tension and darkness out of our world. They describe the same thing with Jesus, except they do so in a more explicit way. In Jesus' case they describe him as doing an action, one of selfless dying, which makes him metaphorically the sacrificial lamb who "takes way the sins of the world." To understand the efficacy of pondering, how carrying and transforming tension helps take tension and sin out of a community, it is helpful to look at how Jesus "took away the sins of the world." This is the ultimate paradigm for how one ponders in the biblical sense.

How did Jesus "take away the sins of the world"? Obviously, some of this is mystery in that there are no clear analogues within human experience with which to ascribe cause and effect here. However, with that being acknowledged, it must be unambiguously stated from the outset that the image of Jesus as the sacrificial lamb, whose blood takes away our sin and washes us clean, is a metaphor. Jesus was clearly not a sheep and what he did in giving his death over in love was not simply some kind of divine magic that can be consigned only to the realm of divine mystery. Partly it is mystery, granted; but partly it is not. How does a sacrificial lamb take away sin and wash others clean? There are some important aspects of this metaphor that can be explicated.

Perhaps a good way to begin to penetrate this metaphor is to ask the question: Why would the first generation of Christians, immediately after Jesus' death, understand his death in this way, that is, as the death of a sacrificial lamb that cleanses the people? Scholars admit that there is no simple answer here because at that time there was not one simple notion of sacrifice, nor of the meaning of sacrificial victims. People at the time of Jesus offered sacrifice in many kinds of ways and under many kinds of understandings. However, one such understanding can be very helpful in shedding light on Jesus' death and on why his followers would, almost spontaneously, ascribe the image of sacrificial lamb to him, and that is the concept of the scapegoat.[17] The Lamb of God who takes away the sins of the world is not just any lamb, he is the scapegoat lamb. What is a scapegoat?

A little anthropological background can be helpful here: anthropologists tell us that, until we can create community with each other at a certain level, that is, on the basis of what we positively and mutually stand for, we create community with each by its opposite, by what we are mutually against. Simply put, we create community by scapegoating, by putting aside our mutual tensions and differences on the basis of some mutual opposition to, anger at, indignation toward, or ridiculing of someone or something that is so different from us that it in effect melts down our differences and brings us into harmony with one another in our mutual distancing from it. And this is not an abstract concept at all. We do it all the time.

Take this example: imagine going out for dinner with a group of colleagues. While there is not necessarily overt hostility among you, there are clear differences and tensions. You would not naturally choose to go out to dinner together, but you've been thrown together by circumstance and are trying to make the best of it. And so you have dinner together, and things, in fact, are quite pleasant. There is banter, humor, and harmony at the table. How do you manage to get on so well, despite and beyond differences? By talking about somebody else! Much of the time is spent talking about others whose faults, eccentricities, and shortcomings we all agree upon. Alternatively, we talk about our shared indignations. We end up having a harmonious time together because we talk about someone or something else whose difference from us is greater than our difference, at least at that moment, from one another. Of course, you are afraid to go to the bathroom because you already know whom they will be talking about when you get up from the table! Your fear is well-founded. That is how scapegoating works.

Until we reach a certain level of maturity, we form community largely around scapegoating; that is, we overcome our differences and tensions by focusing on someone or something about whom or which we share a common distancing, indignation, ridicule, anger, or jealousy. That is the anthropological function of gossip, and a very important one it is. We overcome our differences and tensions by scapegoating someone or something. That is why it is easier to form community against something rather than around something, and why it is easier to define ourselves more by what we are against than by what we are for.

Ancient cultures knew this and designed certain rituals precisely to take tension out of the community by scapegoating. For example, at the time of Jesus, within the Jewish community a ritual existed that essentially worked this way: at regular intervals the community would take a goat and symbolically invest it with the tensions and divisions of the community. They would ritually do this by, among other things, draping the goat with a purple cloth and putting a crown of thorns on its head.[18] The goat was then chased off to die in the desert. Its leaving the community was understood as taking the sin and tension away and the community was seen to be washed clean through its blood, its suffering, its death.

With that as a background it is easy to see why, immediately after Jesus' death, his followers would ascribe that role to him. He is our scapegoat! He is our sacrificial lamb! His sufferings take away our sins! We are washed clean in his blood! His death was understood as doing for them and for the world what a scapegoat did for a given community. Except in their understanding they made a very important distinction: Jesus functions like the sacrificial scapegoat, except he does not take away the tension and sin of the community by some type of psychological transference or spiritual magic, as did the ancient scapegoat. Rather, he takes away the tensions and sins of the community by absorbing them, carrying them, transforming them, and not giving them back in kind. In their understanding, Jesus did this by functioning like a water purifier, a filter of sorts. In looking at his death, they understood this: he took in hatred, held it, transformed it, and gave back love; he took in bitterness, held it, transformed it, and gave back graciousness; he took in curses, held them, transformed them, and gave back blessings; and he took in murder, held it, transformed it, and gave back forgiveness. Jesus resisted the instinct to give back in kind, hatred for hatred, curses for curses, jealousy for jealousy, murder for murder. He held and transformed these things rather than simply retransmitting them. He took away the sins of the world by absorbing them, at great cost to himself.

vii) Highlighting the Metaphor

What does it mean to ponder in the biblical sense? How does this take away tension and the sins of the world? Perhaps it can be summarized in two simple metaphors: the opposite of pondering is amazement, and the metaphor for amazement is that of an electrical cord, a wire that acts as a mindless conduit, simply letting energy flow through it. The metaphor for pondering is that of a water purifier. A filter does not act as a simple conduit for what passes through it. Rather, it takes in water full of toxins, dirt, and impurities, holds the toxins, dirt, and impurities inside of itself, and gives back only pure water. It absorbs what is negative, holds the negative inside itself, and gives back only what is pure. Human energy passes through us in the same way: either we act as a simple conduit, or we act as a filter.

viii) Imitation Rather Than Admiration as Our Response

Moreover, looking at Jesus' sacrificial death and Mary's pondering, what we are invited to is not admiration but imitation. Christian discipleship invites us to imitate their actions, to continue to give them concrete flesh. What is the task? Speaking metaphorically, we are invited to become the water purifier, the toxin-absorbing sponge, within all of our various communities. And we all live in families, circles of friendship, workplaces, churches, and societies that are fraught with tension. There are no perfect human communities, and so our task as mature adults, as elders, as Christian disciples, is to be that place where the amazement, the gossip, the negativity, and the scapegoating stop because, like water purifiers, we take it in, absorb it, transform it, and do not give it back in kind.

In terms of moving toward deeper maturity, of moving from goodness to greatness, this invitation to become the sponge that absorbs tension inside of family, church, and community is perhaps the premier one. Indeed, it is the criterion for adult discipleship.

But it is always to be understood as an invitation, not a command. We are free to do this or not do it. At this level of spirituality, as with the invitation to the rich young man, it is not a question of being good or bad, depending upon whether or not you accept or dodge the invitation. Rather, it is a question of maturity: How mature do you want to be? At what level do you want to carry your discipleship? How adult do you want to be?

ix) Some Caveats

Admittedly, it is not easy to do this. To carry tension is to fill with tension ourselves, and, as we know, this can be unbearable. We do not have God's strength, nor are we devoid of feelings or made of steel. As we try to carry tension for others, what do we do with our own tensions? How do we carry tension without becoming resentful and bitter? How do we carry someone else's cross without, however subtly, sending him or her the bill for its cost?

Carrying tension for others brings with it a series of dangers, as any health professional will tell you. Tension wreaks havoc inside us, physically and emotionally. We can die of high blood pressure or of disappointment. Tension can kill us. We should not be naive as to what is asked of us here. But there are some rules and guidelines that can be of help. Here are some caveats:

First, carrying tension for others does not mean putting up with abuse or not confronting pathological or clinical dysfunction. To love someone does not mean accepting abuse in the name of love for, as we have learned from bitter experience, when we absorb abuse, even with the highest religious motives, we do not take away the sin, we enable it. Jesus confronted dysfunction, even as he gave himself over in love. Sometimes the loving thing to do is not the gentle, accommodating, and long-suffering one. In the face of positive abuse or clinical dysfunction, Christian discipleship can demand hard confrontation and perhaps even a distancing of ourselves from the person or persons who are causing the tension.

Second, we need to find healthy outlets to release our own tensions. However, the rule here is that we should never download them on the same people for whom we are trying to carry them. For example, parents carry tension for their children, but when frustrations build up, they should not angrily vent those frustrations back on the kids themselves. Rather, they should deal with those tensions away from the children, with each other, with friends, when the kids are in bed, over a bottle of wine. The same holds true for every adult who is lovingly trying to carry a tension for someone else: never vent the frustrations on the person or persons for whom you are trying to carry the tension.

Finally, in order to deal with our own tensions, we need, in the midst of them, to be connected to something (a person, a friendship, a hand, a God, a creed, a perspective) beyond ourselves and the situation within which we find ourselves. Scripture offers some wonderful images for this. It tells us, for example, that as the first Christian martyr, Steven, was being stoned to death out of hatred and jealousy, he kept his "eyes raised to heaven."[19] That is not so much a physical description of things, but an artistic image for how Steven kept himself from drowning in the spinning chaos that was assaulting him: He "raised his eyes to heaven"; he stayed connected to a person, a hand, a friendship, an affirmation, a perspective, and a divine power outside of the madness. The crowd who was stoning him, on the other hand, did not have their eyes fixed on anything outside of the madness.

We see the same thing, only a different metaphor, in the story of the three young men who are thrown into the blazing furnace in the book of Daniel.[20] The story tells us that they walked around, right in the midst of the flames, untouched by the fire because they were singing sacred songs. Like Steven, they sustained their love and faith amid madness and hatred by staying connected to something outside of the fiery forces that were consuming everyone else. The lesson is clear: if we volunteer to step into the fire, it is wise not to go there alone, but to stay connected to some hand, some friend, some creed, and some God who will help sustain us in love and faith, right inside the madness and fire.

Thus, the invitation remains, despite its hazards: like Jesus, like Mary, and like everyone else who's ever walked this planet, every adult woman or man will find herself or himself, this side of eternity, inside families, communities, churches, friendships, and work circles that are filled with tensions of every kind. The natural temptation, always, is to simply give back in kind, jealousy for jealousy, gossip for gossip, anger for anger. But the invitation that comes to us from the Gospels, the invitation to move from being a good person to becoming a great person, is the invitation to step forward and help carry and purify this tension, to help take it away by transforming it inside ourselves, by pondering as Mary pondered.

x) One Last Image of Transforming Energy

How does transforming energy and not giving it back in kind take sin out of a community? Here is how a civil rights worker who endured racial hatred and violence while working for justice describes what happened to him. This is part of an interview with him:

"Isn't that dangerous work you are doing?"

"It's true," he said. "The hatred is vicious, and the punishment is violent."

"Have you ever been hurt yourself?"

"Yes, I've been spit upon, beaten with fists, with pipes, with chains and left a bloody mess."

"But you are pretty big. Weren't you able to protect yourself sometimes, to fight back?"

"Yes. At first I did fight back. I made some of them sorry that they had attacked me. But then I realized that by fighting back I wasn't getting anywhere. The hatred coming at me in those fists and clubs was bouncing right off me back into the air, and it could just continue to spread like electricity. I decided not to fight back. I would let my body absorb that hatred, so that some of it would die in my body and not bounce back into the world. I now see that my job in the midst of evil is to make my body a grave for hate."[21]

So Here We Stand

Where do we stand as adult women and men, supposed elders, decent folks, trying to be generous and life giving?

Mostly, we stand in two places. First, we stand almost exactly where the rich young man stood, generous but withholding, ready to give up something but not everything, essentially at peace but harboring a sadness, good of heart but with greatness still eluding us. Beyond that, we stand too much in the amazement of the crowd, too unthinkingly retransmitting the energy that surrounds us, unwilling to carry and transform the tension within our communities.

That is where we stand, but greatness is within reach: we need only to give over those last three rooms and begin to ponder in the biblical sense.

6

DRAWING STRENGTH
FROM PRAYER

The Difference

I got up early one morning and rushed right into the day;
I had so much to accomplish, I didn't have time to pray.

Problems just tumbled about me and grew heavier with each task;
Why doesn't God help me, I wondered; He answered, "You didn't ask."

I wanted to see joy and beauty, but the day toiled on, gray and bleak;
I wondered why God didn't show me—He said, "But you didn't seek."

I tried to come into God's presence; I used all my keys at the lock;
God gently and lovingly chided, "My child, you didn't knock."

I woke up early this morning and paused before entering the day;
I had so much to accomplish that I had to take time to pray.

—GRACE L. NAESSENS[1]

The Need to Draw Strength from Prayer

Our adult years are a marathon, not a sprint, and so it is difficult to sustain graciousness, generosity, and patience through the tiredness, trials, and temptations that beset us through those years. All on our own, relying on willpower alone, we too often fatigue, get worn down, and compromise both our maturity and our discipleship. We need help from beyond, from somewhere even beyond the human supports that help bolster us. We need God's help, strength from something beyond what is human. We need prayer.

The first disciples of Jesus already realized this. They looked at Jesus and sensed that he drew his real strength and his power from a source beyond himself. Nowhere is this more evident than in the Gospel of Luke. In his gospel there are more descriptions of Jesus in prayer than in all the other Gospels combined. Luke gives us glimpses of Jesus praying in virtually every kind of situation: he prays when he is joy filled; he prays when he is in agony; he prays with others around him; he prays when he is alone at night, withdrawn from all human contact. He prays high on a mountain, on a sacred place, and he prays on the level plane, where ordinary life happens. In Luke's Gospel, Jesus prays a lot.

And the lesson is not lost on his disciples. They sense that Jesus' real depth and power are drawn from his prayer. They know that what makes him so special, so unlike any other religious figure, is that he is linked at some deep place to a power outside of this world. And they want this for themselves. That is why they approach him and ask him: "Lord, teach us to pray!"[2] But we must be careful not to misunderstand what constituted their attraction and what they were asking for when they asked Jesus to teach them how to pray. They sensed that what Jesus drew from the depth of his prayer was not, first of all, his power to do miracles or to silence his enemies with some kind of superior intelligence. What impressed them and what they wanted too for their own lives was his depth and graciousness of soul.

The power they admired and wanted was Jesus' power to love and forgive his enemies rather than embarrass and crush them. What they wanted was Jesus' power to transform a room, not by some miraculous deed, but by a disarming innocence and vulnerability that, like a baby's presence, has everyone guarding his or her behavior and language. What they wanted was his power to renounce life in self-sacrifice, even while retaining the enviable capacity to enjoy the pleasures of life without guilt. What they wanted was Jesus' power to be bighearted; to love beyond his own tribe, and to love poor and rich alike; to live inside of charity, joy, peace, patience, goodness, long-suffering, fidelity, mildness, and chastity, despite everything within life that militates against these virtues. What they wanted was Jesus' depth and graciousness of soul. And they recognized that this power did not come from within himself, but from a source outside of him. They saw that he connected to a deep source through prayer, through constantly lifting to God what was on his mind and in his heart. They saw it, and they wanted that depth of connection too, for themselves. So they asked Jesus to teach them how to pray.

Ultimately, we too want and need Jesus' depth and graciousness in our own lives. And like Jesus' first disciples, we also know that we can attain this only through accessing a power that lies beyond our own strength. We know too that the route to that depth lies in journeying inward, in silence, through both the pain and the quiet, the chaos and the peace, that come to us when we still ourselves to pray. In both our more reflective moments and in our more desperate moments, we feel our need for prayer. We cannot sustain ourselves all on our own. We need prayer.

But too often we think of this in pious rather than realistic terms. Rarely do we grasp how much prayer is really a question of life and death for us. We need to pray not because God needs us to pray but because if we do not pray, we will never find any steadiness in our lives. Simply put, without prayer we will always be either too full of ourselves or too empty of energy, inflated or depressed. Why? What is the phenomenology here?

Prayer, as it is understood in all its best traditions, Christian and other, is meant to do two things for us, both at the same time: prayer is meant to connect us to divine energy, even as it makes us aware that this energy is not our own, that it comes from elsewhere, and that we may never identify with it. Authentic prayer, in effect, fills us with divine energy and tells us at the same time that this energy is not our own, that it works through us, but that it is not us. To be healthy, we need both: if we lose connection to divine energy, we drain of energy, depress, and feel empty. Conversely, if we let divine energy flow into us but identify with it, somehow thinking that it is our own, we become grandiose, inflate with self-importance and arrogance, and become selfish and destructive.

Robert Moore offers a very helpful image to illustrate this, that of a small fighter plane having to fuel up inflight. We have all seen video footage of a small fighter jet fueling up while still in the air. Hovering above it is a mother plane with a huge reserve of fuel. The little plane has to fly close enough to the mother plane so that a nozzle from the mother plane can connect with it so as to refill its fuel tank. If it does not make this type of contact, it runs out of fuel and soon crashes. Conversely, if it flies into the mother plane, identifies with it, it goes up in flames.[3] Few images capture as astutely the importance of prayer in our lives. Without prayer, we will forever find ourselves vacillating between being too empty of energy or too full of ourselves. If we do not connect with divine energy, we will run out of gas. If we do connect with divine energy but identify with it, we will destroy ourselves.

Deep prayer is what energizes us and grounds us, both at the same time. We see this, for example, in a person like Mother Teresa, who was bursting with creative energy but was always very clear that this energy did not come from her, but from God, and she was merely a humble human instrument. Lack of real prayer makes for two kinds of antithesis to Mother Teresa: on the one hand, it makes for a wonderfully talented and energetic man or woman who is full of creative energy, but is also full of grandiosity and ego; or, on the other hand, it makes for a man or woman who feels completely empty and flat and cannot radiate any positive energy.

Generativity depends on prayer.

What Is Prayer?

One of the oldest, classical definitions of prayer defines it this way: "Prayer is lifting mind and heart to God." That sounds simple enough, but it is not at all easy to do. It is rare that we actually open mind and heart to God in order to show God what is really there. Mostly, we treat God as a parental figure or as a visiting dignitary and tell God what we think God wants to hear rather than what is actually on our minds and hearts at a given time. Consequently, we have a pretty narrow range of thoughts and feelings that we consider suitable for prayer. Most of what we actually think and feel is considered too base for prayer. We feel we are praying only when we have good thoughts and warm feelings—that is, when we feel like praising God; when we feel altruistic, pure, and centered; when we have positive feelings toward God, others, and nature; when we feel the desire to pray; or when we yearn for moral improvement.

Such warm thoughts and feelings do make for prayer,

but we cannot turn them on when we wish to like a water faucet. Many times, perhaps most times, we experience other thoughts and feelings: boredom, tiredness, dissipation, bitterness, sexual fantasy, and sometimes even a positive distaste for church, prayer, and moral improvement. We do not feel that it is valid to lift these bitter thoughts and impure feelings to God. Instead, we try to conjure up thoughts and feelings we think we should be having when we pray. There is some legitimacy in this, of course. Classically, spiritual masters have distinguished between prayer and distraction. Prayer, they point out, requires an effort of concentration, of attentiveness, an act of will. Prayer is not simply daydreaming or letting a stream of consciousness occur.

But prayer is "lifting mind and heart to God," and that means lifting up, at any given moment, exactly what is there and not what, ideally, might be there. It would be nice if we always felt warm, reverent, altruistic, full of faith, chaste, hopeful, connected with others and nature, happy about who we are and what life has dealt us. But that is not the case. We all have moments and even seasons of doubt, anger, alienation, pettiness, boredom, obsession, and tiredness. Our thoughts are not always holy, and our hearts are not always warm or pure. It is at times like this when we most need prayer and what we need to take to prayer is, precisely, those bitter thoughts and unholy feelings.

All thoughts and feelings are valid material for prayer. Simply put: when you go to pray, lift up what is inside of you at that moment. If you are bored, lift up that boredom; if you are angry, lift up your anger; if you are sexually obsessed, lift up your sexual fantasies; if you are tired, lift up that tiredness; if you feel selfish, do not be afraid to let God see that. Jesus said that we must become like little children to enter the kingdom of heaven. One of the qualities in children to which this refers is precisely their honesty in showing their feelings. Children do not hide their selfishness, sulks, pouts, and tantrums. A good mother handles these rather easily, often with a smile. God is up to the task. In prayer, we can be transparent, no matter how murderous, adulterous, or irreverent our thoughts and feelings might seem.

As well, part of the definition of prayer includes the biblical invitation to "pray always."[4] What does this mean? Obviously, it cannot mean that we should always be at formal prayer, that we should strive to be full-time contemplatives, or even that we should seize every possible occasion we can to pray formally. To "pray always" invites us, rather, to live our lives against a certain horizon. It does not necessarily mean to stop work and go to formal prayer, important though that is at times. The point is that we need to do everything within the context of a certain awareness, like a married man who goes on a business trip and who, in the midst of a demanding schedule of meetings and social engagements, is somehow always anchored in a certain consciousness that he has a spouse and children at home. Despite distance and various preoccupations, he knows that he is "married always." That awareness, more than the occasional explicit phone call home, is what keeps him anchored in this most important relationship.

Our relationship with God is the same. We need to "pray always" by doing everything out of that kind of awareness. Moreover, when we do spend time in formal prayer, we need, like children do, to tell God exactly how we feel and invite God to deal with that. Biblical scholars point out how, in prayer, the great figures of scripture did not always easily acquiesce to God and say: "Thy will be done!" They sometimes fought bitterly and said: "Thy will be changed!" That can be a very good prayer. It lifts mind and heart to God.

Essential Kinds of Prayer

Lifting mind and heart to God is a classical definition of prayer, but it is also a generic one. It needs some qualification because there are different kinds of prayer. There are of course hundreds of different methods of prayer, but within Christian spirituality, there are basically two essential kinds of prayer: *liturgical prayer,* the public prayer of the church, and *private* or *devotional prayer.*

Unfortunately, that distinction is often not clearly made and sometimes not that easy to grasp. For example, five hundred people might be sitting in meditation together in a church or praying the rosary together at a shrine, and this is still private or devotional prayer. Conversely, someone might be praying the Office of the

Church alone at home in an armchair or a priest might be celebrating the Eucharist alone at a kitchen table and this is public, liturgical prayer. The distinction, as we see from these examples, is not dependent upon the number of people participating, or whether the prayer is taking place in a church, or even whether the prayer is being prayed in a group or privately. The distinction is based upon something else. What?

Perhaps a change of names might help us more easily understand the distinction: liturgical, public prayer might more aptly be called *priestly prayer*, while private and devotional prayer might better be termed *affective prayer*. The former is our participation in the prayer of Christ, his praying as priest for the world; while the latter is our own prayer, done by ourselves or with others, within which we ask God from the depth of our own private faith to bless others and ourselves. This distinction can best be explained by highlighting what is contained in each.

i) Priestly Prayer

One of the responsibilities that comes to us from our baptism is that of praying for the world. Like the high priests of old, we need to offer up prayers daily for others. Indeed, we are all priests, ordained by the oils of baptism and consecrated by the burdens of life that have given us wrinkles and gray hair. As adults, elders, priests, we need, as scripture puts it, "to make prayer and entreaty, aloud and in silent tears, for ourselves and for the people."[5] All baptized Christians, lay and cleric alike, are asked to offer up priestly prayer each day for the world.

How do we do that? How do we pray priestly prayer? We pray as priests, as Jesus prayed in the seventeenth chapter of John's Gospel, every time we sacrifice self-interest for the good of others. That defines priestly prayer in its widest sense, as a prayer we do with our actions. However, we pray that prayer, formally and sacramentally, whenever we pray the prayer of the church, namely, the public celebration of the Word of God, the celebration of the Eucharist, or the praying of the Divine Office. This kind of prayer, called *liturgy,* is what keeps incarnate the priestly prayer of Christ.

In priestly prayer we pray not just for ourselves, nor ideally by ourselves, but we pray as a microcosm of the whole world, even as we pray for the whole world. In this kind of prayer we lift up our voices to God, not as a private offering but in such a way as to give a voice to the earth itself. In essence, when we pray during a service of the Word, the Eucharist, or at the Divine Office, we are saying this:

> Lord, God, I stand before you as a microcosm of the earth itself, to give it voice: See in my openness, the world's openness, in my infidelity, the world's infidelity; in my sincerity, the world's sincerity, in my hypocrisy, the world's hypocrisy; in my generosity, the world's generosity, in my selfishness, the world's selfishness; in my attentiveness, the world's attentiveness, in my distraction,

the world's distraction; in my desire to praise you, the world's desire to praise you, and in my self-preoccupation, the world's forgetfulness of you. For I am of the earth, a piece of earth, and the earth opens or closes to you through my body, my soul, and my voice. I am your priest on earth.

And what I hold up for you today is all that is in this world, both of joy and of suffering. I offer you the bread of the world's achievements, even as I offer you the wine of its failures, the blood of all that's crushed as those achievements take place. I offer you the powerful of our world, our rich, our famous, our athletes, our artists, our movie stars, our entrepreneurs, our young, our healthy, and everything that's creative and bursting with life, even as I offer you those who are weak, feeble, aged, crushed, sick, dying, and victimized. I offer to you all the pagan beauties, pleasures, and joys of this life, even as I stand with you under the cross, affirming that the one who is excluded from earthly pleasure is the cornerstone of the community. I offer you the strong and arrogant, along with the weak and gentle of heart, asking you to bless both and to stretch my heart so that it can, like you, hold and bless everything that is. I offer you both the wonders and the pains of this world, your world.

To pray like this is to pray liturgically, as a priest. And we pray like this each time we participate in a service of the Word or the Eucharist or when we, with others or alone, pray the Divine Office of the Church. It is particularly this latter prayer, the Divine Office (also called Breviary or Liturgy of the Hours) that is available daily as the priestly prayer for those who are not ordained ministers in the church. And this is especially true for two of those liturgical hours, Lauds (Morning Prayer) and Vespers (Evening Prayer). They, unlike the other hours, which are more the particular domain of monks and professional contemplatives, are the ordinary priestly prayer of the laity.

What is important in praying them is to remember that these are not prayers that we say for ourselves, nor indeed prayers whose formulae we need personally to find meaningful or relevant. Unlike private prayer and contemplation, where we should change methods whenever praying becomes dry or sterile, Eucharist, Lauds, and Vespers are prayers of the universal church that are, in essence, intended to be communal and priestly. They do not have to be relevant for our private lives. We pray them as elders, as baptized adults, as priests, to invoke God's blessing upon the world. And whenever we do pray them we take on a universal voice. We are no longer just a private individual praying, but are, in microcosm, the voice, body, and soul of the earth itself, continuing the high priesthood of Christ, offering prayers and entreaties, aloud and in silent tears, to God for the sake of the world.

Generativity brings with it a series of responsibilities, and one of these is the invitation to, habitually, join with Christ and the universal church in praying for the world.

ii) Affective Prayer

There is too another kind of prayer that is essential to our lives, *affective prayer*. What is affective prayer?

A number of years ago, I attended a weeklong retreat given by Robert Michel, an Oblate colleague and a highly sought-after spiritual mentor. His approach was disarming. Most of us are forever looking for something novel, at the cutting edge, outside the box, something complex, but what he offered was stunningly simple and down to earth. He spent the whole time trying to teach us how to pray in an affective way.

What exactly does that mean, to pray affectively? In essence, what he told us might be summarized this way: "You must try to pray so that, in your prayer, you open yourself in such a way that sometime—perhaps not today, but sometime—you are able to hear God say to you: 'I love you!' These words, addressed to you by God, are the most important words you will ever hear, because before you hear them, nothing is ever completely right with you, but after you hear them, something will be right in your life at a very deep level."

These are simple words, but they capture a huge part of what we are meant to do when we go to prayer. In the end, prayer's essence, its mission statement, its ultimate intentionality, is simply this: we need to open ourselves to God in such a way that we are capable of hearing God say to us, individually, "I love you!" This might sound pious and sentimental, but it is not. John's Gospel already makes that point. The Gospel of John, as we know, structures itself very differently from the other gospels. John has no infancy narratives or early life of Jesus. In his gospel, we meet Jesus as an adult right on the first page and the first words out of Jesus' mouth are a question: "What are you looking for?"[6] That question remains throughout the rest of the gospel as an undergirding, suggesting that beneath everything else a certain search is forever going on. A lot of things are happening on the surface, but underneath, there remains always the nagging, restless question: What are you looking for?

Jesus answers that question explicitly only at the end of the gospel, on the morning of the resurrection. Mary of Magdala goes looking for him, carrying spices with which to embalm his dead body. Jesus meets her, alive and in no need of embalming, but she does not recognize him. Bewildered but sincere, she asks Jesus where she might find Jesus. Jesus, for his part, repeats for her essentially the question with which he had opened the gospel: "What are you looking for?"[7] Then he answers it: With deep affection, he pronounces her name: "Mary."[8] In doing that, he tells her what she and everyone else is forever looking for—God's voice, one-to-one, speaking unconditional love, gently saying your name.

In the end, that is what we are all looking for and most need. It is what gives us substance, identity, and justification beyond our own efforts to make ourselves lovable, worthwhile, and immortal. We are forever in fear of our own seeming insubstantiality. How to give ourselves significance? We need to hear God, affectionately, one-to-one, pronounce our names: "Carolyn!" "Julia!" "Kern!" "Gisele!" "Sophia!" Nothing will heal us more of restlessness, bitterness, and insecurity than to hear God say: "I love you!"

Moreover, since prayer is meant to be a mutual thing, it is important too that we respond in kind: part of affective prayer is also that we, one-to-one, with affection, occasionally at least, say the same thing to God: "I love you!" In all long-term, affectionate relationships the partners occasionally have to prompt each other to hear expressions of affection and reassurance. It is not good enough to tell a marriage partner or a friend "I love you!" just once. It needs to be said regularly. The relationship of prayer is no different. Prayer is not meant to change God but us, and nothing changes us as much for the good as to hear someone say that he or she loves us, especially if that someone is God.

And hearing that we are loved can give us the strength we need to be virtuous. One of the perennial temptations in our lives is to try to do things on our own, including attempting to live out virtue by our own strength, by willpower alone. Sometimes we even succeed, at least on the surface. We are, in colloquial terms, able to gut it out! But radical fidelity alone, gutting it out, does not necessarily make for generativity or happiness, as we see so clearly in the case of the older brother of the prodigal son. He, precisely, gutted it out, but it did not leave him very happy. We can be doing everything right, and something can still be very wrong. Our virtue, and consequently our generativity, needs to issue forth from a warm heart, from love, from gratitude for first having been loved. We need to serve God as a warm friend, as a lover, not as a cold and commanding moral principle or dogma. Only affective prayer, in some form, can instill this warmth in our hearts. We will not be truly selfless without it.

This insight, so central to the Gospels and to the Christian mystical tradition, has been taken up and made central to Christian discipleship in two very different circles, Roman Catholic devotional spirituality and the emphasis within Evangelical churches on having Jesus as one's personal savior. Both of these circles are often heavily criticized for being too one-sided in how central they place this within their spirituality and practice, but their critics often stand in need themselves of precisely this part of the gospel.

iii) Highlighting the Distinction

Mature Discipleship invites us to two kinds of prayer, priestly and affective: priestly prayer is the prayer of Christ through the church for the world. The Christian belief is that Christ is still gathering us together around his Word and is still offering an eternal act of love for the world. As an extension of that we believe that whenever we meet together, in a church or elsewhere, to gather around the scriptures or to celebrate the Eucharist we are entering into that prayer. This is liturgical prayer—Christ's prayer, not our own. We pray liturgically whenever we gather to celebrate the scriptures, the sacraments, or when we pray, in community or privately, something that is called the Prayer of the Church, or the Office of the Church (Lauds and Vespers).

Affective prayer has a different intent. Though it has many forms, meditation, centering prayer, praying the rosary, devotional prayers of all kinds, it has a single aim, to draw us and our loved ones into deeper intimacy with Christ. In the end, no matter its particular form, all nonliturgical prayer ultimately aims at personal intimacy with God and is ultimately private, even when it is done publicly or in a large group. All private and devotional prayer can be defined in this way: it is prayer that tries, in myriad ways, to open us or our loved ones up in such a way that we can hear God say to us: "I love you!"

It is important to know this distinction when we go to pray: Which kind of prayer are we entering? To confuse the two is to risk doing both badly. For example, the person who feels frustrated because the liturgical ritual and interaction of a congregation inside a church service are felt as a hindrance and distraction to the private devotional prayers he or she would like to be saying is confusing the two forms of prayer and is consequently doing both badly. The function of liturgical prayer is not, first of all, devotional. Or sometimes the confusion leads someone to abandon one form of liturgical prayer altogether. I know a man who, after years of praying the Office of the Church, is substituting his own private prayer in its place because he does not find the ritual prayers personally meaningful. His private meditations now might well be wonderful affective prayer, but he is no longer praying the priestly prayer of Christ when he is praying in this way. We see this sometimes too in well-intentioned, but badly planned, church services when what is intended to be a liturgical service ends up being a guided private meditation, however well done and powerful, which neither uses scripture nor prays for the world.

Churches themselves struggle with this. Roman Catholics, Anglicans, Episcopalians, and main-line Protestant churches have a strong liturgical tradition, sometimes to the detriment of affective prayer. Evangelical and Pentecostal churches, on the other hand, have a strong focus on affective prayer, sometimes to the point of neglecting liturgical prayer.

Perhaps we could all do ourselves a favor by having two prayer shawls, each embroidered separately: *priestly prayer* and *affective prayer*.

iv) A Note on Prayer of Petition

In her autobiography, *The Long Loneliness,* Dorothy Day tells of a very difficult time in her life. She had just converted to Christianity, after a long period of atheism, and then given birth to her daughter. During her season of agnosticism, she had fallen in love with the man who had fathered her child; and she and this man, atheists disillusioned with mainstream society, had made a pact never to marry, as a statement against the conventions of society.

But her conversion to Christianity had turned that

world upside down. The father of her child had given her an ultimatum; if she had their child baptized, he would end their relationship. Dorothy chose to baptize the child but paid a heavy price. She deeply loved this man and suffered greatly at their breakup. Moreover, given that her conversion took her out of all her former circles, it left her with more than a missing soul mate. It left her too without a job, without support for her child, and without her former purpose in life. She felt painfully alone and lost. And this drove her to her knees, literally. One day she took a train from New York to Washington, D.C., and spent the day praying at the National Shrine of the Immaculate Conception. As she shares in her autobiography, her prayer that day was shamelessly direct, humble, and clear. Essentially, she told God, again and again, that she was lost, that she needed a clear direction for her life, and that she needed that direction now, not in some distant future. And like Jesus in the Garden of Gethsemane, she prayed that prayer over and over again.

She took a train home that evening, and when she walked up to her apartment, she saw a man, Peter Maurin, sitting on the steps. He invited her to start the *Catholic Worker*. The rest is history.

Our prayers are not always answered that swiftly and directly, but they are always answered, as Jesus assures us, because God does not withhold the Holy Spirit from those who ask for it. If we pray for guidance and support, it will be given us. In scripture, we see many salient examples of people who, like Dorothy Day, seek out God's guidance in prayer, especially when they are alone and afraid as they stand before some major upheaval or impending suffering in their lives. We see this, for example, in Moses who, when lost in the desert and facing a revolt from his own people, climbs Mount Horeb to ask for God's counsel. And we see it in Jesus, who also climbs Mount Horeb to pray and who spends whole nights in prayer, struggling to find both the guidance and the courage he needs for his mission.

Looking at the prayer of Moses, Jesus, Dorothy Day, and countless other women and men who have prayed for guidance from God, we see that their prayer, especially when they feel most alone and desperate, is marked by three things: honesty, directness, and humility. They lift their own minds and hearts to God, not someone else's. They share their aloneness and fears with shameless honestly. There is no pretense, no rationalization, no hiding of weaknesses. They pour out their fears, their inadequacies, their temptations, and their confusion, as do children, begging for someone's hand to help them.

There is an interesting parallel to this inside some of our classical fairy tales, where the figure of God often appears in the form of an angel, a fairy, a fox, or a horse. Invariably, those who approach that God figure with overconfidence, arrogance, or pretense are denied all counsel and all magic. Conversely, those who approach the God figure in humility and admit that they are lost in their search are awarded with counsel and magic. There is an important prayer lesson in that. All of us, at different times in our lives, find ourselves alone, lost, confused, and tempted toward a road that will not lead to life. At such times we need to approach God with a prayer that is shamelessly honest, direct, and humble. Like Dorothy Day, we need to raise our true fears and insecurities to God, praying, over and over again: "I'm afraid! I feel so alone and isolated in this! I don't want to do this! I'm completely inadequate! I haven't any strength left! I'm full of anger! I'm bitter at so many things! I hate some of the places where my Christian morality has led me! I'm jealous of others who don't have my moral inhibitions! I'm tempted in ways that I'm ashamed to speak of! I need more support than you've been giving me! Send me someone or send me something! If you want me to continue on this road you've got to give me more help! I need this now!"

And then we need to wait, in patience, in advent. Perhaps no Peter Maurin will appear on our doorstep that night, but, with the desert sands having done their work, an angel will come to strengthen us.

v) A Note on Prayer for the Dead

Recently I received a letter from a woman asking me to explain the Christian teaching about praying for the dead. Her son had been killed in an accident, and she had been dissuaded from participating in any special prayers for him. Her question: Does it make sense to pray for the dead?

The Christian answer is unequivocal, yes! It makes sense to pray for the dead, and our Christian faith asks us to do so, both in liturgy and in private.

Why? What possible good can it do? Do we need to remind God to be merciful? God needs no reminders. Do we need to ask God to see a good heart beneath all the struggles of a human life? God does not need a lesson from us on understanding. God is already perfect understanding, perfect love, and perfect forgiveness. A cynic might voice the objection this way: Why pray for the dead? If the person is already in heaven, he or she does not need prayers; if he or she is in hell, our prayers will not be of any help! So why pray for the dead?

For the same reason we pray for anything. We need to pray. It does us good. Objections to praying for the dead might, with equal logic, be raised against all prayers of petition. God already knows everything, and there is no need to remind God of anything. Yet God has asked us to pray and to pray in petition because prayer is meant to change us, not God. Thus, the first reason we pray for the dead is because that prayer helps us, the living. Prayer for the dead is meant to console the living.

Closely tied to this is a second reason: we pray for our dead loved ones to help heal our relationship to them. When someone close to us dies, it is natural, always, to feel a certain amount of guilt, not just because that person died and we go on living, but because, being human, we have had a less-than-perfect relationship with him or her. There is unfinished business between us. In praying for that person, among other things, we help wash clean those things that remain painful between us.

This takes us to the heart of the matter. We pray for the dead because we believe in the communion of saints, an essential Christian doctrine that asks us to believe that a vital flow of life continues to exist between ourselves and our loved ones, even beyond death. Love, presence, and communication reach through death. We pray for the dead to remain in communication with them. Just as we can hold someone's hand as he or she is dying, and this can be an immense comfort to both of us, so too we can hold another's hand beyond death. Indeed, since death washes many things clean, in our prayers for our loved ones who have died, often more so than our conversations with them when they were alive, the connection is purer, the forgiveness is deeper, the perspective is wider, and the distance between us is less. Communication with our loved ones after death is privileged, undercutting much of what kept us apart in this life.

Praying for the dead, our faith assures us, not only consoles us, but also offers real strength and encouragement to the loved one who has died. How? In the same way as loving presence to each other offers strength and consolation here in his life. Picture, for example, a young child learning to swim. The child's mother cannot learn for the child, but if she is present and offering encouragement from the edge of the pool, the child's struggle and learning become easier. Things are more easily borne, if they can be shared. This is true even for a person's adjustment to the life of heaven. By praying for the dead, we share with them the pain of adjusting to a new life. Part of that pain of adjustment (which classically Roman Catholics have called "purgatory") is the pain of letting go of this life. In our prayers for the dead, we offer them our presence and love, as a mother on the edge of the pool, as they adjust to a new life. Purgatory is not a geography, a place distinct from heaven, but the pain that comes from being in heaven without having fully let go of earth. Love, even as we know it in this life, already teaches us that.

From my own experience of having loved ones die, as well as from what others have shared with me, I have found that usually, after a time, we sense that our deceased loved ones no longer need us to pray for them. Now they just want us to connect with them. Prayer for the dead does that, and even though our prayers might still need to be formulated as if we are praying for them, we are now simply connecting with them; what was formerly a cold, cutting absence now becomes a warm, comforting presence.[9]

vi) A Note on Praying While in Crisis

We all have our moments of chaos and crisis. Loss, death, sickness, disappointment, hurt, loneliness, hatred, jealousy, obsession, fear—these come into our lives and often we find ourselves overwhelmed by the darkness they cause. What can we do about them? How can we pull ourselves out of the dark chaos they put us into? The simple answer of course is prayer. But that answer is sometimes given too simplistically. We all have heard the phrases, so true in themselves: "Pray it through! Take your troubles to the chapel! Give it to God! God will help you!" I can speak only for myself, though I suspect that my experience has its parallels in other lives, and I have found that often when I try to pray through some deep hurt, I find no relief and, at times, end up more depressed, more immersed in the chaos, and more obsessively self-preoccupied than before praying. Often I end up sucking God into my obsession rather than opening my obsession to God.

Sometimes when we try to pray when hurting, the prayer serves not to uproot the hurt and obsession, but to root them even more deeply in self-pity, self-preoccupation, and overconcentration. We end up further letting go of God's Spirit and, instead, giving in to more panic, fear, chaos, bitterness, obsession, and resentment. Why? Is God not willing to help? Is it simply a question of patience—God will eventually help, but not yet?

God is always willing to help, and, yes, we must be patient; healing always takes time. But there is more involved. When we pray and our prayers do not help, then we are praying incorrectly. I have learned this painfully, through years of mistakes. Prayer is a focus upon God, not upon ourselves. When we are hurting or obsessed, the problem is that we are able to think about only one thing, the object of our hurt or loss. That concentration becomes depressive, oppressively focusing us so much upon one thing that we asphyxiate emotionally. Obsessions are a form of overconcentration. For this reason, whenever we are caught up in depression, it is important that our prayer be focused upon God and not upon ourselves. If we do what comes naturally when trying to pray through a crisis, too often we will end up wallowing in our own suffering and stewing in our own juices. Instead of freeing ourselves from the sense of loss or obsession, we pull the wound inward, make the pain worse and the depression even more paralyzing. When we try to pray in a crisis, we must force ourselves to focus upon God or Jesus or upon some aspect of transcendent mystery, and we must resist entirely the urge to relate that encounter immediately to our wounded experience.

Let me offer an example: imagine yourself suffering the loss of someone you deeply loved. Hurt, unable to think about anything else, you go to pray. Immediately, the temptation will be to focus upon your heart, your obsession. You will try to talk it through with God, however sincerely. But the result will often be negative. You will find yourself becoming more fixed upon that from which you are trying to free yourself. Your obsession will intensify. Conversely, if you force yourself, and this will be extremely difficult, to focus upon God—for example, as he reveals himself in some mystery of Christ's life—you will have a better chance to break your obsession. You will experience God, slowly but gently, widening again the scope of your heart and mind. With that will come an emotional loosening and freeing. When a wounded child climbs into her mother's lap, she draws so much strength from the mother's presence that her own wound begins to pale. So too with us when we climb into the lap of God through prayer. Our crisis soon domesticates somewhat and slowly leaves us with a more peaceful perspective—not because it goes away, but because the presence of God overshadows us.

But this means we must genuinely climb into the lap of God. Concretely, this means that, when praying in a crisis, we must refuse to think about ourselves at all; we must refuse even to relate the mystery we are mediating to ourselves and our wound. Like a child, we must simply be content to sit and be held by the mother. That will be hard, very hard. Initially, every emotion in us will demand that we focus ourselves back upon our hurt. But that is the key: do not, under the guise of prayer, wallow further in hurt. Focus upon God. Then, like a sobbing child at his mother's breast, in silence, we will drink that which nurtures and brings peace. At the breast of God, we drink the Holy Spirit, the milk of charity, joy, peace, patience, goodness, mildness, long-suffering, faith, chastity, hope, and fidelity. In that nourishment lies peace.

As well, spiritual writers add another major counsel apposite to praying when in a deep crisis, namely, ideally do not enter the darkness alone. To offer just one example of what is meant here: Michael Ford, in his biography on Henri Nouwen, tells us how brutally honest Nouwen was emotionally. Sometimes when loneliness, depression, and chaos would threaten to overwhelm him, Nouwen would go to a friend's house and ask that friend to hold him while he cried. Not an easy thing to do, but in that there is a lesson: when we stare life's chaos and our own demons fully in the face, someone or something had better be holding us, or that darkness can just as easily destroy us as make us stronger.

Often we are naive about this. Today the idea is omnipresent that we must constantly forsake what is safe and move into the unknown, with all the chaos and demons we will meet there. Hence, we hear voices from all sides telling us that it is bad to play it safe, that we must face the chaos, the desert, the dark night, the demons within and around us. This challenge tells us to risk, to abandon safe havens, to face our addictions and fears, to move always toward a greater horizon and thus surrender ourselves beyond the narrow controls of our own wounded, pride-filled egos. Sound advice? Perhaps.

It is quite true that ultimately we must face the chaos. T. S. Eliot once said that home is where we start from, and as we move away the pattern becomes ever stranger and more varied. He is right, and the pain and confusion that result are a necessary part of growth. To grow is to leave the womb, home, all that is secure. To play it safe is eventually to asphyxiate. The Gospels tell us that we can reach eternal life only by undergoing the darkness and death of Gethsemane and the cross. The mystics call this the "dark night of the soul" and assure us that real transformation of soul will not happen at Disneyland but at Calvary. So far the advice is sound.

However, there can be a dangerous naïveté in all this. The idea that you should just let yourself free-fall into the great unknown, with all its darkness and chaos, and that growth and happiness are assured, is not always true—far from it. To enter the darkness, to go into the desert, to face your demons, you must first have the assurance that you will be held by someone or something—God, a loved one, a family, a faith that is strong enough to see you through, while undergoing this journey. To let go of a safe haven without this in place is naive and foolish.

When you let yourself free-fall, two things can happen, and one of them is bad. You can fall apart, pure and simple, with no one and nothing ever to set you back together. In the desert, if you are all by yourself, you can be overwhelmed, lose yourself, and die, literally or figuratively, of depression, dissipation, hopelessness, fear, and loneliness. When you have been through the desert and stand before a mirror and no longer know who you are or can no longer find any positive energy to live, laugh, and love, the journey away from safety has done you no favors. Conversely, of course, the journey through chaos can be paschal; it can bring about a wonderful new resurrection. But to pass through the darkness and chaos, to abandon yourself in trust, you must be sure that you will be held by someone or something when you are free-falling into the darkness.

We see this in Jesus' own paschal journey. He entered the darkness and chaos of Gethsemane and the cross, just as he had once entered the desert, not alone but with another. He was being held by his Father, just as Nouwen, during his depressions, let himself be held by his friends. Jesus was in the dark night, free-falling, but he was not alone. He surrendered himself and jumped over love's cliff, but only because he trusted that someone, his Father, would catch him before he hit the ground. All of us might want to ponder that before we counsel ourselves or others to abandon too hastily safety for chaos, even in the journey of prayer. The journey from Disneyland to Calvary should not be naively undertaken.

It is said that whatever does not kill you makes you stronger. True, though sometimes things will kill you, if you face them alone.

Essential Methods of Prayer

It is easy to be confused regarding methods of prayer, There are almost as many methods of prayer as spiritual authors. Trying to research various methods of prayer is like walking into an overstocked store where the quantity and variety simply overwhelm you. However, within this overwhelming variety of methods, there are, classically within the Christian tradition of prayer, only *two* essential types: *meditation* and *contemplation*.

What are these? The intent here is not to expose in practical detail any one method of prayer but simply to highlight the distinction between the two essential methods of prayer and invite the reader to enter more regularly and deeply into prayer by any method of his or her choosing. Both genres of prayer have the same intentionality—namely, to open our minds, hearts, and souls to a reality beyond our own self-preoccupation; that is, to bring us to a place where we can breathe an air that is transcendent to us. What is the distinction between *meditation* and *contemplation*?[10]

Using the spiritual tradition of the Desert Fathers and that of the great Carmelite mystics, the distinction between the two can be drawn in this way: the Desert Fathers spoke of prayer under the rubric of two Greek words: *praxis* and *theoria*. *Praxis* referred to all the activity we do within our prayer, as opposed to those moments when we sit quietly, passively, and in the mode of receptivity inside of our prayer. *Theoria* referred to being passive and receptive within prayer. In many of the major Christian prayer traditions that followed the Desert Fathers, *praxis* began to be identified with *meditation* and *theoria* with contemplation. Various new names appeared to designate these different methods: *meditation* came to be identified with *lectio divina*,[11] devotional prayers of all kinds, and with most of what is formally done as private, quiet prayer within monasteries and religious houses. *Contemplation*, on the other hand, came to be identified with the prayer of the *cloud of unknowing*,[12] *centering prayer,* and some of the prayer practices within the Buddhist and Zen traditions.[13]

Which method do spiritual writers recommend we use? There is no unanimity here, especially among contemporary spiritual writers. Some fear the practice of *contemplation,* as it has just been defined, and identify it with Buddhism and New Age, but that is an unfortunate and inaccurate judgment. Others, noncritically, recommend a form of *contemplation* for everyone, irrespective of their religious maturity, and this is perhaps a naïveté. Many classical spiritual writers, certainly including John of the Cross, recommend that *meditation* is the more appropriate method of prayer during the earlier stages of the spiritual life, namely, up until we reach the stage of generativity and are beyond the fervor of its first stage. After that initial fervor dies, when the honeymoon is over, be that in our marriage, our prayer life, or our work, these authors recommend that we employ *contemplation* as our method of prayer.

As well, many spiritual mentors today recommend that we do some type of *contemplative* prayer of quiet regularly to help offset the influence of information technology in our lives. Electronic communication has radically changed our lives. While it has made our lives wonderfully efficient, it also demands our attention twenty-four hours a day. Already in the thirteenth century, the poet Rumi complained about having to be available all the time: "I have lived too long where I can be reached!"[14] How much truer is that today in an age of information technology. We can all be reached all the time. There never needs to be any silence and solitude in our lives. And so we end up as good people, but as people who are not very deep: not bad, just busy; not immoral, just distracted; not lacking in soul, just preoccupied; not disdaining depth, just never doing the things to get us there.

Information technology is a powerful narcotic, for good and for bad. It has the power to shield us from pain, to soothe us in healthy ways. That can be good. Sometimes a narcotic is helpful. But it can also be overly intoxicating and too absorbing. It can swallow us whole. There are few better things we can do to find solitude and rest within today's hectic world, where all the news

in the world is available at our fingertips, than to practice *contemplative* prayer, a regular and deep centering
of ourselves in silence, a quiet sitting in one-to-one intimacy with God.

Sustaining Ourselves in Prayer

i) Obstacles Blocking Prayer

It does not take a professional insight to see that our
present culture constitutes a virtual conspiracy against
the interior life. This is not to suggest that somewhere
there are deliberate and conscious forces scheming to
keep us from interiority and prayer, but rather that an
accidental confluence of forces and circumstances in
history are making it difficult for us to live the exam-
ined life. What are these forces? They're simply the daily
headaches and heartaches that beset us.

The first problem we have with prayer is that we're
too busy and too preoccupied to make time for it. There
is never, it seems, a good time for prayer. Always we are
too busy, too stressed, too tired, or too preoccupied to
sit or kneel down to pray. We rise early, groan as our
alarm clocks startle us from sleep, rush through break-
fast, ready things for the day, fight crowds and traffic en
route to work, settle into a task that is demanding and
draining, gulp down a quick lunch, end the workday
tired, commute back home, ready another meal, tend
to the needs of loved ones, share a meal with others
who are just as tired and restless as we are, then, often

enough, have still another meeting or event to attend in the evening. The day simply takes us, consumes us, drains us, and leaves us, in its wake, sitting on the couch before a screen, tired, dissipated, needing still to prepare some things for tomorrow, and wanting a mindless distraction rather than the discipline of prayer. It's hard to pray in our overbusy lives.

But we are not just too busy to pray, we are also too restless. There's a congenital disquiet inside us that is, today, being fanned to a high flame by the culture: one thousand television channels are within our reach, the Internet brings the whole world into our private rooms, and there are always new movies that we have not seen, new songs we have not yet heard, colorful magazines whose covers beckon, sporting events that seem on everyone's mind, and every kind of special event—from the Olympics, to the Academy Awards, to World Cups, to celebrity gossip programs—to distract us. Beyond that, everyone around us seems to be traveling to interesting places, doing interesting things, meeting interesting people. We alone, it seems, are missing out on life, stuck, outside the circle, with nothing interesting to do. It is hard to pray inside of that kind of restlessness. To go to prayer is to miss out on something. Our deepest greed is not for money, but for experience. We hunger for life and rarely connect this hunger to the bread of life. Our restlessness and hunger for experience are huge impediments to prayer.

Finally, beyond the headaches and restlessness, there is the ambiguity of prayer itself. Prayer is not easy. By definition, it is a nonpragmatic, nonutilitarian activity. It is hard to sit still and seemingly do nothing when so many necessary tasks demand our attention and when so much inside us aches for activity and involvement. It is hard to pray when we suffer from the kind of headaches and heartaches that cannot be eased by taking an aspirin. There is indeed a certain conspiracy against the interior life today. But prayer beckons us beyond, asking us to lift even this up to God.

ii) A Canopy Under Which to Pray

Do we ever really understand or master prayer? Yes and no. When we try to pray, sometimes we walk on water and sometimes we sink like a stone. Sometimes we have a deep sense of God's reality, and sometimes we cannot even imagine that God exists. Sometimes we have deep feelings about God's goodness and love, and sometimes we feel only boredom and distraction. Sometimes our eyes fill with tears, and sometimes they wander furtively to our wristwatches to see how much time we still need to spend in prayer. Sometimes we would like to stay in our prayer place forever, and sometimes we wonder why we even showed up. Prayer has a huge ebb and flow.

I remember an incident, years back, where a man came to me for spiritual direction. He had been involved for several years in a charismatic prayer group and had experienced there powerful religious emotions. But now, to his surprise, those emotions had disappeared. When he tried to pray, he experienced mostly dryness and boredom. He felt that there was something wrong because his fiery emotions had disappeared. Here is how he expressed it: "Father, you've seen my Bible, seen how most every line is highlighted with a bright color because the text spoke so deeply to me. Well, right now, I feel like pitching my Bible through a window because none of that means anything to me anymore! What's wrong with me?"

The quick answer could have been: "God is wrong with you!" I pointed him toward the experience of Teresa of Ávila who, after a season of deep fervor in prayer, experienced eighteen years of boredom and dryness. Today, I would have him read the journals of Mother Teresa who, like Teresa of Ávila, after some initial fervor in prayer, experienced sixty years of dryness.

We nurse a naive fantasy both about what constitutes prayer and how we might sustain ourselves in it. And what often lies at the center of this misguided notion is the belief that prayer is always meant to be full of fervor, interesting, warm, carrying spiritual insight, and carrying the sense that we are actually praying. Coupled with this notion is the equally misguided notion that the way to sustain feeling and fervor in prayer is through constant novelty and variety or through dogged concentration. Classical writers in spirituality assure us that, while this is often true during the early stages of our prayer lives, when we are neophytes at prayer and in the honeymoon stage of our spiritual lives, it becomes less and less true the deeper we advance in prayer and spirituality. Much to the relief and consolation of anyone who has tried to sustain a prayer life over a long period of time, the great mystics tell us that once we are beyond the early honeymoon stage of prayer, the single greatest obstacle to sustaining a life of prayer is simple boredom and the sense that nothing meaningful is happening. But that does not mean that we are regressing in prayer. It often means the opposite.

Here is a canopy under which to pray even as we struggle with boredom and the sense that nothing meaningful is happening: imagine you have an aged mother who is living in a nursing home. You are the dutiful daughter or son, and, every night after work, for one hour, you stop and spend time with her, helping her with her evening meal, sharing the events of the day, and simply being with her as her daughter or son. I doubt that, save for a rare occasion, you will have many deeply affective or even interesting conversations with her. On the surface your visits will seem mostly routine, dry, and dutiful. Most days you will be talking about trivial, everyday things, and you will be sneaking the occasional glance at the clock to see when your hour with her will be over. However, if you persevere in these regular visits with her, month after month, year after year, among everyone in the whole world you will grow to know your mother the most deeply and she will grow to know you most deeply because, as the mystics affirm, at a certain deep level of relationship the real connection between us takes place below the surface of our conversations. We begin to know each other through presence.

You can recognize this in its opposite: notice how

your mother relates to your siblings who visit her only very occasionally. During those rare, occasional visits there will be emotions, tears, and conversations beyond the weather and the trivia of everyday life. But that's because your mother sees these others so rarely. Prayer is the same. If we pray only occasionally, we might well experience some pretty deep emotions in our prayer. However, if we pray faithfully every day, year in and year out, we can expect little excitement, lots of boredom, and regular temptations to look at the clock during prayer; but we can also expect through the years an ever deepening intimacy with our God.

iii) Sustaining Ourselves in Prayer Through Ritual and Rhythm

Given what has just been affirmed, that for long seasons in our lives we might suffer boredom and flatness in our prayer, we can learn a lesson from monks. They have secrets worth knowing. Their secret to sustaining a regular life of prayer is ritual and rhythm. They, who pray long hours every day, have long ceased to believe the false notion that prayer needs to be interesting, exciting, intense, and full of energy all the time. That is impossible, nothing is meant to be exciting all the time, including prayer and church services, and nobody has the energy to always be alert, attentive, intense, and actively engaged all the time.

That is important to understand. Too often we do not pray regularly precisely because we simply cannot find within ourselves the energy, time, intensity, and appetite for active participation that we think prayer is demanding of us. But prayer respects that, even if certain spiritual authors and certain liturgists do not. Prayer is meant to respect the natural rhythms of our energy. Praying is like eating, and, as we know from experience, you do not always want a banquet. If you tried to have a banquet every day, you would soon find coming to the table burdensome and would look for every excuse to escape, to sneak off for a quick sandwich by yourself. Eating has a natural rhythm: banquets and quick snacks, rich meals and simple sandwiches, high times with linen serviettes and low times with paper napkins, meals that take a whole evening and meals that you eat on the run. And the two depend upon each other: you can have a high season only if you mostly have ordinary times. Healthy eating habits respect our natural rhythms: our time, energy, tiredness, the season, the hour, our boredom, our taste.

Prayer needs to be sustained by a regular routine. Refuse to be seduced by any spirituality that does not tell you that, because your tiredness will soon enough be your refusal. Prayer cannot always be a high celebration, upbeat, with high energy, with constant variety, and with the naive belief that longer is better than shorter. Time and tiredness must, save on particular occasions, be a consideration. Do not punish yourself for glancing at your watch or falling asleep during prayer. The solution to our struggle, boredom, and lack of energy in prayer is rarely more variety and imagination. Too many people already lack the energy to pray and want to avoid church services.

The rhythm of monastic prayer can be our paradigm here. Monks know that if you pray regularly, boredom and lack of energy will soon begin to wear you down. The answer then is not so much new prayer forms and more variety, but rhythm, routine, and clearly established ritual. For monks, the key to sustaining a daily life is the expected, the familiar, the repetitious, the ritual, the defined prayer form that gives you as well a clearly defined durational expectancy and does not demand of you an energy that you cannot muster on a given day.

There are times of course for high celebration, for variety and novelty, for spontaneity, and for long celebrations. There are also times, and these are meant to predominate just as they do in our eating habits, for ordinary time, for low season, for prayer that respects our energy level, work pressures, and time constraints. It is no accident, I submit, that more people used to attend daily church services when these were shorter, simpler, less demanding in terms of energy expenditure, and gave people attending a clear expectation as to how long they would last. The same holds true for other prayers, such as the Office of the Church and basically all common prayer. What clear, simple, and brief rituals do is carry us: they carry our tiredness, our lack of energy, our inattentiveness, our indifference, and even our occasional distaste. They keep us praying even when we are too tired to muster up our own energy.

There is much to be commended in stressing that prayer, particularly liturgy, should demand of us real energy, real participation, and real celebration. It is meant to be demanding; but sometimes the danger is that we are working too hard at it and are not letting the rituals themselves work hard enough. Dietrich Bonhoeffer had a little mantra he would sometimes use when he was preaching to a young couple on their wedding day. He would tell them: "Today you are young and very much in love and you think that your love will sustain your marriage. It won't. But your marriage can sustain your love!"[15]

That is true too for prayer. We think that good intentions and energy will sustain our rituals of prayer, but they cannot. Rather, our rituals of prayer can sustain our goodwill and our energy.

iv) Our One Great Act of Fidelity—Show Up

No one can decide how he or she gets to feel at a given moment. Feelings come independently of our wanting or not wanting them. What is within our power is how we act in the face of our feelings. Nowhere is this truer than in how we pray and how we are meant to sustain ourselves in prayer through our adult years. The great spiritual writers assure us that, without exception, we will all have seasons within which our prayer is dry, boring, and can be done only on the basis of dogged willpower and commitment. Those same writers then go on to affirm that, because this will be true for everyone, the one, single, nonnegotiable rule for prayer is simply this: show up! Show up regularly, irrespective of feelings and irrespective of method. We cannot guarantee how we will feel on any given day, but we can guarantee that, short of an emergency, we will appear. It is not important which method of prayer we use, only that we pray. We show our fidelity to God not in our feelings but in our commitments.

ITS CROWNING GLORY,
BLESSING OTHERS

Infant Sorrow

My mother groaned! my father wept.
Into the dangerous world I leapt.
Helpless, naked, piping loud:
Like a fiend hid in a cloud.

Struggling in my father's hands,
Striving against my swaddling bands,
Bound and weary, I thought best
To sulk upon my mother's breast.

—WILLIAM BLAKE

Fish aren't the only species that eat their young!

The Full Flower of Maturity—the Capacity and Willingness to Bless Others

What is the mark of deep maturity? What must be manifest in our lives to show that both our person and our virtue are deeply mature?

There are different ways to answer this question. We can, for example, point to Jesus' Sermon on the Mount,[1] or to Paul's description of love,[2] or to Paul's description of life in the spirit.[3] Each of these, in essence, defines human and Christian maturity. But what does that maturity look like concretely? How do we experience someone else's maturity as manifest in our lives? And how do we concretely manifest maturity in relation to those around us?

Again, there are many pictures that might be drawn to show what deep maturity looks like in actual life. For our purposes, I would like to use one image to set forth a picture of the full flower of human maturity, the image of blessing. The mark of a deeply mature man or woman, the mark of a very mature disciple of Jesus, and the mark of someone truly giving his or her life away is this: he or she is a person who blesses others and blesses the world, just as God does and just as Jesus did. What is implied here? What does it mean to bless someone or something?

What Is a Blessing?

i) A Story of Nonblessing

Sometimes things can be better understood by looking at their opposite, and so we might ask the question:

What does it mean not to be blessed and how does that affect our lives? Here is an example: when I was still a very young priest, I once preached a homily on baptism in which I remarked that the words God spoke over Jesus at his baptism (*You are my son, the beloved, my favor rests on you*)[4] are words that God also spoke over each of us at our own baptism and that God speaks over us every moment of our lives. While I was taking off the Eucharistic vestments in the sacristy, I was approached by a young man who was both agitated and irate. He shared with me that he was out of prison on bail, awaiting sentencing, and he had come to church on this Sunday only because he was to appear in court on Monday to be sentenced to prison for several years. Then, in words to this effect, he said: "I came here today because I thought church might give some strength as I go into prison. But I hated it, especially I hated your sermon because it isn't true! You said that God takes delight in us, that he is pleased with us. Well, it is not true! Nobody has ever taken delight in me, least of all my own father!"

It is no surprise that this young man was angry. He was, after all, on his way to prison. He had never been blessed by his own father, and that leaves a deep wound inside someone. Indeed, a good number of anthropologists, psychologists, and spiritual writers today suggest that hunger for the father's blessing is one of the deepest hungers in the whole world, especially among men.[5] Without a blessing from above, and that vitally includes a blessing from our own fathers, we will carry both a deep wound and a deep hunger. There will, in effect, be a constriction around our hearts, a steel band that suffocates in countless ways and helps rob our lives of both color and delight. And that constriction, as we will see later, can be lifted only through being blessed.

ii) What Is a Blessing?

What is a blessing? Dietrich Bonhoeffer once suggested that a blessing is a visible, perceptible, effective proximity of God. That is wonderfully accurate as a definition, but it needs some explication to be understood. What really does it mean to bless someone?

Many of us, particularly Roman Catholics, are familiar with ritual blessings. For example, every Roman Catholic Eucharist ends with the ritual blessing: "I bless you in the name of the Father, and of the Son, and of the Holy Spirit." But what is meant by that exactly? What are those words meant to convey?

Sometimes the etymology of a word can be helpful in our understanding of it, and that is the case with the verb "to bless." The concept captured inside the English verb "to bless" takes its meaning from the Latin *benedicere,* literally meaning "to speak well of" (as in *bene*—meaning well or good, and *dicere*—meaning to speak). Thus, at its root, to bless someone is to speak well of him or her. If someone were to come up to you and say: "You are a wonderful person," that person, if she means what she says, is blessing you. She is speaking well of you.

Biblical Examples of God's Blessing

We see the prototype for a blessing in scripture. Both testaments in scripture open up with a powerful blessing from God, one that sets the tone for the overall story that they will tell. Thus, our Old Testament begins with the story of creation, of God fashioning the world out of nothing, and there we see how at the end of each day, God looked upon what he had done and saw that *it was good!* And this is emphasized even more strongly when, after the sixth day when God had created the man and the woman and completed creation, the scriptures tell us that God looked on all he had done and he saw that it was "indeed very good!"[6] God declared creation very good! This constitutes the original blessing, and, for many Christians, this still constitutes how God looks at us and our world, that is, God is still looking at his creation and saying: "It is indeed very good!"[7]

We see the same kind of blessing, one which colors the rest of Christian history, at the baptism of Jesus. His public ministry is launched with his baptism, and his baptism, as it is described in the Gospels, is the prototype of all blessing. It is wonderfully described in three of the Gospels: Jesus comes to the Jordan River to be baptized by John the Baptist. John immerses him in the river, and as Jesus' head breaks the waters, the heavens open and God's voice is heard to say: This is my beloved son on whom my favor rests.[8]

Rendered in this way, however, some of the richness of this text is lost in translation. First off, the title "beloved" is best translated precisely as "blessed." And the phrase, "on whom my favor rests" is better rendered as "in whom I am well pleased" or "in whom I take delight." Thus, God's words over Jesus at his baptism might more accurately be rendered: "This is my blessed child, in him I take delight!"

As well, scripture scholars alert us to the underlying image inside this text, namely, Jesus' head as breaking the waters is clearly an image of birth, and this highlights how significant this event is in Jesus' life—he is truly being reborn through his father's blessing. And this is so significant in the Gospels that it is impossible to understand Jesus, his consciousness and his vision, without grasping this point. It is as if, after this moment, for the rest of his life, Jesus is hearing his father's voice constantly telling him: "You are my blessed one, in you I take delight!"

That explains why Jesus could invite us to look at our lives and see ourselves always as blessed, no matter how bad our situation is: "Blessed are you when you are poor, when you mourn, when you are hungry and thirsty, when people hate you, when others abuse you, and when you are persecuted."[9] In all those situations, you are still God's beloved, blessed, someone in whom God takes delight. You are always blessed, no matter your circumstance in life. How could Jesus say such an astonishing thing? He could do it on the basis of his own blessing from his father. He had been blessed and he knew his blessedness, felt it; and because of that he could operate out of a blessed consciousness, a consciousness that could look out and see others and the world as blessed. His sense of being blessed formed his eyesight. How?

There's a Buddhist parable that runs something like this: one day as the Buddha was sitting under a tree, a young, trim soldier walked by, looked at the Buddha, noticed his fat, and said: "You look like a pig!" The Buddha looked up calmly at the soldier and said: "And you look like God!" Taken aback by the comment, the soldier asked the Buddha: "Why do you say that I look like God?" The Buddha replied: "Well, we don't really see what's outside of ourselves, we see what's inside of us and project it out. I sit under this tree all day and I think about God, so that when I look out, that's what I see. And you, you must be thinking about other things!"

There's an axiom in philosophy that asserts that the way we perceive and judge is deeply influenced and colored by our own interiority. That's why it is never possible to be fully objective and why five people can witness the same event, see the same thing, yet have five very different versions of what happened. Thomas Aquinas expressed this when he said: "Whatever is received is received according to the mode of its receiver." If this is true, and it is, then, as the Buddhist parable suggests, how we perceive others speaks volumes about what is going on inside of us. Among other things, it indicates out of what kind of consciousness we are operating. Jesus, because he knew his father's blessing, was able to operate out of a positive, blessed consciousness. Sadly, as we shall see later, many of us, because we have not been blessed or do not know our blessing, operate out of a cursed consciousness, one that can only look at the world through the lens of irritation, bitterness, or judgment. When we do this, we do it because we have been more cursed than blessed in our lives.

Blessing as Seen by Its Opposite—a Curse

The opposite of a blessing is a curse. What is a curse? A curse is not the colorful language that comes out of our mouths when we get stuck in traffic, slice our golf ball the wrong way, or lose a few hours of work in a computer meltdown. What we say then may indeed be wrong because it is in bad taste, an aesthetic offense, but it is not a curse. A curse is more pernicious.

Cursing is what we do when we look at someone whom we do not like and think or say: "I wish you weren't here! I hate your presence! I wish you'd go away!" Cursing is what we do when we are affronted by the joyous screams of a child and we say: "Shut up! Don't irritate me!" Cursing is what we do when we look at someone and think or say: "What an idiot" Cursing is what we do whenever we look at another person judgmentally and think or say: "Who do you think you are! You think you've got talent! You don't—you're full of yourself!"

This is the prototype of a curse: imagine a two-year-old child in a high chair who, having just eaten, high on that energy, begins (as do virtually all children that age) to kick her feet, spontaneously shout, and throw leftover bits of food around the room. She is bursting with life, spilling over in zest, shrieking in exuberance;

but that enthusiasm is a source of irritation to one of us in the room, and, in irritation, we say to her: "Shut up! Stop it!"

That is a curse! And that is far more harmful than the colorful language that comes out of our mouths when we have a computer meltdown. In expressing irritation at exuberance, we have just done the very opposite of what God did when he witnessed the original creation and saw the young planet twirling and throwing off mud from its young high chair. God smiled and said: "This is good!" We have also just done the very opposite of what God did when he saw Jesus' head break the waters of the Jordan River and said: "In you I take delight!" Unlike God, we tried to suppress life, deny joy its place, squelch exuberance, and shame enthusiasm. Why do we do that? Why are exuberance and joy an irritation and a threat to us?

No great mystery. We do it because we first have been cursed. When we were young, in the high chair, throwing off mud and food, exuberant, unable to contain our enthusiasm, we were told to shut up! To stop it! As a result, the life principle in us began to depress. If any of us could play back our lives as a video, we would see the countless times, especially when we were young, when we were subtly cursed, when we heard or intuited the words: "Shut up! Who do you think you are! Go away! You aren't wanted here! You're not that important! You're stupid! You are boring! You irritate me!" All of these were times when our energy and enthusiasm were perceived as a threat, and we were, in effect, shut down. The residual result in us is shame, depression. Its phenomenology is what William Blake describes in his poem "Infant Sorrow," whose second stanza might well be rendered: "Hungering for my father's blessing, unsure of my adulthood, feeling a constriction within me, I eventually succumbed to depression."[10] The result of being cursed more than blessed leaves us with a cursed consciousness where, unlike Jesus, we do not see others and the world as blessed. Instead, like the young soldier looking at an overweight Buddha under a tree, our spontaneous judgments are swift and lethal: "You look like a pig!"

Robert Moore, who has made it his life's work to study human energy, submits that, certainly in secularized cultures, most adults live in a state of chronic depression, that this is the result of not being blessed, and that its remedy can be only one thing: blessing.[11] What does he mean by that? What does it mean to be chronically depressed?

What Moore is talking about here is not clinical depression, which is an illness that crosses a certain pathological line and takes one into a realm where professional help is needed. What he is naming here is rather an inchoate grayness, a flatness, a joylessness that permeates life and robs it of color. In his view, depression is best understood by contrasting it with its opposite, delight. The opposite of depression is delight, but delight itself must be astutely defined. Genuine delight may not be confused with the false bravado that we crank up at parties, where we protest how happy we are by singing too loud, drinking too much, and being too boisterous. That is not delight, but rather a badly disguised attempt to keep depression at bay.

For Moore, delight would be defined this way: imagine yourself on an ordinary weekday afternoon, walking to your car after work, after shopping, or after a meeting, and suddenly feeling aware, consciously or unconsciously, of the joy of being alive, of being healthy, of standing inside so rich a life, and spontaneously saying to yourself: *God, it feels great to be alive!* At that moment you are not depressed, you are experiencing delight! But as many of us know from our own experience, we can be wonderfully mature, moral, and generous adults, giving ourselves away in service, and go through years and years of our lives without ever experiencing a moment of genuine delight, where our bodies and souls, in unison, spontaneously sing out: *God, it feels great to be alive!* As we know too, we cannot create a moment like that for ourselves. Delight has to find us! We can help create it for others, but never for ourselves, at least not by directly attempting it. Delight, as we will see later, is a by-product of something else, namely, blessing, giving and receiving blessing.

We need not feel bad that we live with so much chronic depression. Like Freud once said of neurosis, this is the disease of the normal person; in this case, it is the disease of the normal adult. Young children still experience delight. For example, stand outside a kindergarten classroom sometime and listen to the children as they come out for a recess or a lunch break. They simply stand in the sun and shriek! It is unconscious for them, but their bodies and souls, in unison, are saying: *God, it feels great to be alive!* That is what nondepression looks like and sounds like. Our adult lives neither look nor sound like that. Moreover, all too often, those joyous shrieks of children irritate us rather than lift our spirits. Something inside us wants to say: "Shut up! Keep it down!" Why, given that their shouts are probably the only real joy we have witnessed that day? Why our impulse to curse rather than bless that energy? Why do overexuberance and joy threaten us? How might we bless it rather than curse it?

It threatens us because it is, in effect, interfering with our depression and our spontaneous impulse to silence it, saying: "I am a depressed adult. I will not allow your joy to disturb me!" And that is our reaction because, like the soldier calling the Buddha a pig, we are reacting out of a cursed consciousness. We inhaled and internalized the curses we received as children when our own exuberance and life principle threatened those around us and they shut us down. Now we are doing the same thing to others, acting out the very abuse that had been perpetrated on us.

How might we bless that delight we see in these children? Imagine again a child in the high chair, shouting in joy and throwing food around the room: if her parents, depressed adults, tired and struggling with many heartaches in their own lives, could look at each other and, inside of their tiredness and depression, say: "Isn't it marvelous that two depressed people like us could even create someone like this!" They then would be blessing the energy in the room. And that is exactly the challenge, to habitually give off that kind of blessing.

How do we do that, on a larger scale, in our daily lives?

Components of a Blessing

Anthropologists tell us that there are three components to a blessing. To bless someone is to see and admire that person, speak well of him or her, and give away some of your life so that he or she might have more life. What is contained in each of these?

i) Blessing as Seeing Someone

To really see someone, especially a younger person who looks up to you, is to give that person a blessing. In the gaze of true recognition there is a deep blessing. But that implies seeing someone in a way that we do not always see each other, even when we think we do. Perhaps an example can be helpful in illustrating this.

A number of years ago, a couple that I know were going through a difficult time. Their marriage was struggling, and there was talk of separation. The husband, unwilling to submit to counseling, handled his part in the struggle mostly by disappearing and being absent from the home. At one point, their thirteen-year-old daughter went to a mall and shoplifted an item that she neither wanted nor needed and was caught in the act. As well, she was alone, so her little crime was not an attempt to impress friends. The store from which she had stolen the item decided that, while they did not want to press charges, they did want to teach the young girl a lesson, and so they had a policeman come in to talk to her. After lecturing her on the potential seriousness of what she had done, the officer asked her for her parents' phone number so that he could phone her home and have her mother come in to collect her. But the young girl had already prepared a different response: reaching into her pocket, she pulled out a slip of paper with her father's phone number at work, handed it to the officer, and said: "Here's my dad's phone number. I want him to come here and pick me up."

We do not need a degree in psychology to understand what happened here. This young girl was, however unconsciously, forcing her father to see her, and to see her in a way that his absenteeism had obviously prevented him from doing of late. There are different ways of making people see us. As parents, we believe we are seeing our children all the time, but there is a different kind of seeing that happens when you pick up one of your children at a police station. We are often unseen even as we are being seen. That is why it is a blessing to be seen. What is meant by that?

When we walk into a room full of people, two kinds of persons are most aware of our presence, those who love us and those who hate us, in effect, those who are blessing us and those who are cursing us. For the others, even those who know us well, we are part of the crowd

but are individually unseen. We are blessed when someone sees us in such a way that he or she, in word or in
body language, says: "I am glad you are here! You bring
something special into my life! You are not a threat but
a delight in my life!" That is a blessing! Of course, we
experience the opposite as well, a curse, where someone
who does not like us is seeing us and, in his or her body
language, is saying: "I wish you weren't here! Your energy is a threat to me!"

To see someone or be seen by someone else, in a positive light, is a blessing. At a primal level, we see this
need to be blessed by being seen acted out daily on every
playground on earth. The little child is playing at something but is also constantly looking about to see whether
his mother or father is watching: "Mommy, watch me!"
"Daddy, look at what I'm doing!" At another level, we
see this acted out ritually when someone has an audience with a major dignitary like a pope or a queen. In
such an audience, few words are exchanged. The idea is
not so much that you have a real conversation with the
dignitary but that you are seen by him or her. It is only
important that the pope or the queen see you, recognize
you, and have his or her appreciative gaze fall upon you.
There is a blessing imparted when this happens and,
contemporary cynicism notwithstanding, those who
have had such an audience have some feeling for what
that blessing is.

Blessing by seeing is one of the deep archetypal functions of all royalty, all parents, and all who lead others
in any way: God blesses the world by seeing it. Good

kings and queens bless their people by seeing them. A good pope blesses the church by seeing the church. A good president or prime minister blesses the country by seeing the country. A good mother blesses her children by seeing them, as does a good father. A good pastor blesses the parish by seeing its people. A good coach blesses his players by seeing them. A good dean blesses her faculty by seeing them. A good executive blesses the company by seeing his employees. A good friend blesses you by seeing you. And in a good restaurant, at some point in your meal, the owner blesses you by coming around and seeing you.

We are blessed by being seen, and we bless others by seeing them.

ii) Blessing as Speaking Well of Someone

In you I take delight! We bless others when we take delight in them, when we speak well of them, when we feel their presence and energy as a gift rather than a threat. If we can look at another person—man or woman or child—and in full sincerity say: "I am glad you are here! Your presence here brings me life! Your energy doesn't threaten me but adds to the joy of my own life!," then, like God pronouncing the original creation good and telling Jesus at his baptism "In you I take delight," you have blessed someone.

If you are a parent and you sincerely say to a son or daughter: "I'm proud of you!" you have blessed your child. If you are a teacher and say to a student: "Well done!" you have blessed your student. If you are a coach and you say to a player: "Great play!" you have blessed your player. If you are a minister or priest and say to your parish: "I love being here!" you have blessed your parishioners. If you are head of a company and you say to an employee: "Great job!" you have blessed that employee. If at work, you tell a colleague: "It is great working with you!" you have blessed that colleague. Conversely, if you are a parent, teacher, coach, minister, priest, employer, or colleague and are in any way threatened by the energy of your own children, students, players, parishioners, employees, or colleagues, you are probably withholding your blessing or, worse still, subtly cursing.

Blessings need not be articulated in words, though ideally they should be. There are ways beyond words to tell others that we take delight in them, just as there are many ways to communicate to others that we find them a threat or irritation in our lives. We bless more with our body language and our attitudes than we do with our words. How we express our pride and delight in others is not important—but that we do so is.

iii) Blessing as Giving Away Some of Our Own Life So That Someone Else Can Have More Life

To truly see someone and to speak well of that person is to already bless him or her, but to bless someone fully demands still one more component. To bless someone fully is to, in some way, die for him or her. Two examples can help illustrate this, one from the arts and one from scripture.

We see the third component of blessing powerfully

illustrated in the musical adaptation of Victor Hugo's classic *Les Miserables*. At one point in the story, Hugo's hero, Jean Val Jean, goes off in search of a young man, Marius, who is in love with Jean Val Jean's adopted daughter. At this stage of his life, Jean Val Jean is already an old man, and the young man, Marius, constitutes a powerful threat to him because he will take his adopted daughter away from him and in that way rob him of the final joy in his life. Initially, his motivation in going off to search for the young Marius is not first and foremost to bless him. Rather, he wants to see who this young man is and form an opinion of him. So he goes off in search of him.

He finds Marius at the barricades with a group of idealistic, but naive young revolutionaries. And he finds the boy asleep, in a double sense: asleep physically and asleep to the fact the he is almost certain to die in the morning. Then in a very powerful scene, both artistically and morally, the old man, Jean Val Jean, sings a prayer of blessing over the young man, Marius: He begins with an invocation to God, "God, on high, hear my prayer," then, turning to the young sleeping boy, he says: "Look at this boy . . . he is young, he is afraid . . . tomorrow he will die." He finishes the song with a refrain repeated a number of times over within which he asks God to spare the young man's life and take his life instead: "Let him live, let me die—Let him live! Let me die!" His logic is simple: young Marius should live precisely because he is young. He, Jean Val Jean, can die because he is old. The old should give up their lives for the young.

We see this same component of blessing illustrated in the Gospel of Matthew when he tells us how various people reacted to the announcement of Jesus' birth. Matthew sets up a powerful archetypal contrast, blessing and curse, between the reaction of the wise men who bring their gifts and place them at the feet of the new king, and King Herod, who tries to kill him. The wise men, on seeing the new king, place their gifts at his feet. What happens to them afterward? We have all kinds of apocryphal stories about their journey back home, but these, while interesting, are not helpful because their slipping away into anonymity is part of their gift. We do not know what happens to them afterward, and that is integral to the story. They disappear because they can now disappear. They have placed their gifts at the feet of the young king, and like old Jean Val Jean after having blessed young Marius, they can now leave life safely in the hands of the young.

And Herod, how much to the contrary! The news that a new king has been born threatens him at his very core, since he is himself a king. The glory and light that will now shine upon the new king will no longer shine on him. So what is his reaction? Far from laying his resources at the feet of the new king, he sets out to kill him. Moreover, to ensure that his murderers find him, he kills all the male babies in the entire area. A lot of books could be written about this last line. Fish are not the only species who eat their young! But the real point here is the contrast between the wise men and Herod: the former see new life as promise and they bless it; the latter sees new life as threat and he curses it.

To bless another person fully is to give away some of one's own life so that another might be more resourced for his or her journey. And part of that is a dying; we must die so that the other might live. In that sense, a blessing is not just an affirmation, a simple exclamation of "You are a fine young person!" These affirmations are good and life giving but still lack something. To fully bless someone is give up some life for that person, to die for him or her in some real way.

Good parents do that for their children. In all kinds of ways, they sacrifice their lives for their children. They die, but their children live. Good teachers do that for their students, good mentors do that for their protégés, good pastors do that for their parishioners, good politicians do that for their countries, and all good elders do that for the young. They give away some of their own lives to resource the young. Blessing a young person when you are older is as simple as it is difficult: Do you want to bless a young person? Step away and give him or her your job!

This would be more natural for us to do if we were all flowers, as opposed to being people. As we saw earlier, there is a certain anomaly in how human beings arrived at maturity. We can be physically and sexually mature, able to procreate, long before we have the adult maturity required of a parent. Hence, we can procreate and create life without having to bless it. Flowers cannot do this; procreation is necessarily tied to their own death: they can give their seed away only by dying themselves. They bless their young by completely giving up their lives.

In summary, we bless others when we see them, delight in their energy rather than feel threatened by it, and give away some of our own life to help resource their lives. Sadly, the reverse is also true: we curse others when we demand that they see and admire us, when we demand that they speak well of us, and when we use their lives to build up our own. A gesture of blessing feeds others; a cursing gesture feeds off of them.

Two Further Notes

Before offering an example of what a powerful blessing might look like, two things must first be highlighted: blessings are most powerful when they come from the top down and when they take place inside the same gender.

Normally, blessings work from the top down, from someone who has more power to someone who has less. God blesses the world, parents bless their children, teachers bless their students, coaches bless their players, and the old bless the young (at least until that reverses with the diminishments of aging that again reduce us to helplessness). Blessing imparts power, and thus it needs to come from one who has more power to one who has less.

As well, blessings are most powerful within the same gender. Fathers need to bless their sons; mothers need to bless their daughters; old men need to bless younger men; and older women need to bless younger women. Obviously, we need too to bless across gender lines, and these blessings too are powerful. But there is something special about being blessed inside the same gender. Why? The reason is more earthy than theoretical. We are not as threatened in our status and power by members of the other gender. Simply put, if I am a middle-aged man, I am not threatened by younger women but by younger men. The same is true if I am a woman. It is easier to look at a younger person of the opposite gender and say: "In you I take delight!" It is considerably more difficult if that younger person is talented and of our own gender. That is why fathers find it easier to bless their daughters than their sons, and why mothers find it easier to bless their sons than their daughters. We are not as threatened in our status and power by the opposite gender. Hopefully, this will be made clear in the example that follows.

An Example of a Blessing

So what might a simple but powerful blessing look like?

Imagine a man, a gifted teacher, lecturing at a prestigious university. He enjoys an immense popularity with his students, and he fully deserves it. There is no need for him even to receive a Teacher of the Year Award. The honor is his by acclamation. But he is now middle-aged, has lost some of his youthful vibrancy, and despite his ever increasing competence and professional reputation, he is no longer a fresh young face. As he walks into the faculty lounge one day, just as a new school year is about to begin, he is introduced to a new faculty member, Jack. Jack might well have been ordered from a high-end catalogue: he is not yet thirty years old, has a doctorate from a very prestigious university, has already published a well-received book, and is reputed to be a great classroom lecturer. Moreover, he has the looks of a movie star—tall, handsome, great hair, great teeth, great smile. He literally exudes youth and health. Finally, added to all of this, Jack is also a very nice young man, respectful, gracious, humble, not full of himself. The senior faculty member already intuits, and clearly, that Jack's popularity is soon to eclipse his own.

What do you think will be his reaction to Jack becoming his colleague? Will he say: "In you I take delight?" Is he likely, like the wise men who saw Jesus' star, to put his gifts at young Jack's feet and be content to let his own star fall as he sees Jack's star rising? Or, like Herod, will he say: "I will kill you!" meaning: "Just wait! Let him put up with all the garbage that I've had to deal with and in twenty years he will be as jaded and cynical as I am!"

In far too many cases, we know that the response will be that of King Herod rather than that of the wise men, a curse rather than a blessing: I will kill this young life rather than bless it because it is a threat to me. If, however, this middle-aged, soon-to-be-eclipsed man could walk over to young Jack who is such a threat to him, and say: "I am so glad that you are here, glad that you have joined our faculty! You bring so much to us—your excellent research, the great lecturing skills that we have already been told about, that fine book you wrote, not even to mention your youth and your wonderful good looks! I'm going to be retiring in a couple of years, and now I can retire more easily knowing our department is in good hands. If there is anything that I can do to help you—anything at all—let me know. I'm so glad you're here. What a wonderful gift you are to our faculty!"

If he could say these words and truly mean them, even in the face of some natural human jealousy and resentment inside of him, he would be blessing young Jack, and that blessing would have a double effect: on the one hand, it would help free up something inside of Jack, which would forever help make Jack a more secure and blessing person because Jack would be hearing what Jesus heard at his baptism: "You are a blessed one; in you I take delight!" That blessing would help Jack see the world through a blessed consciousness, and it is more likely that, when he is aging and his own star is eclipsing, he will not himself be threatened by young energy. But also, and very importantly, it would help lift some of the chronic depression inside of the man giving the blessing. Not long after blessing young Jack he would, one day, without being conscious of what triggered the feeling, sense deeply the joy of being alive, of being healthy, of standing inside so rich a life, and spontaneously say: *God, it feels great to be alive!* When we act like God, we get to feel like God. Conversely, when we are petty, we get to feel petty. There is a clear cause and effect here: when we do bighearted things, we get to feel bighearted; and when we do small-hearted things, we get to feel small.

Blessing Our Way Out of Depression to Wholeness and Delight

The challenge then is clear: simply put, when we bless others we help lift depression from our lives; when we do not bless others, we deepen that depression.

An image can be helpful in understanding this: when a cow gives birth to a baby calf, the calf emerges from its mother's womb in a certain state of paralysis. It is born enwrapped in a gluelike substance that radically constricts its movement. However, nature provides an answer for this. Its mother turns round and immediately licks this constricting afterbirth off the calf, every inch of it. As soon as the mother has completed this, the calf stands, tests its own legs, and then begins to walk on its own. In the birth of a calf this process does not take very long; it is a question of minutes rather than hours, days, or years.

As human beings we are also born partially paralyzed by a certain constricting afterbirth, except that in our case that constriction fixes itself mainly to the heart, and it takes years to remove. Moreover, we cannot free ourselves of this paralysis all on our own. We need the elders in our lives to turn round, like a mother toward her calf, and metaphorically lick away that constriction. What is that constriction exactly? Our hearts are not free to delight in life because they are habitually partially depressed and asphyxiated by the inchoate sense that we are not deeply loved and not truly wanted, and that our life, health, and energy is a threat to those around us rather than a delight to them. That is the constricting afterbirth that needs to be lifted from us. And that can be done only through blessing. When we are young, the elders in our lives either help lift that constriction from us by blessing us or they tighten its grip by cursing our energies.

Mostly this is an unconscious thing in our lives. We sense that we lack something important, but we do not know what it is or how we can attain it. We do not realize that we are hungry for and in need of blessing. Thus, we look for all kinds of ways to free ourselves. Inside the male psyche, this unrecognized hunger for blessing, especially blessing from one's own father, often takes the form of an unhealthy focus on two things: success and sex. The unconscious belief is that these will bring the blessing we so desperately desire. Sadly, neither of these is an adequate substitute for the father's blessing. The constriction in the heart remains. Only blessing can free up a certain part of the heart.

And too few of us have been sufficiently blessed. It is revelatory for most of us to ask ourselves this question: Can you remember a time in your life when a significant elder—your father, your mother, a teacher, your pastor, your boss, your dean, an uncle, an aunt, or any respected elder, took a true and nonexploitive delight in you, your energies, your talents, your ideas, your looks, your person? Can you remember a time when you heard a significant elder in your life say to you: "In you I take delight!"? For many of us, this type of self-examination results in sadness. Tearfully, we have to confess that it never happened, save for some minor incidents. Is it any wonder then that we are depressed? No one has lifted the constricting afterbirth from our hearts. So what do we do if we have not been sufficiently blessed? What do we do if we had a father who never blessed us or who refuses to bless us? Can we self-bless?

We cannot give ourselves the blessing we need, but we can bless others. It is depressingly revelatory to submit ourselves to a self-examination that asks whether we can remember significant times of blessing in our lives, but it is equally revelatory to ask ourselves a further question: When was the last time I, as an adult man or woman, walked across a room and blessed a younger person, particularly one whose talents are a threat to me? This kind of self-scrutiny also mostly produces a negative answer: it has not happened. And that is a part of our depression.

We cannot force others to bless us, but we can bless others, and in that is our freedom. If we bless others, it will not be long afterward that our hearts will feel an exuberance that will, all on its own, say: *God, it feels good to be alive!* When we act like God, we get to feel like God. And God is never depressed.

Sometimes poets put it best. Here is how William Butler Yeats, writing as an older man, explains why, on a certain day, without being conscious of what triggered the feeling, his own heart is ablaze with an exuberance that literally cries out: *God, it feels great to be alive!*

> *My fiftieth year had come and gone,*
> *I sat, a solitary man,*
> *In a crowded London shop,*
> *An open book and empty cup*
> *On a marble table-top.*
> *While on the shop and street I gazed*
> *My body of a sudden blazed;*
> *And twenty minutes more or less*
> *It seemed, so great my happiness,*
> *That I was blessèd and could bless.*

—WILLIAM BUTLER YEATS, "VACILLATION"[12]

The Difficulty in Doing This

There is a poem by a Chinese American poet, Li-Young Lee, which expresses some of the difficulty that adults, particularly fathers, have in blessing their young. Titled "A Story," the poem ends with the poignant statement that "a boy's supplications and a father's love add up to silence."[13]

It is so important to bless the young, but it is not an easy thing to do. Beyond the fact that their youth and energy are a threat to us, there is also the fact that, on the surface at least, it would seem that mostly they do not want our blessing. The young Jack, we just described above, in his full-blown youth and talents, may well be giving off all kinds of signals that suggest that he does not want your blessing. It is easy to bless a young person if that young woman or man first comes up to you and tells you that he or she admires and respects you. Mostly, that is not the case. Here is a typical example:

Recently at a workshop, as we were discussing the tension that often exists today between younger and older clergy, a middle-aged priest said: "I'd like to bless the younger priests, but they don't want my blessing! They see me as a burned-out middle-aged ideologue, and everything in their attitude and body language tells me that they simply want me to disappear and give them space!"

Many are the parents who feel exactly that way as they stand before their own adolescent or grown children: the mother before her adolescent daughter; the father before his teenage son. That is also true for many others: the teacher before her adolescent students, the priest or minister in the face of a less-than-appreciative congregation, the senior faculty member before the junior member, the coach before his players, and the policeman before a belligerent young man. It is not easy to bless someone who, seemingly, does not want your blessing, before whom it would seem a lie to say what God said to Jesus at his baptism: "In you I take delight!"

But that is the real task! Deeper maturity consists precisely in being bighearted enough to give your blessing, without the young person first admiring you or even realizing that he or she needs your blessing. As scripture puts it, love demonstrates itself in precisely this act, in giving itself over even when it is not appreciated.[14]

Moreover, we distinguish between the various levels at which we want something. On the surface, clearly, young persons often do not want the blessing of their parents, elders, teachers, and clergy. But that is on the surface; they have deeper wants and needs. Someone once said that a true missionary is someone who goes where he or she is not wanted but is needed, and leaves when he or she is wanted but not needed. That is true too for parenting, teaching, coaching, and ministry. We should not identify what someone wants at the surface of life with that which is needed and wanted at a deeper level. Young people may not overtly want the blessing of their elders, but they desperately need it. Later on, after they have matured, they will want that blessing but, paradoxically, then they will no longer need it to the same extent. We should not be put off by the surface of things, where youth, naturally, push their elders away and give the impression the elders have nothing to offer them. But their very aloofness is partly a symptom of the lack of blessing in their lives and a plea for that blessing.

And we need to give that blessing. Admittedly, it is not easy to do. Its cost, as T. S. Eliot once put it, is not less than everything.[15] But this is what it means to act like God. We need to offer our lives for another, particularly for the young, particularly when the cost is high, and particularly too when that other might not even know what you are doing for him or her and might not be grateful for it.

The air we breathe out into the universe is the air we will reinhale. When we bless the young, especially when it seems that they do not want our blessing, we help lift a congenital constriction off of their hearts, and, when we do that, we also lift a huge depression from our own hearts—because when we act like God, we get to feel like God.

Blessing as the Crowning Glory of Mature Discipleship

How might one picture the pinnacle of human maturity, the final stage of adult generativity, and the epitome of Christian discipleship? Generally, this is pictured as martyrdom, dying for another person, and this is then held forth as the ultimate that one person can do for another. Indeed, that is the supreme act of love. As Jesus himself says, there can be no greater love than to lay down one's life for others.[16]

But martyrdom is not an end but a passage, and an unnatural and unintended one at that, toward a final state. The glory and joy are not in being a martyr, the glory and joy lie on the other side of the struggle. Heaven will not be a celebration of martyrdom, a postvictory party at which we eternally congratulate one another for how well we fought the good fight and how much of ourselves we were willing to sacrifice. The fight was necessary to get there, but the fight is over and it was never the end. We were born for something else, eternal Sabbath, taking delight in God and in each other. Getting there involves struggle and sometimes martyrdom, but these are only a means to an end.

The final stage of everything, including maturity, generativity, and discipleship, lies beyond martyrdom, on the other side, in a place beyond pain and struggle, in a garden of delight, in heaven. The final picture then of human and Christian development is not that of the suffering martyr; that lies next to the final picture. The final picture rather is that of a blessing grandmother or a blessing grandfather, not suffering but joyful, smiling and beaming with pride at the life and energy of the young, basking in that energy and radiating from every pore of his or her being the words of the Creator: "It is good! Indeed, it is very good! In you I take delight!"

SIMPLIFYING OUR SPIRITUAL VOCABULARY: TEN COMMANDMENTS FOR THE LONG HAUL

Life has served me as it serves everyone, sometimes well and sometimes ill, but I have learned to be grateful for the gift of it, for the love that began it and the other loves with which I have been so richly endowed.

—MORRIS WEST[1]

Can a single moral or religious issue become the litmus test in terms of defining the very essence and the nonnegotiable heart of Christian discipleship? Yes. In the Gospels the moral heart of discipleship is articulated by Jesus, and this challenge lies at its center: Can you love and forgive your enemy?

When you carry someone's cross, don't send them the bill!

Simplifying Our Spiritual Vocabulary

In his autobiography, *A View from the Ridge,*[2] novelist Morris West suggests that at a certain age our lives simplify and we need have only three phrases left in our spiritual vocabulary: *Thank you! Thank you! Thank you!* He is right, providing we understand fully what is implied in living out gratitude. Gratitude is the ultimate virtue, undergirding everything else, even love. It is synonymous with holiness.

Gratitude not only defines sanctity, it also defines maturity and is the ultimate fuel for generativity. We are mature to the degree that we are grateful. But what brings us there? What makes for a deeper human maturity? What does genuine gratitude look like in its full bloom?

From all that is best and noble within human wisdom, from all that is best within world religions, from all that is best within the Judeo-Christian scriptures, and especially from the wisdom and example of Jesus, we can draw out a number of major principles that reside inside human and Christian maturity and ultimately define them. And since the number ten is hallowed in the scriptures as constituting and signifying a certain wholeness and completeness, I would like to synthesize those moral principles around ten commandments, commandments for maturity and generativity.

What are those commandments? I beg the reader's pardon here since some of these themes and concepts have been mentioned before, but this will be an attempt to bring them together into a brief, synthetic package:

Ten Commandments for Mature Living

A Synthetic Listing

The Ten Commandments given us in scripture are warnings intended to keep us from falling into sin and into places where we should not be. They are not the standard for holiness, but a lowest common denominator, the minimal requirement for morality, the benchmark below which someone should not fall. Hence, each of them is prefaced with the command: "Thou shalt not!" The series of commandments proposed here for mature discipleship have a different intent, to invite us to a higher place, a deeper maturity, and a more intimate relationship with God and one another. Hence, they are invitations more than commands, and consequently, each begins with a positive invitation:

1. Live in gratitude and thank your Creator by enjoying your life.
2. Be willing to carry more and more of life's complexities with empathy.
3. Transform jealousy, anger, bitterness, and hatred rather than give them back in kind.
4. Let suffering soften your heart rather than harden your soul.
5. Forgive—those who hurt you, your own sins, the unfairness of your life, and God for not rescuing you.
6. Bless more and curse less!
7. Live in a more radical sobriety.
8. Pray, affectively and liturgically.

9. Be wide in your embrace.

10. Stand where you are supposed to be standing,
and let God provide the rest.

Some Elaboration

What is implied in each of these invitations? The task of
this entire book has been precisely to try to name and
flesh out what is implied in these invitations. Hence, the
attempt here will be to more sharply synthesize what
this book as a whole has been trying to say. What are the
core principles both for a more mature Christian discipleship and a deeper generativity within our adult lives?

*1. Live in gratitude and thank your Creator
by enjoying your life.*
When I was eighteen, while playing soccer at the seminary, I injured one of my knees rather seriously. The in-
jury required a weeklong stay in a local hospital. While
there, I shared a ward with three other patients, one of
them a fiftysomething truck driver who was suffering
from an abdominal disorder. Whatever the specifics of
his illness, it caused him a great deal of pain; he would
often wake at night in pain, and his groaning would
wake the rest of us. Eventually, a nurse would come and
give him a painkiller to help him go back to sleep.

One night, deep into the night, I was wakened by
his groaning. Eventually, he pushed his buzzer, and the
nurse came into the ward. She washed his face with a

cool towel, and then, using a syringe, administered a painkiller to him. After some minutes, the medication took effect, and he relaxed considerably. Just as the nurse turned to leave the room, he said to her in a clear, firm voice: "I really appreciate you doing this for me!" She replied simply: "No need for thanks. I'm only doing my job!" But he answered: "Ma'am, it's nobody's job to take care of me! So when you do this for me, I need to say thanks!"

It is not anybody's job to take care of us, and so we should be grateful when someone does. There is a lot of wisdom in that simple statement. Gratitude, both in terms of our recognition of our need for it and our expression of it, is ultimately the basis of all virtue. Søren Kierkegaard said that to be a saint is "to will the one thing," namely, God and the life of service to which faith in God calls us. As excellent as that definition is, it needs some qualification in terms of our motivation for willing that one thing. To be a saint, one must also be fueled by gratitude. To be a saint is to recognize, as did that truck driver with whom I once shared a hospital ward, that nobody owes us life, a living, service, or love—and when we are given these, we need to be grateful.

Gratitude is the basis of all holiness. The holiest person you know is the most grateful person you know. That is true too for love: the most loving person you know is also the most grateful person you know because even love finds its basis in gratitude. Anything we call love, but that is not rooted in gratitude, will, at the end of the day, be manipulative and self-serving. If our love and service of others does not begin in gratitude, we will end up carrying peoples' crosses and sending them the bill.

We are all familiar with T. S. Eliot's famous dictum that the last temptation that is the greatest treason is to do the right thing for the wrong reason.[3] Gratitude is the true reason for love, and when we try to root our love in anything else (shared ideology, ethnicity, gender, pity, cause, religion, or anger), it will invariably be more self-serving than life giving. Real love roots itself in gratitude, and gratitude roots itself in the recognition, expressed so well by the truck driver just quoted, that nothing is owed to us—"It's nobody's job to take care of me!" Jesus tries to teach this to us in a mini-parable that, on the surface, sounds rather awful but, underneath, carries a profound lesson: "Which of you, with a servant ploughing or minding the sheep, would say to him when he returned from the fields, 'Come and have your meal immediately'? Would he not be more likely to say. 'Get my supper laid; make yourself tidy and wait on me while I eat and drink. You can eat and drink yourself afterward'? Must he be grateful to the servant for doing what he was told? So with you: when you have done all you have been told to do, say, 'We are merely servants: we have done no more than our duty.'"[4]

What Jesus is doing in this parable is drawing the distinction between what comes to us *by right* as opposed to what comes to us *as gift*. If each of us were given only what is owed to us, we would live like that servant just described. But we are given more, infinitely more. The real task of life then is to recognize this, to recognize that everything is a gift and that we need to keep saying thanks over and over again for all the things in life that we so much take for granted, recognizing always that it is nobody's job to take care of us.

As well, our gratitude is meant to carry something else: enjoyment of the gift that is given to us. The highest compliment we can give a gift giver is to enjoy the gift thoroughly. We owe it to our Creator to appreciate things, to be as happy as we can be. Life is meant to be more than a test, and so we might add this to our daily prayer: give us today our daily bread, and help us to enjoy it without guilt.

Our level of maturity and generativity is synonymous with our level of gratitude—and mature people enjoy their lives.

2. Be willing to carry more and more of life's complexities with empathy.

Few things in life, including our own hearts and motives, are black or white, either/or, simply good or simply bad. Maturity invites us to see, understand, and accept this complexity with empathy so that, like Jesus, we cry tears of understanding over our own troubled cities and our own complex hearts and, like Jesus too, we can forgive others, the world, and ourselves for this complexity and imperfection. A mature person watching the news at night and seeing the world's wars, violence, and wounds responds with empathy because she already recognizes within herself that same complexity, neediness, pride, greed, and lust that lie at the root of all that unrest. Deep maturity is very much synonymous with empathy.

Empathy is predicated too in part on being able to accept the limitations and innate frustrations in our lives; but, as Karl Rahner once suggested, that is not an easy maturity to attain. In his view, maturity here finds us by way of conscription: "In the torment of the insufficiency of everything attainable we come to understand that here, in this life, all symphonies remain unfinished."[5]

What does it mean to be tormented by the insufficiency of everything attainable? We all experience this daily. This torment is generally an undertow to everyday life: beauty makes us restless when it should give us peace; the love we experience with others does not fulfill our deep longings; the relationships we have within our families seem too domestic to be fulfilling; our job is inadequate to the dreams we have for ourselves; the place we live seems "small town" in comparison to other places; the ideal we have for our lives habitually crucifies the reality of our lives and makes us too restless to sit peacefully at our own tables, to sleep peacefully in our own beds, and be at ease within our own skins. Our lives seem too small for us, and we are always waiting for something or somebody to come along and change things so that our real lives, as we imagine them, might begin.

Accepting our limitations is not just diagnostic, it

is prescriptive too. To accept that we cannot have the full symphony gives us permission to have a bad day, a lonely season, a life that somehow never fully gets free of tension and restlessness. It gives us permission as well not to be too hard on ourselves and, more importantly, it tells us to stop putting unfair pressure on our spouses, families, friends, vacations, and jobs to give us something that they cannot give—namely, happiness without a shadow, the full symphony. We move beyond the cancer of frustration and restlessness by precisely accepting that here, in this life, there is no finished symphony.

We carry the infinite inside ourselves. We are Grand Canyons without a bottom. Nothing, short of union with all that is, can ever fill in that void. To be tormented by complexity and restlessness is to be human. To make our peace with that is to come to peace, and we are mature to the degree that our own restlessness is no longer the center of our lives.

3. Transform jealousy, anger, bitterness, and hatred rather than give them back in kind.

Any pain or tension that we do not transform we will retransmit. As we saw in an earlier chapter, in the face of jealousy, anger, bitterness, and hatred we must be like water purifiers, holding the poisons and toxins inside of us and giving back only the pure water, rather than being like electrical cords that simply pass on the energy that flows through them.

The natural, instinctual temptation in the face of jealousy, anger, bitterness, and hatred is to give back in kind: you hate me so I will hate you! But we are in-vited to something higher. At the very heart of the gos-pel of Jesus, at its moral center, lies the invitation to go beyond, far beyond, our natural instincts on this so as to meet hatred with love, bitterness with graciousness, jealousy with affirmation, and murder with forgiveness. Indeed, if one is looking for a litmus test as to what sin-gle issue is the test for Christian morality, perhaps more than anything else, this would be the test: Can we move beyond instinct so as not to give back in kind? Can we love an enemy? Can we, despite the rebellion of our own emotions, forgive a murderer? Can we resist giving back in kind? Can we love and forgive beyond those whom we deem as deserving of that love and forgiveness?

This challenge is what sets Jesus' moral teaching apart from others and gives it its unique character, and its real teeth. And the litmus test, more broadly under-stood, is not one, single moral issue but rather a whole way of living that radiates more charity than selfishness, more joy than bitterness, more peace than factionalism, more respect than negative judgment, more empathy than anger, and more willingness to sweat the blood of sacrifice than to give in to the sway of our natural emotions.

As we saw earlier, the Gospels present Mary, the mother of Jesus, as a paradigm for this. In the language of the gospels, she was able *to ponder,* that is, to hold, carry, and transform tension rather than to give it back in kind. This quality, perhaps more than any other, de-fines maturity and spawns generativity.

4. *Let suffering soften your heart rather than
harden your soul.*

Several years ago, at a conference that I was attending,
the keynote speaker challenged his audience in this way:
all of us, he pointed out, are members of various communities—we live in families, are part of church con-
gregations, have colleagues with whom we work, have
a circle of friends, and are part of a larger civic community. In every one of these there will come a time when
we will get hurt, when we will not be honored, when
we will be taken for granted and treated unfairly. All
of us will get hurt. That is a given. However, and this
was his challenge, how we handle that hurt, with either
bitterness or forgiveness, will color the rest of our lives
and determine what kind of person we are going to be.

Suffering and humiliation find us all, and in full
measure, but how we respond to them will determine
both the level of our maturity and what kind of person
we are. Suffering and humiliation will either soften
our hearts or harden our souls. The dynamic works
this way:

There is no depth of soul without suffering. Human
experience has long ago taught us this. We attain depth
primarily through suffering, especially through the kind
of suffering that is also humiliating. If any of us were to
ask ourselves the question: What has given me depth?
What has opened me to deeper perception and deeper
understanding? Almost invariably, the answer would be
one of which we would be ashamed to speak: we were
bullied as a child, we were abused in some way, some-

thing within our physical appearance makes us feel inferior, we speak with an accent, we are always somehow the outsider, we have a weight problem, we are socially awkward, the list goes on, but the truth is always the same. To the extent that we have depth we have also been humiliated; the two are inextricably connected.

But depth is not all of a kind. Humiliation makes us deep, but it can make us deep in very different ways. It can make us deep in understanding, empathy, and forgiveness, or it can make us deep in resentment, bitterness, and vengeance. The young men who shot their classmates in Columbine and the young man who indiscriminately gunned down students at Virginia Tech University had, no doubt, suffered more than their share of humiliation in life, and that had made them deep. Sadly, in their case, it made them deep in anger, bitterness, and murder.

We see the opposite in Jesus in how he faces his crucifixion. Crucifixion, as we know, was designed by the Romans as capital punishment, but they had more than mere capital punishment in mind. Crucifixion was also designed to do two other things: to inflict the optimal amount of pain that it was possible for a person to absorb and to utterly and publicly humiliate the one undergoing it.

As Jesus prepares to face his crucifixion and the shameful humiliation within it, he cringes before the challenge and asks God whether there is another way of getting to the depth of Easter Sunday without having to undergo the humiliation of Good Friday. Eventually, but only after sweating blood, does he accept that there is no other way than to undergo the humiliation of crucifixion. But we get the real lesson only if we really understand what was at stake in Jesus' choice here. The agonizing choice that he is making is not the choice: Do I submit to death or do I invoke divine power and walk free? He was condemned to death and felt as helpless as would any other human in that situation. Invoking divine power or not invoking it as a means of escape was not the issue about which he was anguishing. The issue was not whether to die or not die. It was about *how to die.* Jesus' choice was this: Do I die in bitterness or in love? Do I die in hardness of heart or softness of soul? Do I die in resentment or in forgiveness?

We know which way he chose. His humiliation drove him to extreme depths, but these were depths of empathy, love, and forgiveness.

That is the issue that is perennially at stake in terms of our own maturity. In our humiliations, do we give ourselves over to bitterness or love, resentment or forgiveness, hardness of heart or softness of soul? And we have to make that choice daily: every time we find ourselves shamed, ignored, taken for granted, belittled, unjustly attacked, abused, or slandered we stand between resentment and forgiveness, bitterness and love. Which of these we choose will determine both our maturity and our happiness.

And, ultimately, for all of us, as was the case with Jesus, we will have to face this choice on the ultimate playing field: in the face of our earthly diminishment and death, will we choose to let go and die with a cold heart or a warm soul?

5. Forgive—those who hurt you, your own sins,
the unfairness of your life, and God for not
rescuing you.

As we age, we can begin to trim down our spiritual vocabulary, and eventually we can get it down to three words: *Forgive, forgive, forgive!* To die with a forgiving heart is the ultimate moral and religious imperative. We should not delude ourselves on this. All the dogmatic and moral purity in the world does little for us if our hearts are bitter and incapable of forgiveness.

We see this in the Gospels, for instance, in the sad figure of the older brother of the prodigal son. He stands before his father protesting that he has never wandered, never been unfaithful, and that he has stayed home and done the family's work. But, and this is the issue, he stands outside the father's house, unable to enter into joy, celebration, the banquet, the dance. He has done everything right, but a bitter heart prevents him from entering the father's house just as much as the lustful wanderings of his younger brother took him out of that same house. Religious and moral fidelity, when not rooted inside of gratitude and forgiveness, are far from enough. They can leave us just as much outside the father's house as sin and infidelity. As Jesus teaches forcefully in the Lord's Prayer, a nonnegotiable condition for going to heaven is forgiveness.

But the struggle to forgive others is not easy and may

never be trivialized or preached lightly. In the end, it is our greatest psychological, moral, and religious struggle. It is not easy to forgive. Most everything inside of us protests. When we have been wronged, when we have suffered an injustice, when someone or something has treated us unfairly, a thousand physical and psychological mechanisms inside of us begin to clam up, shut down, freeze over, self-protect, and scream in protest, anger, and rage. Forgiveness is not something we can simply will and make happen. The heart, as Pascal once said, has its reasons. It also has its rhythms, its paranoia, its bitter spots, and its need to seal itself off from whatever has wounded it.

Moreover, all of us have been wounded. No one comes to adulthood with his or her heart fully intact. In ways small or traumatic, we have all been treated unjustly, violated, hurt, ignored, not properly honored, and unfairly cast aside. We all carry wounds, and, with those wounds, we all carry anger, bitterness, and some nonforgiveness.

But as we know, forgiveness is not easy, and, indeed, sometimes it seems impossible. The famous line from the poet Alexander Pope is now a standard axiom in the English language: "To err is human; to forgive, divine." Given the truth of this, and given our own bitter experience, how can we move toward forgiveness? There are no easy answers here, and perhaps true forgiveness can only be divine in origin, the operation of a special grace inside us. However, deeper insight born of empathy can also be helpful. Let me offer two examples:

In one of James Carroll's early novels, he offers this poignant image: a young man is in the delivery room watching his wife give birth to their baby. The delivery is a difficult one, and she is in danger of dying. As he stands watching, he is deeply conflicted: he loves his wife, is holding her hand, and is frantically praying that she not die. Yet the impending birth of their child and the danger of his wife's death conspire to make him acutely aware that, deep in his heart, he has not forgiven her for once being unfaithful to him. He has expressed his forgiveness to her, but he realizes now, at this moment of extreme crisis, that in his heart he still has not been able to let go of the hurt and that he has not truly forgiven her.

As his wife hovers between life and death, he sees in her face a great tension, a struggle to give birth to someone even as she desperately struggles not to die. Her agony accentuates the deeper lines in her face, and he sees there a dual struggle, to give birth and not to die. Seeing this, he is able to forgive her in his heart. What moves him is not simple pity but an empathy born of special insight: his wife's struggle to give birth, while wrestling to stay alive, highlighted by the agony of her situation, is like a light shining on her whole life helping to explain everything, including her infidelity. Forgiveness can be born from that.

The second example comes from the autobiography of Doris Lessing.[6] During her marriage to Gottfried Lessing, it became evident to both of them at a point that they were simply incompatible as a married couple and that they would eventually have to seek a divorce. However, for practical reasons, they decided to live together, as friends, until they could both move to England, at which time they would file for a divorce. Their marriage was finished, but unexpectedly their friendship began to grow. They had accepted their incompatibility as a fact and as something that didn't call for resentment from either of them. Why be angry at someone just because he or she feels and thinks differently than I do? One night, lying in their separate beds in the same room, both smoking and unable to sleep, Gottfried said to her: "This kind of incompatibility is more of a misfortune than a crime."[7]

That is a mature insight: it is not a crime or a sin to be incompatible; it is only unfortunate. Gottfried Lessing was an agnostic and a Marxist, not an easy friend to Christianity. But we who vow ourselves by our baptism to empathy and forgiveness should be strongly and healthily challenged by his insight and understanding: it is not a sin or a crime to be incompatible; it is only unfortunate! Forgiveness can rise out of that insight.

The major task, psychological and spiritual, for the second half of our lives is to forgive: we need to forgive those who have hurt us, forgive ourselves for our own failings, forgive life for not being fully fair, and forgive God for seemingly being so indifferent to our wounds. We need to do that before we die because ultimately there is only one moral imperative: not to die an angry, bitter person, but to die with a warm heart.

6. Bless more and curse less!

We are mature when we define ourselves by what we are for rather than by what we are against. The capacity to praise more than to criticize defines maturity. The crowning glory of maturity and discipleship, as we saw, is the capacity and willingness to bless others, particularly the young. The ultimate picture of maturity and generativity is not that of a warrior or martyr, dying for a cause, noble as that may be. Ultimate maturity is seen in the picture of a blessing elder, a grandmother, a grandfather, a parent, a teacher, a coach, a mentor, or anyone else with power and authority standing before the life and energy of the young and, like the Creator at the original creation and like the Father at the baptism of Jesus, basking in that energy and saying: "It is good; it is very good! In you I take delight!"

The opposite, of course—the picture of immaturity—is that of the threatened elder, King Herod threatened by the young Jesus, the parent threatened by the exuberant energies of his own child, the aging man or woman threatened by the health and good looks of the young, the teacher threatened by the intelligence of his students, the tired man walking home from work irritated by the joyous shrieks of children in a playground, and the cynical adult looking at someone else's life and energy and saying: "Who does she think she is!"

Nothing so much depresses us as cursing others, just as nothing brings as much joy into our lives as blessing others. When we act petty, we get to feel petty. When we act like God, we get to feel like God—and God is never depressed.

7. *Live in a more radical sobriety.*

We are as sick as our sickest secret, but we are also as healthy as we are honest. We need, as Martin Luther once put it, "to sin bravely and honestly." Maturity does not mean that we are perfect or faultless, but that we are honest.

A recovering alcoholic once told me: "Sobriety is only 10 percent about alcohol or a drug; it's 90 percent about honesty. You can drink, if you can do it honestly. Indeed, you can do anything, if you don't have to lie about it." As a moral principle that requires some qualifications, but it covers a lot of ground: Could you cheat someone, be sexually unfaithful, slander someone, or commit a sin of any kind and feel comfortable in sharing that openly with those who are closest to you? The need to hide some action from others is a strong moral nudging. If we are walking in grace, we do not need any other commandment: we can do anything as long as we do not have to lie about it.

And there is a further insight in this. When we do something wrong and then cover it up and lie, it is not so much the particular thing that we did wrong that harms us, it is the lying about it afterward that does the real damage. We are all weak, we all fall, and we all commit sin. God understands this, and it is not so much the sin itself that harms us. What causes the real harm is lying, covering up, sneaking around, not being transparent, living a dishonest life. Why is lying the ultimate moral canker? Lying ultimately destroys us because the human spirit is not made to live in dishonesty and duplicity. When we do wrong, we either have to stop doing what we are doing, or in honesty and contrition admit our weakness; otherwise, our spirits will spontaneously begin to harden and to warp. Such is the anatomy of the soul; it cannot tolerate moral duplicity for long without having to reshape and distort itself.

Indeed, that is how the unforgivable sin against the Holy Spirit, the one infamous sin that cannot be forgiven, can happen. It begins with lying, rationalization, cover-up, and dishonesty. When we sustain a lie for any length of time, we begin to warp our conscience and the sin eventually can become unforgivable, not because God does not want to forgive but because we no longer see any need to be forgiven. Lying, especially to ourselves, hardens and corrupts the spirit. That is why Satan is called the prince of lies rather than the prince of weakness. That is also what is contained in Martin Luther's famous axiom: "Sin bravely!" The invitation, in Luther, is not that we should have the courage to sin without flinching, but that, if we do sin, we should have the courage not to lie or rationalize about it after the fact.

Sobriety is ultimately not about alcohol or some drug. It is about honesty and transparency. And like honesty and transparency, it is not all or nothing but has degrees. We are all sober more or less, according to the degree that our lives are an open book with nothing hidden in the closet.

In biblical terminology, living in honesty is called *living in the light,* but that concept is easily misunderstood. We tend to think that to live in the light means that there should be a kind of special sunshine inside of us, a divine glow in our conscience, a sunny joy inside us that makes us constantly want to praise God, an ambience of sacredness surrounding our attitude. But that is overly romantic piety. To live in the light means to live in honesty, pure and simple, to be transparent and not have part of us hidden as a dark secret. All conversion and recovery programs worthy of the name are based on bringing us to this type of honesty. We move toward health precisely by flushing out our sickest secrets and bringing them into the light. Sobriety is more about living in honesty and transparency than it is about living without a certain chemical, gambling, or sexual habit. Moreover, it is the hiding of something—the lying, the dishonesty, the deception, the resentment we harbor toward those who stand between us and our addiction— that does the real damage to us and to those we love.

Maturity and generativity lie in honesty and transparency. We see a wonderful example of this in the case of Cardinal Joseph Bernardin. When he was falsely accused of sexual abuse, he was able to stand publicly before the world and say, with credibility: "Everyone who knows me knows that this accusation is false because *my life is an open book*." Everyone who knew him believed him precisely because of the transparency evident in his life, the radical sobriety manifest in his person.

One further point on sobriety, honesty, and transparency: one of the constants within the writings of classical spiritual writers is the idea that spirituality and morality are all of one piece. Every area affects every other area and all areas are important. Nothing may be deemed exempt. These spiritual masters go on to affirm that one cannot progress beyond a certain point of maturity if any one area of life, however small, remains unredeemed because of conscious exemption. John of the Cross, for example, uses an interesting image here. He states that the soul is like a bird, and that a bird is bound to the ground just as effectively by a light thread as by a heavy chain. In either case it cannot fly.[8] He is right: morality is all of a piece. No one part is enhanced when another is made exempt.

Maturity is radically predicated on honesty. This does not mean we will always hit the moral mark, that we will not sin and betray, but it does mean that we must admit those moral failures precisely as failures, that we need to sin honestly. Only a saint can afford a saint's persona. The rest of us have to live in the kind of honesty that is forever owning its betrayals and humbly asking for forgiveness for a life of weakness.

8. Pray, affectively and liturgically.

The fuel we need to resource ourselves for our journey in life does not lie in the strength of our own willpower, but in grace and community. We access that through prayer. We are mature to the degree that we open our own helplessness and invite in God's strength and to the degree that we pray with others that the whole world will do the same thing.

The classical definition of prayer, as we saw earlier, simply defines prayer as "lifting mind and heart to God." But as we also saw, Christian spirituality has always divided that into two distinct kinds of prayer: liturgical prayer, the public prayer of the church, and private or devotional prayer, more aptly called affective prayer. As mature men and women and as adult Christian disciples we are covenanted by our baptism to pray *through* the church *for* the world. That constitutes liturgical prayer and is prayer that we pray not for ourselves but, with others, for the world. However, to sustain ourselves and our loved ones through the ups and downs of life, we need too to pray privately, deeply, and affectively, asking God to do for us what we cannot do for ourselves, namely, give ourselves affirmation, meaning, community, substance, and immortality.

Beyond formal prayer, we are also asked to make our very lives a prayer. Many things are implied here, but perhaps the most important way that we can make our lives a prayer is by living always in respect, graciousness, and love. These are the nonnegotiable essentials within Christian charity. They are also part and parcel of all that is noble within humanity. Whenever we step outside of these, as we often do in our discourse with those who are not of our political or ecclesial mind-set, we should not delude ourselves into thinking that the high cause we think we are serving justifies this fundamental lapse in our humanity and charity. Whenever our words or our actions show disrespect, we are not serving God or truth, no matter how high the canopy under which we put our reasoning. Rather, we are serving some ideology or, worse still, working out some personal angers and pathologies.

We perennially live in bitter, highly polarized times, both inside of society and inside of our churches. The causes are real and what is at stake is critical: war, injustice, abortion, poverty, ecology, racism, immigration, the economy, democratic principles, law and order, freedom of speech, proper authority, proper dogma, proper ecumenism, legitimacy within ministry, Christians relating to other religions, and the proper freedoms and limitations within secularity itself. All of these are, in the end, life and death issues that, precisely because of their importance, are invariably emotionally inflamed. Anyone who has any real concern for the world and the church and their future will sometimes find himself or herself at odds with others, sometimes bitterly so.

Thus, the perennial temptation, especially when the issue at stake is a critical one, is to bracket the essentials (respect, graciousness, and love) on the basis of cause and, in essence, fall into a way of thinking that says: This issue is so important that I need not be respectful, gracious, and loving in this instance. I may demonize an opponent, assassinate character, name-call, and use everything in my power, perhaps even violence, to have my truth win out. Because I am right, and this is so important, I can bracket basic respect.

What is wrong with that? Beyond deluding ourselves that lack of charity and respect may be justified in the name of the gospel, all that is best within our humanity and all that is best within Christian principle call for the exact opposite: the urgency of a situation and the bitterness already inherent within it call for more, not less, care in our rhetoric and in the actions we undertake. The more we encounter anger, hatred, disrespect, demonizing, name-calling, refusals for a real conversation, and spoken and unspoken threats, the more we are called to bear down on the essentials of charity: respect, graciousness, openness, and the offer of a true, mutual conversation. Because in the end, we are not life giving by winning a battle with someone, we are life giving by winning someone over. True prayer is, at a point, synonymous with respect, graciousness, and love.

Maturity and generativity cannot be sustained by willpower alone. We need help from beyond, and that help is found in prayer.

9. Be wide in your embrace.
There is a Chinese greeting that works as both a blessing and a curse: *May you live in interesting times!* We live in such times, and, indeed, it is both a blessing and a curse. We are constantly being overwhelmed by otherness. Nothing is safe for long. More than any previous generation, we are being stretched beyond what is familiar. Often that is painful and disorienting. It is not easy to have our boundaries, values, and ideas under constant redefinition, especially when we believe that God has revealed certain reliable truths to us. But as we know, while perfect truth exists, we cannot know it perfectly. We have truth in part, in small pieces. That is why we need to be content to live with a lot of mystery and humility. Moreover, and this is the point, a lot of the pieces we still need to fill in the mysteries of our lives

lie precisely in what is foreign to us, in what is other, strange, different.

David Tracy, the eminent intellectual, submits that perhaps the biggest challenge confronting us today is that of facing our differences, of truly accepting otherness. This challenge confronts us at every level.

Here is how he describes this:

> For anyone in this troubled, quarrelling center of privilege and power (and as a white, male, middle-class, American, Catholic, professor and priest I cannot pretend to be elsewhere) our deepest need, as philosophy and theology in our period show, is the drive to face otherness and difference. Those others must include all the subjugated others within Western European and North American culture, the others outside that culture, especially the poor and the oppressed now speaking clearly and forcefully, the terrifying otherness lurking in our own psyches and cultures, the other great religions and civilizations, the differences disseminating in all the words and structures of our own Indo-European languages.[9]

But accepting what is foreign is not easy, despite our rhetoric to the contrary. Most of us claim to accept otherness and difference, but we are there more in desire than in actuality. We claim openness to multiculturalism, ethnic diversity, global community, gender equality, wide religious tolerance, alternative lifestyles, and befriending our shadow; but, as we all admit when we are honest, the reality is not as easy as the rhetoric. The simple fact is that otherness frightens us and often brings out the worst in us. It is not easy to be comfortable with, at home with, and welcoming to, what is other, different, and often seemingly deviant. More often than not we try to put up walls against it.

We see this today in the rise of fundamentalism and paranoia of every kind. Everywhere, on both sides of the ideological and political spectrum, there seems to be an excessive pressure to circumscribe, to rein in, to exclude, and to punish anyone or anything that does not fit our mold. For all the talk of global community, wide tolerance, and acceptance of differences, there is, almost everywhere, a growing obsession with boundaries and with protecting one's own kind in terms of ethnicity, culture, language, religion, gender, ideology, and lifestyle.

Not that all of this is bad. True community can be predicated only on the strong self-identity of those who enter it, and true ecumenism can never be rooted in people abandoning their own cherished values and beliefs. True acceptance of otherness and difference means something only if someone first has a strong identity, complete with real boundaries and cherished borders to protect. Fundamentalism arises precisely when human beings feel adrift, cut off from their own roots, without clear boundaries. We need to protect what we cherish.

But protecting cherished values and defending necessary boundaries are a good place from which to start.

Ultimately, we must move on to face and accept otherness, strangeness, difference, what is foreign. Our survival depends upon it. We can no longer live just among our own. Sooner or later, given that the planet is both limited and round, we will find it impossible to avoid what is foreign to us. What is strange to us will soon enough be part of our neighborhood, our home, our church, and our perspective on things.

Moreover, welcoming what is other and different is, in fact, a key biblical challenge. In the scriptures of all the great religions, Christianity no exception, we see that God is defined precisely as "Other," as what is beyond imagination, outside the realm of the familiar. This is what scripture means when it calls God *holy*. Biblically, *holy* is not primarily a moral quality but an ontological one—namely, otherness and different from us.

Thus, biblically, we have the tradition within which revelation from God is understood to come mostly through the stranger, the foreigner, the unexpected, in the unfamiliar, in what is different, in the surprise. For this reason the scriptures insist on the importance of welcoming strangers. Since God is Other, strangers, among all others, are the most likely to be carrying God's revelation. As Parker Palmer puts it:

> The role of the stranger in our lives is vital in the context of Christian faith, for the God of faith is one who continually speaks truth afresh, who continually makes all things new. God persistently challenges conventional truth and regularly

upsets the world's way of looking at things. It is no accident that this God is so often represented by the stranger, for the truth that God speaks in our lives is very strange indeed. Where the world sees impossibility, God sees potential. Where the world sees comfort, God sees idolatry. Where the world sees insecurity, God sees occasions for faith. Where the world sees death, God proclaims life. God uses the stranger to shake us from our conventional points of view, to remove the scales of worldly assumptions from our eyes. God is a stranger to us, and it is at the risk of missing God's truth that we domesticate God, reduce God to the role of familiar friend.[10]

Some of this truth is expressed in the wonderful richness of the word *catholic*. The opposite of a Catholic is not a Protestant, an Evangelical, or even a non-Christian. The opposite of a Catholic is a fundamentalist. The word *catholic* means universal, wide, embracing everyone. Jesus defines the word in this way: "In my father's house there are many rooms!"[11] In saying this, he is not describing a celestial mansion, but rather the scope of God's heart. God's heart is not a house with one room. God has a catholic heart, a nonfundamentalist heart. In a fundamentalist's house there is only one room, it might even be a good room, but it is a single room with no place for anyone not of its own kind. A true catholic heart has a room for everyone.

But our hearts are complex and, even while they yearn for a wide embrace, they also huddle in fear and are forever locking doors against what looks strange and threatening. We see a powerful image of this in the first disciples of Jesus, as they huddled together in fear behind locked doors while waiting for Pentecost. When we look at the story of how the first disciples of Jesus reacted to his death, we see a lesson to be learned as well as a great irony. Frightened by what had happened to Jesus in his death, they retreat to a room, lock the door against the outside, and huddle together in fear.[12] However, and this is the great irony, while they were in that room so huddled in fear of what was outside, they were not really in community with one another, nor was there much that was life giving flowing out from them. They were a group of frightened persons, ganging up against the world and consoling one another within their fragility, but nothing life giving flows from that. Conversely, when Pentecost does happen and they receive God's spirit, they unbolt the doors, throw them open, and burst out of those narrow confines, ablaze with a new fire and courage. Their narrowness and fear give way to an inclusivity that enables them to speak all the languages of the world. Their real discipleship and their generativity begin at precisely that point.

We grow in maturity to the degree that we come out from behind the doors we have locked because of fear and begin to define family in a way that is ever more ecumenical, interfaith, postideological, and nondiscriminatory. We are mature only when we are compassionate as God is compassionate—namely, when our sun shines both on those we like and on those we do not. There comes a time when it is time to turn in our cherished moral placards for a basin and a towel.

10. Stand where you are supposed to be standing, and let God provide the rest.

A number of years ago, one of my cousins died in an industrial accident. He had been helping load some railway cars at a grain terminal when a cable pulling the cars away snapped, sprang back with thousands of pounds of tension, and literally cut him in half. He died en route to the hospital. He was young, in the prime of his life, and a talented athlete who enjoyed playing sports on a number of local teams.

Tragic and sad as was his death, his family and loved ones had some consolations: his last days had been good, his last touches had been warm. He had dropped in for lunch with his mother just a few days prior to his death, enjoyed a great visit, and, on leaving, had kissed her a warm good-bye, assuring her of his affection. Several weeks earlier, he had taken his youngest brother, who idolized him, on a short vacation to watch baseball games. He had, as far as anyone knew, parted on peaceful terms with everyone, and he had died doing his job. Loading grain cars was his job, and when that cable snapped and killed him, he was standing where he was supposed to be standing at that moment. Indeed, had he not been there, someone else would have been, and that person would have suffered his fate. He died at his post, doing his job, working honestly, earning a living, a victim of contingency, standing where he was supposed to be standing.

Ultimately, that is all we can try to assure for ourselves. We can try to be standing where we are supposed to be standing. All of us, without exception, irrespective of age and health, are vulnerable, contingent, mortal, one heartbeat away from leaving this planet, one stroke away from losing control of our lives, one accident way from knowing how illusory is the sense of our own strength, and one broken cable away from dying in an ambulance. We can be careful with our lives, live prudently, try to ensure our own safety and the safety of our loved ones, but ultimately we are inadequate. We cannot ensure our own continued heartbeat. So what can we do?

We can live prudent lives, care for our health and safety, and, if we have faith, we can pray for God's protection and providence. These are good, no doubt. But we can do something else too, something even more important. We can try always to be standing where we are supposed to be standing. We can try always to keep our touches warm, in case they are our last ones. We can have lunch with our mother and assure her of our affection. We can take a loved one to a ball game, and we can try to be on peaceful terms with everyone. In essence, we can be faithful, true to those whom we love and true to what we believe in. We can be at our post, in commitment, love, and duty.

In the end, that is all we can do, and in the end, that

is enough. Awareness of our vulnerability and mortality is not meant to make us fearful, morbid, timid about life, or guilty about enjoyment. Nor is it meant to make us otherworldly at the cost of denigrating this life. Conversely, it is not meant to drive us to hedonism because life is short and unpredictable. It is an invitation to be faithful; to try always to stand where we are supposed to be standing, in warmth, love, duty, and enjoyment. John Powell once wrote that there are only two potential tragedies in life, and that dying young is not one of them. These are the two potential tragedies: To live and to not love and to love and to never express that affection and appreciation.[13] How true.

Not a single year will pass, perhaps not even a single month, when you will not experience the death of someone you love. And not a year goes by within which we do not become more aware of how fragile is life. More superficially, this challenges us to look at our health: Are we taking proper care of ourselves? Exercising enough? Eating properly? Resting enough?

More deeply, however, this should challenge us to look at our wider health: Are we standing where we are supposed to be standing? Are we being faithful enough to who we are and what we believe in so as to be comfortable that, if today is our last day, we are doing what we are supposed to be doing? Have our recent touches been warm?

We need to try to be faithful—to pray, to go to church, to be warm to people, to do the job as best we can do— knowing that if we do these things, we are standing where we are supposed to be standing, and that we can then enjoy this wonderful life without guilt or fear, ready, standing in honesty, should the cable snap.

In the end, we are all vulnerable, contingent, and helpless both to protect our loved ones and ourselves. We cannot guarantee life, safety, salvation, or forgiveness for ourselves or for those we love. Maturity depends upon accepting this with trust rather than anxiety. We can only do our best, whatever our place in life, wherever we stand, whatever our limits, whatever our shortcomings, and trust that this is enough, that if we die at our post, honest, doing our duty, God will do the rest.

A Final Word—Living Under a Prodigious God

A couple of years ago, Barbara Kingsolver wrote a book titled *Prodigal Summer*.[14] It tells the story of a young woman who got pregnant during a summer within which everything seemed to be dangerously fertile. From the plants, to the insects, to the animals, to the people—everything seemed to be teeming with fecundity, overactive, overabundant in seed. Life seemed to be bursting forth everywhere. The title of the book is a good metaphor for what she describes, a summer overabundant in fertility.

Nature is like that, teeming with everything, prodigal, fertile, overabundant, wasteful. Why else do we have 90 percent more brain cells than we need, and why else is nature scattering billions of seeds, of virtu-

ally everything, all over the planet every second? And
if life is so prodigal, what does this say about God, its
author? God, as we see in both nature and in scripture,
is overgenerous, overlavish, overextravagant, overpro-
digious, overrich, and overpatient. If nature, scripture,
and experience are to be believed, God is the absolute
antithesis of everything that is stingy, miserly, frugal,
narrowly calculating, or sparing in what it doles out.
God is prodigal.

Dictionaries define *prodigal* as "wastefully extrava-
gant and lavishly abundant." That certainly describes
the God that Jesus incarnates and reveals. We see this
in the parable of the Sower.[15] God, the sower, goes
out to sow, and he scatters his seed generously, almost
wastefully, everywhere—on the road, among the rocks,
among the thorns, on bad soil, and on rich soil. No
farmer would ever do this. Who would waste seed on
soil that can never produce a harvest? God, it seems,
does not ask that question but simply keeps scattering
his seed everywhere, overgenerously, without calculating whether it is a good investment or not in terms of
return. And it seems that God has an infinite number of
seeds to scatter, perpetually, everywhere. God is prodi-
gious beyond imagination.

Among other things, this speaks of God's infinite
riches, love, and patience. For us, there is both a huge
challenge and a huge consolation in that. The challenge,
of course, is to respond to the infinite number of invitations that God scatters on our path from minute to
minute. The consolation is that, no matter how many

of God's invitations we ignore, there will always be an infinite number of others. No matter how many we have already ignored or turned down, there are new ones awaiting us each minute. When we have gone through thirty-nine days of Lent without praying or changing our lives, there is still a fortieth day to respond. When we have ignored a thousand invitations, there is still another one waiting. God is prodigal, and so are the chances God gives us.

If we look back on our lives with honesty, we have to admit that of all the invitations that God has sent us, we have probably accepted and acted on only a fraction of them. There have been countless times we have turned away from an invitation. For every invitation to maturity we have accepted, we have probably turned down a hundred. But that is the beauty and wonder of God's richness. God is not a petty Creator, and creation, itself, is not a cheap mechanism with barely enough energy and resources to keep it going. God and nature are prodigal. That is plain everywhere. Millions and millions of life-giving seeds blow everywhere in the world, and we need only to pick up a few to become pregnant, fecund, to be capable of newness, maturity, and of producing life.

God is prodigal, abundant, generous, and wasteful beyond our small fears and imaginations. And that invites us to be generous: when we have a sense of God's abundance, we can risk having a bigger heart and a generosity beyond the instinctual fear that has us believe that, because things seem scarce, we need to be more calculating. In the Gospels we read that, while Jesus warns about the dangers of riches, he also makes a distinction between the generous rich and the miserly rich. The former are good because they radiate and incarnate God's abundance and generosity while the latter are bad because they belie God's abundance, generosity, and huge heart.

Jesus assures us that the measure we measure out is the measure that we ourselves will receive in return. In essence, that says that the air we breathe out will be the air we will reinhale. That is not just true ecologically. It is a broad truth for life in general. If we breathe out miserliness, we will reinhale miserliness; if we breathe out pettiness, we will breathe in pettiness; if we breathe out bitterness, then bitterness will be the air that surrounds us; and if we breathe out a sense of scarcity that makes us calculate and be fearful, then calculation and fearfulness will be the air we reinhale. But if, aware of God's abundance, we breathe out generosity and forgiveness, we will breathe in the air of generosity and forgiveness. We will reinhale what we exhale.

From God's abundance we get a universe that is too huge and prodigal to be imagined. That is a challenge not just to the mind and the imagination, but especially to the heart, to become huge and generous.

Part Three

RADICAL DISCIPLESHIP: THE STRUGGLE TO GIVE OUR DEATHS AWAY

I've seen two deaths in a series of lithographs that the German artist Käthe Kollwitz made between the wars. One drawing represents death as a terrifying, skeletal figure, snatching a young child from its mother's clutching arms. In another drawing, titled Death Recognized as a Friend, *an old woman reaches out with joy and release to a dark figure. I noticed that expression at times in my [own] mother's eyes. It spoke of a quiet acceptance I couldn't understand.*

—BELDEN C. LANE[1]

RADICAL DISCIPLESHIP: ANTICIPATORY INCOMPLETIONS

*Now you are no longer caught
in the obsession with darkness,
and a desire for higher love-making
sweeps you upward.*

*Distance does not make you falter,
now, arriving in magic, flying,
and finally, insane for the light,
you are the butterfly and you are gone.*

—GOETHE, "THE HOLY LONGING"

*There is such a thing as a good death. We are
responsible for the way we die. We have to choose
between clinging to life in such a way that death
becomes nothing but a failure, or letting go of life
in freedom so that we can be given to others as a
source of hope.*

—HENRI NOUWEN[1]

A Deeper and Final Generativity—Giving Our Deaths Away

Christian spirituality, except for a few parts of scripture, the theology of martyrdom, and the writings of mystics, has not, until quite recently, reflected much on the question of what we are meant to do after our retirement years: What lies beyond generativity as we normally define this? How is the final season of our life meant to be one within which we integrate generativity with dying?

Perhaps these questions were largely ignored within theology and spirituality, as indeed they were too in the human sciences, because until very recently in history most people, in fact, died while they were still trying to give their lives away. There was no need to develop a spiritual vision for what lay beyond retirement. Today, as our life expectancy is ever increasing and many people are staying healthy and active long after their retirement, these questions are taking on a new importance. What is the final stage of our lives meant to look like? How are we meant to live out our final years so that our death is part of our gift to others? As outlined in Chapter One, there are three major stages of Christian discipleship: the struggle to get our lives together, the struggle to give our lives away, and, ultimately, the final stage, the struggle to give our deaths away. But this last concept is largely foreign to us. How does one give his or her death away? How can it matter to others how you or I face and undergo our deaths? In the last years before his death, Henri Nouwen began to focus more of his reflections and writings on the theme of dying, particularly on how our death is meant to be our last and greatest gift to our loved ones. There comes a time in life, he submits, when the real question is no longer: How can I live now so that my life still makes a contribution? Rather, the question becomes: How can I live now so that when I die, my death is an optimal blessing to my family, my friends, the church, and the world?[2] With those words he, in essence, defines what the final state of Christian discipleship asks of us, namely that we give our deaths away as we once gave our lives away. But how do we do that? And what value is there for the world in how we die? To answer that we turn to the passion and death of Jesus, a death we understand as redemptive, as pouring out life-giving blood and water onto an entire planet, and a death we understand precisely as Jesus' last and greatest gift to us.

The Passion of Jesus as the Paradigm of How We Are Meant to Give Our Deaths Away

i) An Important Distinction

We speak of Jesus both as living for us and as dying for us. He gave us a double gift, his life and his death. As mentioned earlier, too often, however, we do not distinguish between the two, lumping them together into one act when, in fact, other than in metaphor, they were two quite distinct things: Jesus gave his life for us in one way, through his activity; he gave his death for us in another way, through his passivity, his passion.

ii) Jesus' Passion as Passivity

It is easy to misunderstand what the Gospels present to us as the *passion of Jesus*. The English word *passion*, in this case, is a false friend because we spontaneously grasp its meaning in relation to the wrong thing. When we use the word *passion* in relationship to Jesus' suffering, we spontaneously connect it to the idea of passion as pain, the pain of the crucifixion, the scourging, the whips, the nails in his hands, the humiliation before the crowd. And indeed, the passion of Jesus does refer to this, but the word needs a different focus here. The English word *passion* takes its root in the Latin *passio,* meaning "passivity," and that is its primary connotation here: what the passion narratives describe for us is Jesus' passivity. He gives his death to us through his passivity, just as he had previously given his life to us through his activity.

Indeed, each of the Synoptic Gospels can be neatly divided into two distinct parts. We could take each gospel and split off everything that is narrated until Jesus' arrest in the Garden of Gethsemane and call this part of the gospel: the Activity of Jesus Christ. Then we could take the section of the Gospels that we call "the passion" and call that section: the Passivity of Jesus Christ.[3] This would, in fact, help clarify an important distinction: Jesus gave his life for us through his activity; he gave his death for us through his passivity. And that is clear in the Gospels. Up until his arrest, the Gospels describe Jesus as active, as doing things, in charge, preaching, teaching, performing miracles, consoling people. Then, after his arrest, all the verbs become passive: he is led away, manhandled by the authorities, whipped, helped in carrying his cross, and ultimately nailed to the cross. After his arrest, like a patient in palliative care, he no longer does anything; others do it for him and to him. He is passive, a patient.[4] And in the manner that he endured that passivity, he gave his death for us.

This then becomes the paradigm for how we are meant to give our own deaths away. But how is that meant to be understood?

Henri Nouwen, in trying to explain this, shares this story: once he went to a hospital to visit a man dying of cancer. The man was still relatively young, in his sixties, and had been a very hardworking and generous person. He was the father of a family and provided well for them. He was the chief executive officer in a large company, and he took good care of both the company and his employees. Moreover, he was involved in many other organizations, including his church, and, because of his leadership abilities, was often the one in charge. But now, this once so active and generous man, the person who was used to being in control of things, was lying on a hospital bed, dying, unable to provide for himself even some of his most basic needs.

As Nouwen approached the bed, the man took his hand. It is significant to note what particular frustration he expressed and what particular thing he asked for:

"Father, you have to help me! I'm dying, and I am trying to make peace with that, but there is something else too: You know me, I have always been in charge. I took care of my family. I took care of the company. I took care of the church. I took care of things! Now I am lying here, on this bed, with tubes in me, and I can't even take care of myself. Nurses have to bring me a bedpan, I can't even go to the bathroom! Dying is one thing, but this is another! I'm helpless! I can't do anything anymore!"[5] Despite his exceptional pastoral skills, Nouwen, like any of us in a similar situation, was left rather helpless in the face of this man's plea. The man was undergoing his passion, his passivity. He was now a *patient*. (Notice that this word too comes from the Latin *passio*.) Just like Jesus, he had once been active, the one in charge; and now, just like Jesus in the hours leading up to his death, he was reduced to being a patient, one who is ministered to by others. Nouwen, for his part, tried to help the man see the connection between what he was undergoing and what Jesus endured in his passion, especially how this time of helplessness, diminishment, passivity, and dying is meant to be a time when we give to those around us a deeper gift, the gift of our death. Among other things, Nouwen read the passion narratives aloud to him.[6]

In our passivity we can give to others a gift that we cannot give in our activity. This is a mystery of how we give and receive, but it is not an entirely abstract thing. Allow me a personal example: I had a sister, Helen, who was an Ursuline nun, and a very happy one. She entered the convent at the age of eighteen and died of cancer, as a nun, more than thirty years later. During most of those thirty years as a religious sister, she worked at a high school for girls run by her order. It was a residential school, and the young women attending lived in convent residence during the school year. Helen was in charge of taking care of their needs outside of the classroom, and these young women leaned on her for many things. She became a surrogate mother to them, tending to their many needs, and she loved every minute of it. She had the perfect temperament for the part. She was an extrovert and more of a natural doer than a natural contemplative. She loved activity, loved organizing things, had great common sense, and loved being with people. She also played that role in our family, after our parents died. She was a person who took charge. That was her temperament. And she was much loved for it.

And then she was diagnosed with cancer, and, after some initial surgery and treatment, it seemed as if she had beaten it. She went back to work, to her busy life, to the activities she so loved and within which she so thrived. But the cancer eventually came back and claimed her. Moreover, it played a mean trick on her. For the last nine months of her life, she, this once so active woman, lay in bed, paralyzed from the waist down, unable even to prepare her own food, unable to go to the bathroom on her own, and unable to do all those life-giving things she had done for others her entire adult life. For nine months before she died, the exact length of time it takes to gestate new human life, she lay in bed as a patient, in a frustrating passivity, unable to be in charge even of her own basic needs.

But there was a great irony and stunning biblical parallel in this: during those last nine months, when she was unable to do things for others as she had always done, she, in some deep but real way, was able to give more to those around her than she was able to give during all those years of her busy activity. And in that, her life and death, in their own humble way, paralleled the life and death of Jesus. For most of her life, like Jesus during his active life, she was the active one, busy, generous, doing things for others. In all that activity, she gave her life away. Then, in those months when she lay paralyzed in bed unable to do things for others, she was passive, undergoing her passion, and like Jesus in his passivity, giving her death away.

Our passivity and dying can potentially be our last and greatest gift to others. There is a deep truth in this which, unfortunately, we stand in danger of losing. Today, certainly within secular culture, we tend to identify value with utility, with action, with work. In a culture that is driven by health and pragmatism we find it almost impossible to see what value there is in people who, because of age, health, or handicap, cannot visibly and actively contribute something. So we ask ourselves: What is the value of someone living with Alzheimer's? What is the value of people continuing to live on in palliative care when there is no chance of recovery or improvement and they have already slipped away from us mentally? What is the value of the life of a person who is so mentally or physically challenged that by normal standards he or she cannot contribute anything? The answer to that lies in the mystery of the passion or, more widely framed, in the mystery of passivity. Simply put, sometimes in our helplessness and passivity we can give something that is deeper than what we can give through our strength and activity. A culture that is speaking more and more of euthanasia clearly is beginning to lose sight of this and will be significantly impoverished, humanly and spiritually, for that loss.

James Hillman, in a brilliant book on aging, *The Force of Character and Lasting Life,* highlights the poverty that besets a culture that no longer understands what it receives through the passivity of those whose contribution is of another kind. He asks the question: What is our value to others once our practical usefulness, and perhaps even our sanity, are gone? What do people bring to the table once they can no longer bring what society deems as useful? His answer: character. Not just their own. They help give character to others:

> Productivity is too narrow a measure of usefulness, disability too cramping a notion of helplessness. An old woman may be helpful simply as a figure valued for her character. Like a stone at the bottom of a riverbed, she may do nothing but stay still and hold her ground, but the river has to take her into account and alter its flow because of her. An older man by his sheer presence plays his part as a character in the drama of the fam-

ily and neighborhood. He has to be considered, and patterns adjusted simply because he is there. His character brings particular qualities to every scene, adds intricacy and depth by representing the past and the dead. When all the elderly are removed to retirement communities, the river flows smoothly back home. No disruptive rocks. Less character too.[7]

Another parallel between what occurred in Jesus' passion and what often occurs in our own diminishment and death is also worth highlighting. Jesus died by crucifixion. Crucifixion was a death designed by Romans as a version of the death penalty. But in designing crucifixion, they had more than simple capital punishment in mind. They wanted, at the same time, to inflict the optimal amount of suffering that is possible for a person to endure. Hence, the death was to be slow and torturous. Beyond that, crucifixion was also meant to totally and publically humiliate the person being executed. Hence, among other things, the person was stripped naked and hung on a cross with his genitals exposed. In addition, often at the moment of death, or even before, his bowels would loosen in a further humiliation. Crucifixion was not a pretty sight! Neither is death through old age, cancer, dementia, AIDS, multiple sclerosis, amyotrophic lateral sclerosis, and countless other diseases. Like death by crucifixion, terminal illnesses also inflict intense pain and, worse still, utterly humiliate the body. They also are not a pretty sight. Terminal illnesses mimic the crucifixion. This should not surprise us since our diminutions, powerless moments, humiliations, and illnesses are our passion, the passivity through which we are asked to give our deaths away. And how are our deaths received? What is the effect of our passivity on others, if it is given over in a loving manner? If we speak of giving our deaths away, then we must speak too of how they are received by others. How is a good death received? What is its effect on others? Again, Jesus is the paradigm. The Gospel of John tells us that at the moment of Jesus' death "blood and water" flowed from his dead body.[8] This is a stunning image carrying several levels of meaning. First of all, the image is clearly one of birth—blood and water accompany the newborn out of the womb. Jesus' death is understood to be giving birth to something in the world. What is being born? The answer is in the symbols, blood and water: What is blood? Blood is the life principle inside us. We are alive when blood flows through us. What is water? Water does two things for us: it quenches thirst and it washes us clean. When we combine these concepts, we begin to get a sense of what the gospel is trying to teach us here. It is telling us what Jesus' disciples experienced inside of themselves in the face of his death. They felt an outpouring of blood and water, that is, a deeper and richer flow of life within themselves and a sense of being both nurtured and cleansed in a new way. They felt something flow out from Jesus' death that made them freer, less guilty, and more open to life than ever before. They felt washed, cleansed, and nourished.

This sounds abstract and quasi-magical, but it is anything but that. We too have the same experience when someone we know and love dies in such a way so as to give his or her death to us. Again, an example can help explicate this. If someone were to ask me this question—What were the happiest occasions that you have been present to within the last ten years?—my answer would at first glance seem unreal: a number of funerals. The happiest occasions that I have been present to within the last decade were a number of specific funerals, funerals of persons, women and men, who, in the way they died, figuratively set off a flow of blood and water from their caskets.

To cite one such example: a couple of years ago, I went to visit a man who was already in palliative care, dying of cancer. He was a young man, still in his fifties, but he was dying well because he was dying in the same way as he had lived his life, without bitterness and without enemies. He spoke to me of the intense loneliness of dying: "I have a wonderful wife and kids, and they are holding my hand every minute, but I'm 'a stone's throw away from everyone,' like Jesus in the Garden. I'm loved, but I'm alone in this. Nobody can be truly with you as you're dying!" Then he shared this: "I've had a good life and I've no regrets. I don't think I have an enemy, at least I don't know of one. And I want to do this right. I want to die with a dignity that makes my wife and kids proud of me. I want to do this right for them and for everyone else." He died some days later, and his family and everyone else who knew him were deeply saddened.

But inside that sadness, there was also something else, an outflow of blood and water. After his funeral, as we walked out of church to a small reception, there was not one person who knew this man well, including his grieving wife and children, who, at a level deeper than the sadness of the moment, did not feel freer, less guilty, and more open to life than ever before. He wanted to do his death right, and he did, and that reinforced everything good he had done in his life so that what he wanted to give to us came to us—the goodness of his life and the love he showed in his death. Blood and water flowed from his casket, to all of us and not least to his family. Less happily, this is also sometimes true in its opposite: not every death is a gift to those who knew that person. All of us have also been to funerals where, because of the manner in which the person lived or died, we did not feel blood and water flowing from the casket but rather felt as if the very oxygen was being drawn out of the room. Instead of feeling freer, less guilty, and more open to life, we felt guilty about the very act of breathing and guilty about enjoying anything in life. How we live and how we die leaves behind a spirit, a blessing or a curse, after we are gone. Our caskets will either emit a flow of life-giving and guilt-freeing blood and water, or they will suck some of the oxygen from the room and hearts of those who knew us.

The final human and Christian challenge of our lives is the struggle to give our deaths away.

Other Images for the Struggle

BIBLICALLY, Jesus' death is, of course, the prime paradigm of how we give our deaths away, but scripture offers us other images for this. We have the image, explored earlier, of wrestling with God, the struggle in late life to forgive and let go. Giving our deaths away is also the image that underlies the challenge in this famous line from the book of Job: "Naked I came from my mother's womb and naked I shall depart. The Lord gave and the Lord has taken away, may the name of the Lord be praised."[9] Our childhood, adolescent, and adult years are a lot about accumulating (a name, a self-image, a language, an education, a home, a career, a certain amount of security). Our final years are more about shedding, about returning to God as naked as we were born. Finally, scripture offers us too the very rich image of Abraham and Sarah who, after biological generativity becomes an impossibility, set out into the unknown to get pregnant in a new and deeper way.[10] Their story will be picked up later in this text.

MYTHICALLY, the struggle of late life is captured in the image of *having to leave home again*. T. S. Eliot gives this poetic expression in his famous line in "Little Gidding": "The end is where we start from."[11] As well, the invitation to give one's death away receives powerful poetic expression in Goethe when he suggests that at a certain age and level of maturity a higher kind of sanity should kick in and make us "insane for the light."[12]

MYSTICALLY, as we saw earlier, the struggle to give

our deaths away is expressed in the concept of the "dark night of the spirit." We shall see shortly how the mystics understood this. In Hindu spirituality, as we have also already seen, the final human struggle, the struggle to give our deaths away, is contained in the idea of becoming a holy beggar, a sannyasin. In recent Christian spirituality, Richard Rohr has given varied and rich expression to this, ranging from how he defines the task of the last half of life to his concept that the final stage of discipleship invites us to become "holy old fools."[13] For Rohr, aging and the diminishments that accompany it will eventually reduce all of us, without exception, to being "old fools." That part is nonnegotiable, it will find us all. By the standards of youth, health, sexual attractiveness, status in the culture, and productivity, all of us will eventually find ourselves radically marginalized, "old fools." However, where we do have a choice is in what kind of "old fool" we want to be. Here are the options: I can become a "pathetic old fool," someone who is futilely trying to cling to my youth; I can become an "embittered old fool," someone who while fully aware of my age and diminishments is bitter rather than accepting about that; or I can become a "holy old fool," someone who accepts age and diminishment without bitterness and without clinging, seeing it as a necessary condition for my next journey. James Hillman, in the book we cited earlier, has his own language for expressing how the final task of our lives is to give our deaths away. He asks the question: What can nature and God have had in mind when they designed the aging process?

Why is it that just when our mental prowess, our human maturity, and our emotional freedom are at their peak, that the body begins to fall apart? He answers with a metaphor: "The best wines have to be aged in cracked old barrels."[14] The last years of our lives are meant to mellow the soul and most everything in our biology conspires together to ensure that this happens. There is an intelligence in life, he asserts, that intends aging just as it intends growth in youth. It is a huge mistake to read the signs of aging as indications of dying rather than as initiations into another way of life.[15] Each physical diminishment (from why we have to get up at night to go to the bathroom to why our skin sags and goes dry) is designed to mature the soul. And they do their work without our consent, relentlessly and ruthlessly.[16] The aging process, he asserts, eventually turns us all into monks and that, indeed, is its plan, just as it once pumped all those excessive hormones into our bodies to drive us out of our homes at puberty. And God again is in on this conspiracy. But there is a wonderful beauty in the process, as aging deliteralizes biology. As Hillman puts it: "Perhaps 'usefulness' needs to be regarded aesthetically. Must the soul be properly aged before it leaves? We can imagine aging as a transformation in beauty as much as in biology. The old are like images on display that transpose biological life into imagination and art. The old become strikingly memorable, ancestral representations, characters in the play of civilization, each a unique, irreplaceable figure of value. Aging: an art form?"[17] Increasingly, as we age, our task is not productivity, but reflection. In Hillman's words: "Earlier years must focus on getting things done, while later years consider what was done and how."[18] The former is a function of mature discipleship, when we are trying to give our lives away; the latter is a function of radical discipleship, when we are trying to give our deaths away.

Giving Our Deaths Away—a Fantasy Journey into the "Dark Night of the Spirit"

Still the question remains: How concretely can we give our deaths away? How might we live so that our death is a gift to our families, our church, and world? The paradigm, as we saw, is Jesus' death, but the language within which this is expressed is so entangled with other things that it is difficult to extrapolate exactly what made his death so special a gift. For this reason, it can be helpful to turn to another rich well within the Christian tradition—that of the mystics—to help explain how someone can give his or her death away.

In the mystical tradition of John of the Cross, radical discipleship, that time in our lives when we give our deaths away, is understood to be the journey that one makes through something John calls the "dark night of the spirit."[19] What is the dark night of the spirit? The concept is complex and, since it is not a commonsense idea, difficult to explain. But in essence, the dark night of the spirit in the tradition of John of the Cross works this way:

The Function of the "Dark Night of the Spirit"

Once someone has attained a true maturity within his or her discipleship, one that has been tested over time, that person stands before the invitation to enter the final, and most radical, phase of discipleship, the dark night of the spirit. The purpose of the journey through this dark night is not so much to deepen one's maturity, as was the case earlier in life with the dark night of the senses. The purpose now is rather to purify one's natural attachments so as to connect oneself to the world, to others, and to God more radically through faith alone, rather than through understanding; through hope alone, rather than through security; and through charity alone, rather than through possessiveness. One does that, John submits, by doing a radical act which totally cuts one's attachments and securities on the basis of raw faith alone—that is, on the basis of the written promise and word of God. Such an act, John says, in effect mimics what we will have to do at the moment of our deaths. It metaphorically puts us into palliative care. It is also how we imitate the way Jesus gave his death to the world.

i) A Fantasy Trip Through the "Dark Night of the Spirit"

Perhaps this can be best explained with an example. Here is what a journey through the dark night of the spirit might look like in its ideal type: imagine John and Martha as a married couple approaching their seventy-fifth birthdays. They enjoy good physical health, have a solid marriage, are very involved in their church and their community, are proud of their grown children—all of whom seem to be doing well—and take particular delight in their grandchildren. They are also financially secure enough to enjoy a comfortable retirement. One day they approach their parish priest and ask for his guidance, and this is the story they share: "Father, we have been long-standing and faithful parishioners here, and you know us well. We're retired, we're comfortable, we're still enjoying good health, and we're really enjoying our grandchildren. In fact, John has just built a huge deck off of our living room so that we have more space for our family when they drop round. There are so many options still open to us, so many things we would still like to do in our lives. But . . . but . . . we have been praying together, and praying a lot over the story of Abraham and Sarah and how when they were old, done with their childbearing years, God called them to set out for an unknown place and how it took them ten years to get there and then, when they arrived there, with them now well over eighty years old, Sarah got pregnant in some new way, and how that, this gray-haired and impossible pregnancy, became their real gift to the world . . . . Well, we have been praying over this for a long time and we feel called in this way, like Abraham and Sarah. We feel that God is calling us into the big, big unknown as he did them. We have mulled over this for a long time and this is our plan: What we want to do is to sell our house and, after buying two one-way airline tickets, give the rest of money to the food bank (because Jesus said to sell everything and give the money to the poor). The one-way tickets we would buy would be for Pakistan. We feel that God is calling us to spend the rest of our lives as missionaries to Islam in Pakistan. We picked Pakistan because there is so much tension today between Christians and Muslims, and there is a need for more understanding between us. Our plan is to go there with no money and to live simply with the poor there, and to die there. We presented this plan to our children, and they were beyond belief, stunned and horrified. They think we are insane and demanded that, among other things, we talk to you. So what do you think of this idea?"

The priest, unless he was John of the Cross, would most certainly side with the view of their children: "You're crazy! This is dangerous fundamentalism! This is the ultimate in naïveté!" But being a trained pastoral minister, he would attempt to dissuade them and bring them to their senses through logic. His first objection would be this: "You shouldn't do this. You are needed here! Your children, your grandchildren, the church, the community, we need you! There is still so much that you can do. You're still young, still healthy. You may not do this!" But John and Martha are ready for this objection, having already thought this through: "We appreciate your saying that, and it's nice to be wanted. But, radically, we are not needed. What we have to give we have already given through the last fifty years. We did the work, we provided for our kids, and we love them deeply. But in going to Pakistan and ending our lives in this way, we want to give our kids and grandkids something else, something deeper, something that can be given only in spirit. We have already given them what we can give them humanly. We are doing this for them! They will miss us and we will miss them terribly, but that's the price for this. Besides, yes, we are healthy, but we are no longer young. Either or both of us could be struck down by cancer or a stroke or something else, and we would be gone in any case. In twenty years, we'll both most likely be gone, so we may as well do this of our own volition, when we can make it mean something deep." Dissatisfied but undaunted, the priest would move on to his second argument: "And how do you intend to live in Pakistan, once you have given all your money away? How will you eat? Where will you live? What will you do if you get sick and need a hospital?" But again, John and Martha are ready for those questions: "That's the real point of this. If we took along credit cards and had return tickets tucked away in case of an emergency, that would defeat the real purpose of this. We need to do this on blind trust. We won't starve, we'll live somehow, we'll beg, we'll live off peoples' kindness. We know this sounds utterly naive, but God will provide for us somehow! Don't think that we haven't thought of this, and don't think that we aren't scared. We're very scared; we don't even know what we are going to do immediately after we get off the plane. But that is the point of this!"

With that response staring at him, the priest plays

his last card: "Besides, the whole thing is wrong from the top down. You know nothing about Pakistan, nothing about the Islamic religion. Moreover, the last thing we need in the church and the world today is a couple of naive, misguided missionaries, thinking they can save the world! You will do more harm than good!" John and Martha have also already thought about this: "You're right. We are naive, and maybe we are misguided. We don't know anything about Pakistan and Islam, other than some rather superficial things we've picked up by reading a couple of books. But again, that is the point. We are going there as sheep. We're not going there to preach or to convert anyone. We just want to live among the people there and try to understand and love them. Maybe we will get killed, but we hope not. We are not going there to try to save the world; it's more ourselves and our kids and grandkids whom we are trying to save!" Now imagine what would happen if neither their family nor the priest could talk them out of their plan and they indeed went to Pakistan, stayed there, and died there. What would be the reaction of their family ten years after their deaths: "Our parents were crazy!"? More likely the reaction would be: "We had extraordinary parents! They did this incredible faith thing when they retired! What an incredible witness they gave us! What an incredible memory we have of them!" And if they could articulate this in more religious terms, they might phrase it like this: "What a freeing and life-giving spirit they left us! They gave us their deaths as a gift!"

ii) What Happens When We Do Not Risk This Kind of Raw Faith?

This fantasy might seem pretty fanciful and far-fetched. Who would ever do something like this? John of the Cross would, I suspect, answer the question this way: You may as well risk this kind of radical journey, because if you do not do this of your own volition, it will be done to you. Sometime, and it will happen to us all, we will walk into a doctor's office and be given a death sentence. Or death will catch us even more unexpectedly in a heart attack, stroke, or accident. At that moment, metaphorically, we will have been handed our one-way ticket to the greatest of all unknowns and, from this journey, there will be no coming back. Palliative care awaits us all, and palliative care is a one-way ticket. We can enter it on our own, on purpose, or we can wait to be eventually taken there against our will. Either way, we will now stand before the same choice that Jesus had to make in the Garden of Gethsemane: How am I going to give my death over? In freedom or in clinging? In graciousness or in bitterness? In anger or in forgiveness? The particular spirit that our death leaves behind, our final gift to the ones left behind, will be determined on how and what we choose in our dying.

iii) Our Struggle to Do This

For most of us, no doubt, entry into the dark night of the spirit will be by conscription rather than through a premeditated, voluntary choice of something that mimics what happens to us in our death. And that is okay too. In fact, Jesus' entry into his passion was also by conscription. He did not choose the cross, he only accepted it. It was his attitude in accepting what was imposed upon him that made his death redemptive. The same can be true for us. We need not choose the dark night of the spirit, but how we accept it is important. Still John of the Cross would, ideally, invite us to do some kind of voluntary palliative journey late in life, like that of John and Martha to Pakistan. Obviously, "Pakistan" is used here as an image, a metaphor. We need not leave home or country to do this. Perhaps one's giving up of one's house and car and moving into an assisted-living center more than suffices. The key is only that whatever it is we choose, it must displace us from our normal securities in as radical a way as going to Pakistan would do for John and Martha or as something as debilitating as a serious stroke or terminal cancer would do. It needs to be a journey into palliative care, not just a trimming down, no matter how radical, of our lifestyle. In our culture, entering into the dark night of the spirit deliberately will be hard to do for a number of reasons: First, culturally and even in our spiritualities, we have little vision of what life might mean beyond generativity. Next, and connected to the first reason, we lack competent spiritual directors for this stage of the spiritual life. Not many spiritual mentors have a vision of what ideally should happen post-generativity, and not everyone gets to have a John of the Cross as his or her spiritual director. Finally, in trying to discern what we might do in our final years so as to give our deaths away more deliberately, we are left too much alone, without a community vision and without real mentors, and this is the consequence: Many seniors feel an inchoate nagging inside of them, gently trying to push them beyond the golf course and the bridge table to something deeper, but they are unable to respond to that voice because they have no idea of where to go with it. So they simply keep doing what they are doing and hanging on to generativity as long as they can. Culturally and spiritually, we have little to help them. What we are lacking inside of secular culture and in our churches is any kind of meaningful ritualization or institutionalization of a concept that the Hindus call "forest dwelling." Simply put, we have no universities or seminaries to prepare us for the last stage of our lives. Hindu spirituality does. It proposes an intermediate stage between generativity and giving your death away (by living as a "holy beggar"). They call this intermediate state "forest dwelling," a metaphor for leaving behind one's home, going into the deep forest, and apprenticing yourself to some elders who can then teach you what the next step in your life should be. In their vision, we need to be initiated into the final stage of our lives in a manner analogous to the way we were once prepared for the personal and professional tasks of adulthood. And this is precisely where, in our Christian cultures, we have a massive lacuna. We go through years of schooling and training to prepare us for our careers, but we have no schools, universities, seminaries, or novitiates to prepare us for the final stage of our lives, postretirement.

We are alone, mostly without preparation, without a vision, without mentors, and without communal support. Small wonder we dodge the inchoate nagging inside of us that would want us to do something of greater depth during our final years.

A Final Image—John Paul II

Perhaps one final image can be helpful in explaining what it means to give one's death away: whether a fan of Pope John Paul II or not, everyone has to admit that his death spoke to the world as few other deaths ever have. The outpouring of love and affection at this death has few equals in history. Why did so many millions and millions of people sense some special spirit at his death and react with so much love and affection? Indeed, his long papacy had its share of controversies, and he had his share of detractors. Why such an outpouring of love at his passing?

John Paul II spent the last years of his life, in effect, living out his death publicly before the whole world, a broken and dying man, and in doing that, John Paul II, the broken, was able to give to the world something that John Paul II, the handsome athlete, could not give— namely, his death.

The Mystery of Giving and Receiving Spirit

How we give our deaths to one another is deeply entwined inside the mystery of how we give and receive spirit, and that mystery is itself entwined inside the mystery of how we are present and absent to one another.

For example, when Jesus is saying farewell to his disciples, he tries to explain to them some of the deep paradoxes inside the mystery of presence and absence. He tells them that it is better for them that he go away because, unless he does, he will be unable to send them his spirit. He assures them too that the heaviness and grief they will feel at his leaving is really the pain of giving birth and that this heartache will eventually turn warm and nurturing and bring them a joy that no one can ever take from them.

That is the language of Ascension and Pentecost—not just as it pertains to Jesus leaving this earth and sending his spirit, but also as it pertains to the mystery of giving and receiving spirit in all our good-byes, including the good-bye inside our own death. Among other things, it points to that perplexing experience we have of fully understanding and appreciating others only after they go away, just as others can fully understand us and let themselves be fully blessed by us only after we go away. Like Jesus, we can really send our spirits only after we go away.

We experience this everywhere in life: a grown child has to leave home before her parents can fully understand and appreciate her for who she is. There comes a day in a young person's life when she stands before her parents and, in whatever way she articulates it, says the words: "It is better for you that I go away! Unless I go, you will never really know who I am. You will have some heartache now, but that pain will eventually become warm because I will come back to you in a deeper way." Parents say the same thing to their children when they are dying.

We only really grasp the essence of another after he or she has gone away. When someone leaves us physically, we are given the chance to receive his or her presence in a deeper way. And the pain and heartache we feel in the farewell are birth pangs, the stretching that comes with giving new birth. When someone we love has to leave us (to go on a trip, to begin a new life, or to depart from us through death), initially that will feel painful, sometimes excruciatingly so. But when that leaving is necessitated by duty or by life itself, then, no matter how hard it is, even if it is death itself that takes away our loved one, eventually he or she will come back to us in a deeper way, in a presence that is warm, nurturing, and immune to the fragility of normal relationships. Many of us, I suspect, have experienced this in the death of someone whom we loved deeply. For me, this happened at the death of my parents. My mother and father died three months apart, when I was twenty-three years old. They were young, too young to die in my view, but death took them anyway, against my will and against theirs. Initially, their deaths were experienced as very painful, as bitter. My siblings and I wanted their presence in the same way as we had always had it, physical, tangible, bodily, real. Eventually, the pain of their leaving left us, and we sensed that our parents were still with us, with all that was best in them, our mom and dad still, except that now their presence was deeper and less fragile than it had been when they were physically with us. They were with us now, real and nurturing, in a way that nobody and nothing can ever take away.

Our presence to one another physically, in touch, sight, and speech is no doubt the deepest wonder in all of life, sometimes the only thing we can appreciate as real. But wonderful as that is, it is always limited and fragile. It depends upon being physically connected in some way, and it is fragile in that separation (physical or emotional) can easily take someone away from us. With everyone we love and who loves us (parents, spouse, children, friends, acquaintances, colleagues), we are always just one trip, one misunderstanding, one accident, or one heart attack away from losing their physical presence. This was the exact heartache and fear that the disciples felt as Jesus was saying good-bye to them, and that is the heartache and fear we all feel in our relationships. We can easily lose one another. But there is a presence that cannot be taken away, that does not suffer from this fragility, that is, the spirit that comes back to us whenever, because of the inner dictates of love and life, our loved ones have to leave us or we have to leave our loved ones. A spirit returns and it is deep and permanent and leaves a warm, joyous, and real presence that nobody can ever take from us.

Recently, I was at a funeral of a woman who was much loved by family, friends, and community, deservedly so. She had a large family and a large heart. She took care of her own, and she helped take care of others.

She was one of those women who fed the neighborhood and tried to feed the world. Her life and her love had had a wide embrace. By any standard she was a great person. Just before her body was taken out of the church, four of her children each gave a short eulogy. Her eldest son gave a brief sketch of the major chronological events in her life; her eldest daughter then shared about her generosity and her propensity to feed every person and dog in the neighborhood; another of her sons shared about some of the wonderful rituals she had developed within their family around birthdays and other celebrations; and finally, her youngest daughter gave a final eulogy. Her sharing was brief and poignant. She simply stated what we all already knew, this woman, her mother, was an exceptional person. Then, addressing herself more directly to her siblings and her nephews and nieces, the woman's grandchildren, she said: "Our mother, your grandmother, was a great woman. But we don't really know that yet, but someday we will. Someday we will know this because she will come to us, she will come back to each of us, in her own way, respecting who we are, respecting what our lives are, and we will *get* her— get who she really was, get what she gave us in her life and in how she died, get how blessed we are to have had her, and get that we have this exceptional, wonderful person as our mom and our grandmother! In receiving her spirit we will drink more fully from her depth."

In receiving Jesus' spirit, his disciples drank more fully from his depth. That is true too for us as his disciples. We too only can fully drink in Jesus in all his depth through his spirit. And that is also true for how we receive the spirit of our loved ones after they die and how others will receive our spirit after our own death. Some form of Ascension and Pentecost occur after every death. I sometimes tell parents who are distressed because their own children are not able to appreciate the faith and virtue they see in them, their parents, that someday those children will appreciate them, but that this will probably occur after they, the parents, have died and left their spirits.

If we die well, without bitterness and without regret, the spirit we leave behind will be one that is nurturing, warm, and cleansing—biblical blood and water.

Part One
Chapter One

1. Nikos Kazantzakis, *Report to Greco*, trans. P. A. Bien (New York: Simon and Schuster, 1965), p. 222.

Though less directly relevant for the purposes of this book, a remarkable conversation, highlighting the different struggles of the young and the old, follows immediately upon this exchange. Kazantzakis continues his questions:

"Yours is a hard life, Father. I too want to be saved. Is there no other way?"

"More agreeable?" asked the ascetic, smiling compassionately.

"More human, Father."

"One, only one."

"What is that?"

"Ascent. To climb a series of steps. From the full stomach to hunger, from the slaked throat to thirst, from joy to suffering. God sits at the summit of hunger, thirst, and suffering; the devil sits at the summit of the comfortable life. Choose."

"I am still young. The world is nice. I have time to choose."

Reaching out, the old monk touched Kazantzakis' knee and said:

"Wake up, my child. Wake up before death wakes you up."

The young Kazantzakis shuttered and said:

"I am still young."

"Death loves the young," the old man replied. "The inferno loves the young. Life is like a lighted candle,

easily extinguished. Take care—wake up!" (Kazantzakis, pp. 222–23).

2. Henry David Thoreau, *True Harvest: Readings from
Henry David Thoreau for Every Day of the Year*, ed.
Barry Andrews (Boston: Skinner House Books, 2006),
entry for July 14, 1851.

3. For an excellent analysis of this, see Alice Miller's famous work *The Drama of the Gifted Child: The Search
for the True Self*, trans. Ruth Ward (1979; repr.: New
York: Basic Books, 2007).

Among other things, Miller's thesis holds that, because
the life force is so strong in us when we are young, we are
able to more easily live with our wounds then, even our
deep ones. However, beginning with midlife (sometime
in our thirties), our wounds begin to break through, and
this creates, particularly in sensitive people (the "gifted"
ones), a "drama," namely, a sense of the depth of our
own wounds and a sense of how those wounds take their
root in our having been cheated and treated unfairly. And
how is this drama to be resolved? Through tears, through
properly grieving our wounds. For Miller, the major psychological and spiritual tasks of midlife and beyond is to
grieve until the old foundations of our lives are shaken
and altered.

4. This parable is given twice in the Gospels: Matthew
25:14–30 and Luke 19:12–27.

5. Richard Rohr is particularly insightful in articulating
this and that concept lies very close to the heart of his
challenge to us in the second half of our lives. See, for
example: Richard Rohr, *Falling Upward: A Spirituality
for the Two Halves of Life* (San Francisco: Jossey-Bass,
2011).

6. Luke 10:38–42.

7. Matthew 7:24–27.

8. I particularly recommend the work of Richard Rohr,

Robert L. Moore, Paula D'Arcy, and Bill Plotkin apposite to this. Rohr offers a full and coherent structure for understanding the two halves of life. Moore, drawing insights from a variety of disciplines, offers both an analysis of our struggles toward maturity and a recipe for achieving maturity that, to my mind, outside of perhaps some of the major classics in spirituality, is the most penetrating and challenging analysis available. Paula D'Arcy offers valuable insights on loss and grieving and how to let them help us to maturity and mellowness of soul. Bill Plotkin offers a powerful challenge vis-à-vis how nature can (and should) play an important role in helping to mature and mellow the soul.

9. For an excellent and thorough historical analysis of this, see Charles Taylor, *A Secular Age* (New York: Random House, 2007).

10. Kazantzakis, *Report to Greco*, p. 16.

11. Richard Rohr, who has done extensive work in this area, employs a different set of categories. His categorization divides the human and spiritual journey into just two seasons, the *first half of life* and the *second half of life*. His categories, though, perfectly complement what is presented here. Indeed, I have occasionally worked with Rohr in presenting workshops and lectures on this and, when doing that, have simply melded my categories into his. In Rohr's categories, the transition from the first half of life to the second half of life takes place sometime within the mid- to late stage of generativity in life and is normally more developmental than dramatic. The lack of exactness here has the advantage of affording his categories more flexibility than many of the classical categories. How my categories relate to those of John of the Cross will be outlined briefly, later, in the text itself.

There are, of course, numerous other ways of categorizing the different phases of the spiritual life; for example, there are the classical categories (used by a vast variety of writers, though not always in the same way, which speak of the *Purgative*, *Illuminative*, and the *Unitive* stages of the spiritual life. Because of the variety of ways in which these categories have been used, and because linguistically today these words might confuse more than clarify, I chose not to employ them here.

An interesting contemporary venturing out into a new set of categories can be seen in the early writings of the British Carmelite Ruth Burrows, where she speaks of three islands we journey across: Ruth Burrows, *Guidelines for Mystical Prayer* (Denville, NJ: Dimension Books, 1976).

12. *Generativity* is a word coined by Erik Erikson; he used it to connote "a concern for establishing and guiding the next generation." In essence, it means having the capacity to act beyond selfish concerns, the idiosyncratic preference, and the pleasure principle as the source of our motivation, so as to have our actions help generate more life for others. There are numerous commentaries on Erickson and on how he defines generativity. I recommend one here: *Make It Count* by John Kotre. In this book, Kotre lays out eight steps that walk us along the path of generativity.

13. Henri Nouwen: *Life of the Beloved* (New York: Crossroad, 1992), pp. 92–93.

Nouwen develops this theme elsewhere in his works, particularly in his book *Our Greatest Gift: A Meditation on Dying and Caring* (New York: HarperCollins, 1994), where he writes: There is such a thing as a good death. We are responsible for the way we die. We have to choose between clinging to life in such a way that death becomes nothing but a failure, or letting go of life in freedom so that we can be given to others as a source of hope . . . . The real question before our death, then, is not, how much can I still accomplish, or how much influence can I still exert? But, how can I live so that I can continue to be fruitful when I am no longer here among my family and friends?

14. The complete works of John of the Cross, in their most critical translation, can now be purchased in one volume: *The Collected Works of St. John of the Cross*, trans. Kieran Kavanaugh and Otilio Rodriguez (Washington, D.C.: ICS Publications, 1991).

15. Ronald Rolheiser, *The Holy Longing: The Search for a Christian Spirituality* (New York: Doubleday, 1999).

Chapter Two

1. Anthropologists and other experts on initiation agree that, for the most part, our society is good at this initial initiation process, i.e., of initiating an infant into childhood. The one warning they do sound, however, is this: the energies of a baby are very raw and undisciplined. In initiating those energies we must be careful not to shame those energies as a way of trying to direct them. For example, if you see a child eating messily with her fingers, don't try to correct that behavior by saying, "Don't eat like a pig!" That clearly does direct the energy, but also shames it. Energy must be honored, even as it is directed. When we are shamed in our energies as a child, this will have negative consequences later, particularly, as we will see in Chapter Seven, in a "cursed consciousness" that will struggle to bless others. As well, when our innate energies are shamed when we are a child, we will often, later on in life, struggle with our concept of God and church.

2. Anthropologists who study initiation rites in tribal cultures tell us that, in essence, the initiation of adolescent energy (which is especially raw and fiery at puberty) consists in teaching a young man or woman how to link together four powerful energies inside them so as to make those energies function for the larger good, the community. What are those four energies (so raw and powerful at puberty)? Simply put, we stand at puberty powerfully charged in the heart, the groin, the muscles, and the head, not knowing either how to link those energies to one another or how to link them to the greater good of the community. A good initiation rite teaches young men and young women, in a way that transforms both their vision of things and changes their behavior, what their head is for, what their muscles are for, what their sexuality is for, and what their hearts are for—and gives them a sense as well of how head, muscles, groin, and heart fit together. On the issue of the initiation of adolescents into adulthood, I especially recommend the work of Michael Meade.

3. Bill Plotkin, *Soulcraft: Crossing into the Mysteries of Nature and Psyche* (Novato, CA: New World Library, 2003).

4. Johann Wolfgang von Goethe, "The Holy Longing." See a translation by Robert Bly in *The Rag and Bone Shop of the Heart: A Poetry Anthology*, ed. Robert Bly, Michael Meade, and James Hillman (New York: Harper-Perennial, 1993), p. 382.

5. For more of an elaboration on the different aspects of eros, see "A Spirituality of Sexuality," in Ronald Rolheiser, *The Holy Longing: The Search for a Christian Spirituality* (New York: Doubleday, 1999). pp. 192–212, particularly p. 196.

6. William Stafford, "A Ritual to Read to Each Other."

See *The Rag and Bone Shop of the Heart*, Bly, Hillman, and Meade.

The actual lines in Stafford's poem read this way:

> *For there is many a small betrayal in the mind,*
> *a shrug that lets the fragile sequence break*
> *sending with shouts the horrible errors of childhood*
> *storming out to play through the broken dyke.*

7. For a brief definition and theology of sexuality, see Rolheiser, *The Holy Longing*, pp. 192–212.

8. The *full bloom* of sexuality takes on many life-giving forms. See Rolheiser, *The Holy Longing*, pp. 196–98.

9. Karl Rahner, *Servants of the Lord* (New York: Herder and Herder, 1968), p. 152.

10. Ecclesiastes 3:10–11.

11. Jill Alexander Essbaum, "Easter," *Poetry Magazine*, January 2011.

12. Matthew 6:24–34 and Luke 12:24–27.

13. Luke 10:17–20.

14. Christopher de Vinck, *Only the Heart Knows How to Find Them: Precious Memories for a Faithless Time* (New York: Viking Books, 1991).

15. Dennis Lee, "Juniper and Bone," quoted by J. S. Porter, *Spirit Book Word: An Inquiry into Literature and Spirituality* (Ottawa: Novalis, 2001), p. 151.

16. Soren Kierkegaard once defined a saint as someone "who can will the one thing."

17. Henri Nouwen, *The Genesee Diary* (Garden City, NY: Doubleday, 1976. Reprint, Garden City, NY: Image Books, 1981.)

18. See Robert Bly, *The Sibling Society* (New York: Random House, 1996). Also see Marie-Louise Von Franz, *The Problem of the Puer Aeternus* (Toronto: Inner City Books, 2000).

19. See the key works of Robert L. Moore: *King, Warrior, Magician, Lover: Rediscovering the Archetypes of the Mature Masculine* (San Francisco: Harper, 1990); *The King Within: Accessing the King in the Male Psyche* (New York: William Morrow, 1992); *The Warrior Within: Accessing the Knight in the Male Psyche* (New York: William Morrow, 1992); *The Magician Within: Accessing the Shaman in the Male Psyche* (New York: William Morrow, 1993); *The Lover Within: Accessing the Lover in the Male Psyche* (New York: William Morrow, 1993); *The Archetype of Initiation: Sacred Space, Ritual Process, and Personal Transformation* (Philadelphia: Xlibris, 2001); *The Magician and the Analyst: The Archetype of the Magus in Occult Spirituality and Jungian Analysis* (Philadelphia: Xlibris, 2002); *Facing the Dragon: Confronting Personal and Spiritual Grandiosity* (Wilmette, IL: Chiron Publications, 2003).

20. John of the Cross graphs out the journey toward Essential Discipleship in what he calls the journey through the "dark night of the senses." This can be found in his works: *The Ascent of Mount Carmel*, Book I and *The Dark Night*, Book I. See, *The Collected Works of St. John of the Cross*, trans. Kieran Kavanaugh and Otilio Rodriguez (Washington, D.C.: ICS Publications, 1991).

21. Rolheiser, *The Holy Longing*, pp. 45–70.

22. Matthew 6:1–6, 16–18.

23. Matthew 6:5–6

24. John 14:15.

25. Luke 14:12–14.

26. Matthew 25:31–46.

27. A line attributed to James Forbes, pastor of an Interdenominational Church in New York City.

28. The distinction between private charity and social justice is, today, generally understood and accepted, but

for some elaboration on it, see Rolheiser, *The Holy Longing*, pp. 167–91.

29. 1 John 4:20.

30. T. S. Eliot, *Murder in the Cathedral* (New York: Harcourt Brace, 1935).

31. John of the Cross, *The Ascent of Mount Carmel* in *The Collected Works of St. John of the Cross*, trans. Kavanaugh and Rodriguez.

32. Ibid., chapter 13, number 11.

33. That is how John of the Cross would define initial maturity. For him, it is attained at the end of the "passive night of the senses" when our motivation has finally shifted from "What's in it for me?" to "I need to do this because it is the right thing to do." Indeed, for John, the ultimate purpose of the "dark night of the senses" is to break our innate motivational instinct, i.e., the pleasure principle.

Part Two
Chapter Three

1. Luke 10:38–42.

2. Joan Chittister, *Winds of Change: Women Challenge the Church* (Kansas City, MO: Sheed and Ward, 1986), pp. 153–55, shortened and condensed from its original.

3. It is ironic that, although we are in this phase of our lives for the bulk of our years, John of the Cross spends very little time focusing explicitly on proficiency. Most of his writings are devoted to explaining how we get there and what we are invited to once we get there in terms of moving into the last, more radical, stage of discipleship. However, in mapping out the route to proficiency (which he does in *The Ascent of Mount Carmel*, Book I and *The Dark Night*, Book I), particularly when he describes

what happens to us in the "passive night of the senses," he touches on most of the struggles and challenges that face us as proficients. His explicit section on proficiency is found in *The Dark Night*, Book 2, chapters 1–3. See *The Collected Works of St. John of the Cross*, trans. Kieran Kavanaugh and Otilio Rodriguez (Washington, D.C.: ICS Publications, 1991), pp. 395–400. Also see Wayne Teasdale *A Monk in the World: Cultivating a Spiritual Life* (Novato, CA: New World Library, 2002).

4. What it might mean to be a "forest dweller" and a "sannyasin" within Christian discipleship will be explored somewhat in Chapter Nine. For a quick, accurate, for-the-novice insight into Hindu spirituality, I heartily recommend the books of Huston Smith.

5. James Hillman, *The Soul's Code: In Search of Character and Calling* (New York: Random House, 1996), pp. 34–35.

6. John of the Cross, "The Living Flame of Love," commentary on stanza 2, numbers 13–15, *The Collected Works of St. John of the Cross*, trans. Kavanaugh and Rodriguez, pp. 662–63. John is very nuanced in his explanation of this, explaining at length how, depending upon what degree of maturity we have, the effects of the spirit flowing into our bodies will vary greatly, i.e., when we still lack a deep maturity, during the night of the senses and our years of proficiency, the effect of the spirit flowing into the senses is experienced in a much more problematic way, that is, as stimulating and over-stimulating our "grandiosity" (the image and likeness of God inside of us). At this earlier stage, the experience can be far from "pure" and can help trigger the issues with sexuality mentioned. However, when a person has attained a much deeper level of maturity (in what John calls "the living flame" experience) the inflow will be

pure and will not trigger the temptations that were triggered earlier. Instead, we will feel that inflow as pure joy, a pure foretaste of heaven, and we will be moved to be the smiling, blessing grandparent, beaming at a grandchild, full of joy at the beauty of it all. And it is interesting to note that, for John, when this happens at the full level of maturity that "flowing of the spirit into the senses" will be evident in our bodies and will enhance our physical attractiveness.

7. This concept of what kind of disillusionment happens when a honeymoon ends will be more fully explained in the later chapters of this book.

8. Note how Dorothy Day titled her autobiography, within which she detailed her long years of struggle as a disciple of Jesus: *The Long Loneliness*.

9. For an excellent and very detailed analysis of this, see Kathleen Norris, *Acedia and Me: A Marriage, Monks, and a Writer's Life* (New York: Riverhead Books, 2008).

10. Evagrius Ponticus, *The Praktikos,* quoted in ibid., preface.

11. Ibid.

12. Alice Miller, *The Drama of the Gifted Child: The Search for the True Self*, trans. Ruth Ward (1979; repr.: New York: Basic Books, 2007).

13. Luke 18:9–14.

14. See, for example: Ruth Burrows, *Guidelines for Mystical Prayer* (Denville, NJ: Dimension Books, 1976), pp. 154–55.

15. Ibid., p. 77.

16. Matthew 20:1–16.

17. Burrows, *Guidelines for Mystical Prayer*, pp. 16, 79–80.

18. Thérèse of Lisieux, *Her Last Conversations* (Washington, D.C.: ICS Publications, 1977), p. 111.

19. John of the Cross, *The Dark Night*, Book II, in *The Collected Works of St. John of the Cross*, trans. Kavanaugh and Rodriguez, chapter 2, number 2, p. 397.

20. Wayne Muller, Sabbath: *Finding Rest, Renewal, and Delight in Our Busy Lives* (New York: Bantam Books, 1999), p. 3.

21. Matthew 5:28.

22. James Hillman, *The Force of Character: And the Lasting Life* (New York: Random House, 1999), p. 112.

Chapter Four

1. Quoted by Kurt Vonnegut, *A Man Without a Country* (New York: Random House, 2005), p. 14.

2. Lee Gutkind, ed., *In Fact: The Best of Creative Nonfiction* (New York: Norton, 2004).

3. Comment made by Edward Schillebeeckx at a workshop at the American College, Louvain, Belgium, March 1983.

4. Luke 24:13–35.

5. Historians and scripture scholars have been unable to establish with any certainty where this town of Emmaus was located. A number of possible sites have been proposed, but there is no universal consensus as to where the town of Emmaus of Luke's Gospel exactly was and, with that uncertainty, what its precise symbolic meaning is for Luke. One possibility, however, as to its symbolic value, is that one of the locations proposed as a possible site was also the site of some hot springs that were reported to have healing powers, i.e., a spa. My own interpretation as to the symbolic meaning of Emmaus, as an escape from one's crucified faith dream and a movement toward some kind of worldly consolation, was triggered by the possibility that the disciples were

walking toward a spa, but is based as well on the over-all thrust of the text.

6. Psalm 14:1.

7. John 6:52–69.

8. John 6:53.

9. John 6:67–68.

10. C. S. Lewis, *Surprised by Joy: The Shape of My Early Life* (New York: Harcourt Brace, 1955), pp. 228–29.

11. Mark 7:25–30 and Matthew 15:21–28.

12. Matthew 5:48 and Luke 6:27–38.

13. John 13:1–17.

14. John 13:2–5.

15. Luke 15:8–10.

16. John Shea, *On Earth as It Is in Heaven: The Spiritual Wisdom of the Gospels for Christian Preachers and Teachers, Matthew: Year A* (Collegeville, MN: Order of Saint Benedict, 2004), p. 34.

17. Luke 24:49 and Acts 1:12–14.

Chapter Five

1. Leon Bloy: See Daily Quote from Leon Bloy, January 18, 2011. Available at www.integratecatholiclife.org/2011/01/daily-quote-from-leon-bloy. Article Source: http://EzineArticles.com/282550.

2. Mark 10:17–22, Luke 18:18–30, and Matthew 19:16–30.

3. Benedicta Ward, *The Sayings of the Desert Fathers: The Alphabetical Collection* (Kalamazoo, MI: Cistercian Publications, 1984), p. 103.

4. Bloy, Daily Quote from Leon Bloy.

5. Margaret Halaska, OSF, *Review for Religious*, May/June, 1981.

6. Matthew 19:23–26.

7. This is true for the "Synoptic Gospels," namely, the

Gospels of Matthew, Mark, and Luke. In them, Mary, the mother of Jesus, is given the role of premier disciple. In John's Gospel, however, she is assigned a different role and is depicted as the mother of all creation, as Eve, and the paradigm for discipleship is modeled for us by two other disciples: the beloved disciple of Jesus and Mary of Magdala.

8. Matthew 12:47–48.

9. Luke 11:27–29.

10. Lamentations 3:25–29.

11. Rainer Maria Rilke, "Sonnets to Orpheus IV," trans. Robert Bly, *The Rag and Bone Shop of the Heart: A Poetry Anthology*, ed. Robert Bly, Michael Meade, and James Hillman (New York: HarperPerennial, 1993), p. 100.

12. Michael Maginn, "Huntsville," in *Prayers from Life (Newry, Co. Down: Carmelite Publications*, 2010), p. 81. The emphases are his own.

13. Matthew 5:20.

14. Matthew 5:43–48, but also all the verses from 20–48 make the same point. Translation taken from the Jerusalem Bible. I took the liberty to change the word *sons* in verse 45 to *children*.

15. Can you love an enemy? Can you forgive a murderer? Christian opposition to the death penalty is ultimately based on this challenge from Jesus. The argument from Jesus is not that capital punishment is wrong—*it may be done in strict justice*. The argument is rather that *it should not be done* because Jesus invited us to something higher, namely, to forgive murderers . . . as he so explicitly forgave those who killed him.

16. Luke 1:12–28.

17. The notion of the scapegoat has been most famously articulated in the writings of René Girard. For a popu-

larized, though still deeply insightful, analysis of this, I recommend Gil Bailie, *Violence Unveiled: Humanity at the Crossroads* (New York: Crossroad, 1995).

18. Notice how Jesus is vested in exactly these symbols when Pilate shows him to the crowd and pronounces the famed words: "Ecco homo . . . Behold your scapegoat!" John 19:5.

19. Acts of the Apostles 7:55–60.

20. Book of Daniel, chapter 3.

21. Jerome Kodell, "The Good Fight: How Christians Suffer, Die, and Rise with Jesus," *America*, April 25, 2011, pp. 15–18.

Chapter Six

1. Grace L. Naessens, "The Difference" Available at uk.answers.yahoo.com/question/index?qid=20070222124127AA6Pf9b.

2. Luke 11:1–4.

3. Robert Moore, *Jungian Psychology and Human Spirituality: Liberation from Tribalism in Religious Life.* CDs or MP3 downloads. Available at www.robertmoore-phd.com/downloads/RMresource.pdf.

4. Luke 21:36.

5. Hebrews 5:1–10.

6. John 1:38. Newer translations of this gospel sometimes render the question this way: What do you want? (E.g., the New International Version.)

7. John 20:11–18.

8. Ibid.

9. A note on purgatory is in order here: Catholics and Protestants have long had a dispute over the existence of purgatory. Many Protestants reject the notion because scripture is clear that, after death, there are only

two places to which we can go, heaven or hell. So where does purgatory fit in? Perhaps some of the distance between Roman Catholics and Protestants on the question of purgatory might be bridged by conceiving it not as a place separate from heaven, but as our initial struggle, in heaven itself, to adjust to full light and full love. Allow me to risk an analogy here: imagine being born blind and living into adulthood without ever having seen light and color. Then, through some miraculous operation, doctors are able to give you sight. What would you feel immediately upon opening your eyes? Wonder? Bewilderment? Ecstasy? Pain? Some combination of all of these? We now know the answer to that question. This kind of sight-restoring operation has been done and is being done, and we now have some indication of how a person reacts upon opening his eyes and seeing light and color for the first time. What happens might surprise us. Here is how J. Z. Young, an authority on brain function, describes what happens: "The patient on opening his eyes gets little or no enjoyment; indeed, he finds the experience painful. He reports only a spinning mass of light and colors. He proves to be quite unable to pick up objects by sight, to recognize what they are, or to name them. He has no conception of space with objects in it, although he knows all about objects and their names by touch. 'Of course,' you will say, 'he must take a little time to learn to recognize them by sight.' Not a little time, but a very long time—in fact, years. His brain has not been trained in the rules of seeing. We are not conscious that there are any such rules; we think we see, as we say naturally. But we have, in fact, learned a whole set of rules during childhood." (See Emilie Griffin, *Souls in Full Sail* [Downers Grove, IL: IVP Books, 2011], p. 143–44.)

Might this be a helpful analogy for what happens to us in what Roman Catholics call purgatory? Could the purification we experience after death be understood in this very way—namely, as an opening of our vision and hearts to a light and a love that are so full as to force upon us the same kind of painful relearning and reconceptualization that have just been described? Might purgatory be understood precisely as being embraced by God in such a way that this warmth and light so dwarf our earthly concepts of love and knowledge that, like a person born blind who is given sight, we have to struggle painfully in the very ecstasy of that light to unlearn and relearn virtually our entire way of thinking and loving? Might purgatory be understood not as God's absence or some kind of punishment or retribution for sin but as what happens to us when we are fully embraced, in ecstasy, by God.

10. A clarifying note is in order here: Not all schools of thought use these words in the same way; e.g., in the Carmelite tradition, the tradition of John of the Cross and Teresa of Ávila, *meditation* refers to everything we do within prayer that is active, as opposed to being passive and in a posture of receptivity. And *contemplation* refers to prayer that is largely or wholly passive and receptive in nature. In essence, in the Carmelite tradition, *contemplation* is the wider genus for what is today commonly called *centering prayer.* In the tradition of the Jesuits and their renowned founder, Ignatius of Loyola, the words are used differently, i.e., both *meditation* and *contemplation* refer to active prayer, which is *meditation* in the Carmelite sense. In the Ignatian tradition *meditation* connotes more of an intellectual entry into prayer, and *contemplation* connotes more of a heart entry into it. But there is no opposition in substance between the two schools, only a different use of words.

11. *Lectio divina* (Latin for "divine reading") is a traditional Benedictine practice of scriptural reading, meditation, and prayer intended to promote communion with God and to increase the knowledge of God's Word. It does not treat scripture as texts to be studied, but as the Living Word. Traditionally, *lectio divina* has four separate steps: read, meditate, pray, and contemplate. First a passage of scripture is read, then its meaning is reflected upon. This is followed by prayer and contemplation on the Word of God.

12. James Walsh, ed., *The Cloud of Unknowing* (New York: Paulist Press, 1981).

13. I recommend the works of Thomas Keating for two things here: (i) an explication of the distinction between meditation and contemplation and the history of that distinction within Christian spirituality. Particularly, I recommend his 1986 work, *Open Mind, Open Heart: The Contemplative Dimension of the Gospel*, 3rd ed. (New York: Crossroad, 2009). And (ii) his masterful exposé of *centering prayer* as *contemplation*. Keating has numerous exposés on centering prayer, but his mature thought is wonderfully synthesized in his recent work *Manifesting God* (New York: Lantern Books, 2005).

14. See Rumi Quotes. Available at www.higher-self-improvement.com/rumi-quotes.html.

15. See "A Wedding Sermon" by Dietrich Bonhoeffer. Available at lutheranweddings.blogspot.com/2007/10/wedding-sermon-by-dietrich-bonhoeffer.html.

Chapter Seven

1. Matthew 5–7.
2. 1 Corinthians 13.
3. Galatians 5:22–24.

4. Luke 3:21–22, Mark 1:9–11, and Matthew 3:16–17.

5. I point you toward the work and the writings of Robert Moore, Richard Rohr, James Hillman, Robert Bly, and Michael Meade, among others. I single out particularly the writings of Robert Moore and the pastoral work of Richard Rohr. But the central insight that one of our deepest wounds, perhaps the deepest one of all, is the absence of blessing in our lives is everywhere present within the literature and the healing practices of those working in healing ministries today.

6. Genesis 1.

7. Roman Catholic and Anglican thought differs from classical Protestant thought on the effect of original sin on God's original blessing: In classical Reformed theology, original sin corrupts the world in a way that in essence eclipses the original blessing. In Roman Catholic and most Anglican/Episcopalian theology, original sin flaws the original creation without fully corrupting it and thus does not fully eclipse the original blessing, so that right at this present moment God is still looking at the world and saying: *It is good!*

8. Luke 3:21–22, Mark 1:9–11, Matthew 3:16–17.

9. Matthew 5:1–10 and Luke 6:20–23.

10. William Blake, "Infant Sorrow."

11. I am very indebted to Robert Moore for his insights here. Indeed, what I am presenting here is largely a popularization of his work and a commentary on it. His major works are listed in the bibliography. I recommend all of them but, for this particular section, recommend more specifically: *The King Within: Accessing the King in the Male Psyche* (New York: William Morrow, 1992).

12. William Butler Yeats, "Vacillation."

13. Li-Young Lee, "A Story."

14. Romans 5:8.
15. T. S. Eliot, "Little Gidding." Available at en.wikiquote .org/wiki/Four_Quartets.
16. John 15:13.

Chapter Eight

1. Morris West, *A View from the Ridge: The Testimony of a Twentieth-Century Christian* (London: HarperCollins, 1996), p. 2.
2. Ibid.
3. T. S. Eliot, *Murder in the Cathedral* (New York: Harcourt Brace, 1935).
4. Luke 17:7–10.
5. Karl Rahner, *Servants of the Lord* (New York: Herder and Herder, 1968), p. 152.
6. Doris Lessing, *Under My Skin: Volume One of My Autobiography, to 1949* (London: HarperCollins, 1994).
7. Lessing, *Under My Skin,* p. 358.
8. John of the Cross, *The Ascent of Mount Carmel* in *The Collected Works of St. John of the Cross* Kieran Kavanaugh and Otilio Rodriguez, trans. (Washington, D.C.: ICS Publications, 1991), book 1, chapter 11, number 4.

   Here is how John words it: "As long as he continues this attachment, it is impossible for him to make progress in perfection, even if the imperfection may be very small. It makes little difference whether a bird is tied by a thin thread or by a cord. For even if tied by thread, the bird will be prevented from taking off just as surely as if it were tied by a cord—that is, impeded from flight as long as it does not break the thread. Admittedly, the thread is easier to rend, but no matter how easily this may be done, the bird will not fly away without first doing so. That is the lot of a man who is attached to something, no matter how much virtue he has he will not reach the freedom of divine union."

9. David Tracy, *On Naming the Present: Reflections on God, Hermeneutics, and Church* (Maryknoll, NY: Orbis, 1994), p. 4.

10. Parker Palmer, *The Company of Strangers: Christians and the Renewal of America's Public Life* (New York: Crossroad, 1983), p. 59.

11. John 14:2.

12. John 20:19–23 and Acts 1 and 2.

13. John Powell, *Unconditional Love* (Niles, IL: Argus Communication, 1978).

14. Barbara Kingsolver, *Prodigal Summer* (New York: HarperCollins, 2000).

15. Mark 4:1–20, Matthew 13:3–23, and Luke 8:4–15.

Part Three

1. Belden C. Lane, *The Solace of Fierce Landscapes* (New York: Oxford University Press, 1998), p. 95.

Chapter Nine

1. Henri Nouwen, *Life of the Beloved* (New York: Crossroad, 1992), pp. 94–95.

2. Henri Nouwen, *With Burning Hearts: A Meditation on the Eucharistic Life* (1994; repr., Maryknoll, NY: Orbis Books, 2003). For Nouwen's exact words, see chapter 1, footnote 13.

3. This is true for the Synoptic Gospels, namely, for Matthew, Mark, and Luke. Things are very different in John's Gospel. Throughout his entire gospel, John emphasizes the divinity of Jesus, to the point of leaving almost no humanity in him. This carries through to John's narrative of the passion, where he has Jesus in full control, showing no human weaknesses whatsoever. John's passion narrative puts emphasis on the trial of Jesus and

John writes it up in such a way that everyone else is on trial—including us the reader—except Jesus.

4. For an excellent, detailed, and scholarly analysis of this, see W. H. Vanstone, *The Stature of Waiting* (New York: Morehouse Publishing, 2006).

5. Henri Nouwen, *A Spirituality of Waiting: Being Alert to God's Presence in Our Lives* (Notre Dame: Ave Maria Press, 2006), audiocassette. The dialogue here is not verbatim but a "rendering" of the substance of the conversation.

6. Nouwen also read aloud to him: Vanstone, *The Stature of Waiting*.

7. James Hillman, *The Force of Character: And the Lasting Life* (New York: Random House, 1999), p. 16.

8. John 19:34.

9. Job 1:21.

10. Genesis 12 and following.

11. T. S. Eliot, "Little Gidding." Available at en.wikiquote .org/wiki/Four_Quartets.

12. Goethe, "The Holy Longing." See a translation by Robert Bly in *The Rag and Bone Shop of the Heart: A Poetry Anthology,* ed. Robert Bly, Michael Meade, and James Hillman (New York: HarperPerennial, 1993), p. 382.

13. Richard Rohr, *Falling Upward: A Spirituality for the Two Halves of Life* (San Francisco: Jossey-Bass, 2011). This is just the latest of Rohr's many articulations of this. I recommend too his other works, as well as his many audio and video presentations. Among contemporary Christian writers no one has done more work on this question than Rohr.

14. Hillman, *The Force of Character: And the Lasting Life,* preface.

15. Ibid., pp. 59–60.

16. Ibid., pp. 72–77. To cite just one example that Hillman offers regarding how our physical diminishments even-

tually make monks out of us all. He takes up the issue of how, at a certain age, we cannot sleep fully through the night but have to get up to go to the bathroom. Why does nature do that to us? It is turning us into monks! Monks get up during the night to do an exercise that they call "vigils." They could, radically, do this during the day, but they choose to do it at night because darkness and night bring with it a special ambience, a mood, a spirit, some angels of the hour. We are in a different reflective state in the middle of the night. So nature eventually forces the rest of us, nonmonks, to do the same. We get up at night to go to the bathroom and return to our beds, but sleep does not come at once. Instead, the mythical goddess of night, Nyx, surrounds the bed, along with her children (old wounds, grudges, bitterness, unresolved anger), and we are forced to deal with her and with them in a way that we need not during our daylight hours. Such is nature's wisdom.

17. Ibid., p. xv.

18. Ibid., p. 56.

I recommend here too the insights of Germaine Greer in her book *The Change: Women, Aging, and Menopause* (New York: Ballantine Books, 1993). She sees five distinct stages to a woman's life: *infancy, nubility, wifehood/parenthood, menopause, crone,* and she submits that, certainly in our secular cultures today, women are valued only in the first three stages, particularly in the second stage. Then, sadly, after menopause, they become, in Greer's words, invisible. Her challenge, of course, as the thesis of this chapter, is that, as we age, we must begin to ground ourselves in meaning beyond biology, youth, and sexual attractiveness.

19. John's theology of the "dark night of the spirit" as mentioned earlier, is contained in these books (and is to be read in that order): *The Ascent of Mount Carmel,* Books II and III, and *The Dark Night,* Book II.

SELECT BIBLIOGRAPHY

Bailie, Gil. *Violence Unveiled: Humanity at the Crossroads.* New York: Crossroad, 1995.

Bloy, Leon. Daily Quote from Leon Bloy, January 18, 2011, Available at www.integratedcatholiclife.org/2011/01/daily-quote-from-leon-bloy. Article Source: http://EzineArticles.com/282550.

Bly, Robert, James Hillman, and Michael Meade (eds.). *The Rag and Bone Shop of the Heart: A Poetry Anthology.* New York: HarperPerennial, 1993.

Bly, Robert. *The Sibling Society.* New York: Random House, 1996.

Bonhoeffer, Dietrich. "A Wedding Sermon." Available at lutheran-weddings.blogspot.com/2007/10/wedding-sermon-by-dietrich-bonhoeffer.html.

Burrows, Ruth. *Guidelines for Mystical Prayer.* Denville, NJ: Dimension Books, 1976.

Chittister, Joan. *Winds of Change: Women Challenge the Church.* Kansas City, MO: Sheed and Ward, 1986.

de Vinck, Christopher. *Only the Heart Knows How to Find Them: Precious Memories for a Faithless Time.* New York: Viking Books, 1991.

Eliot, T. S. "Little Gidding." Available at en.wikiquote.org/wiki/Four_Quartets.

———. *Murder in the Cathedral.* New York: Harcourt Brace, 1935.

Essbaum, Jill A. "Easter." *Poetry Magazine.* January 2011. Available at www.poetryfoundation.org/poetrymagazine/poem/240934.

Greer, Germaine. *The Change: Women, Aging, and Menopause.* New York: Ballantine Books, 1993.

Gutkind, Lee, ed. *In Fact: The Best of Creative Nonfiction.* New York: Norton, 2004.

Halaska, Margaret, OSF. *Review for Religious.* May/June 1981.

Hillman, James. *The Force of Character: And the Lasting Life.* New York: Random House, 1999.

———. *The Soul's Code: In Search of Character and Calling.* New York: Random House, 1996.

Kavanaugh, Kieran, and Otilio Rodriguez, trans. *The Collected Works of St. John of the Cross*. Washington, D.C.: ICS Publications, 1991.

Kazantzakis, Nikos. *Report to Greco*. New York: Simon and Schuster, 1965.

Keating, Thomas. *Manifesting God*. New York: Lantern Books, 2005.

——. *Open Mind, Open Heart: The Contemplative Dimension of the Gospel*, 3rd ed. New York: Crossroad, 2009.

Kingsolver, Barbara. *Prodigal Summer*. New York: HarperCollins, 2000.

Kodell, Jerome. "The Good Fight: How Christians Suffer, Die, and Rise with Jesus." *America*, April 25, 2011.

Lessing, Doris. *Under My Skin: Volume One of My Autobiography, to 1949*. New York: HarperCollins, 1994.

Lewis, C. S. *Surprised by Joy: The Shape of My Early Life*. New York: Harcourt Brace, 1955.

Maginn, Michael. "Hunstville" in *Prayers from Life*. Newry, Co. Down: Carmelite Publications, 2010.

Miller, Alice. *The Drama of the Gifted Child: The Search for the True Self*. Translated by Ruth Ward. 1979. Reprint, New York: Basic Books, 2007.

Moore, Robert. *The Archetype of Initiation: Sacred Space, Ritual Process, and Personal Transformation*. Philadelphia: Xlibris, 2001.

——. *Facing the Dragon: Confronting Personal and Spiritual Grandiosity*. Wilmette, IL: Chiron Publications, 2003.

——. *Jungian Psychology and Human Spirituality: Liberation from Tribalism in Religious Life*. CDs or MP3 downloads. Available at www.robertmoore-phd.com/downloads/RMresource.pdf.

——. *King, Warrior, Magician, Lover: Rediscovering the Archetypes of the Mature Masculine*. San Francisco: Harper, 1990.

——. *The King Within: Accessing the King in the Male Psyche*. New York: William Morrow, 1992.

——. *The Lover Within: Accessing the Lover in the Male Psyche*. New York: William Morrow, 1993.

——. *The Magician and the Analyst: The Archetype of the Magus in Occult Spirituality and Jungian Analysis*. Philadelphia: Xlibris, 2002.

——. *The Magician Within: Accessing the Shaman in the Male Psyche*. New York: William Morrow, 1993.

——. *The Warrior Within: Accessing the Knight in the Male Psyche*. New York: William Morrow, 1992.

Muller, Wayne. *Sabbath: Finding Rest, Renewal, and Delight in Our Busy Lives.* New York: Bantam Books, 1999.

Naessens, Grace. "I Didn't Have Time to Pray." Available at uk.answers .yahoo.com/question/index?qid=20070222124127AA6Pf9b.

Norris, Kathleen. *Acedia and Me: A Marriage, Monks, and a Writer's Life.* New York: Riverhead Books, 2008.

———. *The Cloister Walk.* New York: Riverhead Books, 1996.

Nouwen, Henri. *The Genesee Diary.* Garden City, NY: Doubleday, 1976. Reprint, Garden City, NY: Image Books, 1981.

———. *Life of the Beloved.* New York: Crossroad, 1992.

———. *Our Greatest Gift: A Meditation on Dying and Caring.* New York: HarperCollins, 1994.

———. *A Spirituality of Waiting: Being Alert to God's Presence in Our Lives.* Read by the author. Notre Dame: Ave Maria Press, 2006. Audiocassette.

———. *With Burning Hearts: A Meditation on the Eucharistic Life.* 1994. Reprint, Maryknoll, NY: Orbis Books, 2003.

Palmer, Parker. *The Company of Strangers: Christians and the Renewal of America's Public Life.* New York: Crossroad, 1983.

Plotkin, Bill. *Soulcraft: Crossing into the Mysteries of Nature and Psyche.* Novato, CA: New World Library, 2003.

Porter, J. S. *Spirit Book Word: An Inquiry into Literature and Spirituality.* Ottawa: Novalis, 2001.

Powell, John. *Unconditional Love.* Niles, IL: Argus Communication, 1978.

Rahner, Karl. *Servants of the Lord.* New York: Herder and Herder, 1968.

Rohr, Richard. *Falling Upward: A Spirituality for the Two Halves of Life.* San Francisco: Jossey-Bass, 2011.

Rolheiser, Richard. *The Holy Longing: The Search for a Christian Spirituality.* New York: Doubleday, 1999.

Rumi. Rumi Quotes: www.higher-self-improvement.com/rumi-quotes .html.

Shea, John. *On Earth as It Is in Heaven: The Spiritual Wisdom of the Gospels for Christian Preachers and Teachers: Matthew, Year A.* Collegeville, MN: Order of Saint Benedict, 2004.

Taylor, Charles. *A Secular Age.* Cambridge, Mass.: Harvard University Press, 2007.

Teasdale, Wayne. *A Monk in the World: Cultivating a Spiritual Life.* Novato, CA: New World Library, 2002.

Thérèse of Lisieux. *Her Last Conversations.* Washington, D.C.: ICS Publications, 1977.

Thoreau, Henry David. *True Harvest: Readings from Henry David Thoreau for Every Day of the Year,* ed. Barry Andrews. Boston: Skinner House Books, 2006.

Tracy, David. *On Naming the Present: Reflections on God, Hermeneutics, and Church.* Maryknoll, NY: Orbis, 1994, p. 4.

Vanstone, W. H., *The Stature of Waiting.* New York: Morehouse Publishing, 2006.

Von Franz, Marie-Louise. *The Problem of the Puer Aeternus.* Toronto: Inner City Books, 2000.

Vonnegut, Kurt. *A Man Without a Country.* New York: Random House, 2005.

Walsh, James, ed. *The Cloud of Unknowing.* New York: Paulist Press, 1981.

Ward, Benedicta. *The Sayings of the Desert Fathers: The Alphabetical Collection.* Kalamazoo, MI: Cistercian Publications, 1984.

West, Morris. *A View from the Ridge: The Testimony of a Twentieth-Century Christian.* London: HarperCollins, 1996.

ABOUT THE AUTHOR

RONALD ROLHEISER, O.M.I., is a Roman Catholic priest, a member of the Missionary Oblates of Mary Immaculate, and president of the Oblate School of Theology in San Antonio, Texas. He is a community-builder, lecturer, and writer. His books are popular throughout the English-speaking world and his weekly column is carried by more than seventy news-papers worldwide. He is the author of the prizewinning *The Restless Heart* as well as *Forgotten Among the Lilies, Our One Great Act of Fidelity, The Shattered Lantern, Against an Infinite Horizon,* and *Prayer: Our Deepest Longing.* His book *The Holy Longing* has more than a quarter of a million copies in print.